Taking the Long View

Taking the
Long View

Christian Theology in Historical
Perspective

DAVID C. STEINMETZ

OXFORD
UNIVERSITY PRESS

OXFORD
UNIVERSITY PRESS

Oxford University Press, Inc., publishes works that further
Oxford University's objective of excellence
in research, scholarship, and education.

Oxford   New York
Auckland   Cape Town   Dar es Salaam   Hong Kong   Karachi
Kuala Lumpur   Madrid   Melbourne   Mexico City   Nairobi
New Delhi   Shanghai   Taipei   Toronto

With offices in
Argentina   Austria   Brazil   Chile   Czech Republic   France   Greece
Guatemala   Hungary   Italy   Japan   Poland   Portugal   Singapore
South Korea   Switzerland   Thailand   Turkey   Ukraine   Vietnam

Published by Oxford University Press, Inc.
198 Madison Avenue, New York, New York 10016

www.oup.com

Oxford is a registered trademark of Oxford University Press.

Library of Congress Cataloging-in-Publication Data
Steinmetz, David Curtis.
Taking the long view : Christian theology in historical perspective / David C. Steinmetz.
p.   cm.
Includes bibliographical references and index.
ISBN 978-0-19-976893-6; 978-0-19-976894-3 (pbk.)
1. Theology, Doctrinal—History.   I. Title.
BT21.3.S74 2011
230.09—dc22   2010034821

9 8 7 6 5 4 3 2 1

Printed in the United States of America
on acid-free paper

Contents

Introduction, vii

1. The Superiority of Pre-Critical Exegesis, 3
2. Miss Marple Reads the Bible: Detective Fiction and the Art of Biblical Interpretation, 15
3. Inclusive Language and the Trinity, 27
4. Creator God: The Debate on Intelligent Design, 37
5. Mary Reconsidered, 45
6. The Catholic Luther: A Critical Reappraisal, 53
7. Starting Over: Reformation and Conversion, 69
8. Forgiving the Unforgivable Wrong, 79
9. The Domestication of Prophecy in the Early Reformation, 81
10. The Learned Ministry Revisited, 91
11. Marriage, Celibacy, and Ordination, 103
12. Christ and the Eucharist, 115
13. World Christianity under New Management?, 127
14. Religion in the Public Square, 131
15. The Necessity of the Past, 137
16. Taking the Long View, 147
17. Concluding Notes for a Pilgrim People, 157

Appendix: Footnotes to an Old Complaint, 161
Notes, 169
Scripture Index, 175
General Index, 177

Introduction

The first essay in this book—"The Superiority of Pre-critical Exegesis"—might not have been written at all, had I not been invited to deliver the Kearns lecture at Duke University in 1979. Under the terms of the lectureship, I was expected to speak on a subject of general interest to biblical, historical, and theological students. It occurred to me at the time that it might be useful to raise some questions about the methods then followed by biblical scholars in the practice of their craft.

The lecture addressed a problem that the Church experiences every Sunday, when ministers, who have been taught to use historical-critical tools in biblical interpretation and never to allegorize, often allegorize when they preach and even appear reluctant to use historical-critical tools with a lay audience. Some critics assume the problem is primarily with the ministers themselves, who need to change their approach to the Bible to match the theory they learned in school. My own contention is that the problem is less with ministers than with the theory they have been taught.

From the very beginning the historical-critical method insisted that a biblical text had one meaning and one meaning only: namely, what the human author of the text had in mind when he wrote it. Older exegesis thought it probable that many texts had more than one legitimate meaning, without arguing that a text could mean anything the interpreter wanted it to mean. I suggested that older exegesis was correct in its view of multiple meanings, at least of some texts. If so, modern interpreters were woefully wrong to insist on one meaning and one meaning only, especially if that meaning were recoverable solely by the application of the historical-critical method. When the lecture appeared in print in *Theology Today*, it created a minor firestorm, the brush fires of which are still smoldering.

This essay was in its own way an illustration of the thesis that shapes my argument throughout this collection of essays. The thesis, simply put, is that memory of the past is essential to proper functioning in the present. Without a knowledge of the past, the Church knows neither where it has been or where it is going. Worse yet, it does not know where it should go. One would think that this generalization is a shining and obvious truth known to all Christians. After all, the Church is one of the oldest and most enduring institutions in the world. The office of Archbishop of Canterbury, for example, is far older than either the British monarchy or the British parliament.

However, the impression the Church often gives is of an institution that is suffering from collective amnesia. The American Protestant churches in particular, with their passion for action over thought, frequently appear to be sounding boards for causes whose connection to the Christian gospel is tenuous at best. Agendas set by secular culture, however worthy in themselves, are adopted without serious theological reflection on their place and significance in the larger Christian mission.

I do not want to be misunderstood as arguing that the Church cannot do new things in changed circumstances or that the Christian past should be allowed to lock the Church into traditional patterns of thought and action. The Christian past, like the Christian present, is subject to the judgment of the gospel. It is not only something to be celebrated; it is also in certain respects something to be overcome. Therefore memory has an important negative as well as positive theological function. It reminds ordinary Christians of mistakes to be avoided, of roads we ought not to choose, and of bitter culs-de-sac from which there is no easy or honorable exit.

The purpose of the Church is to confess by word and deed the good news of God. That mission may involve the Church in experimental social ministries or in political action. It will certainly require the Church to continue its traditional ministry of preaching, teaching, celebration of the sacraments, and generous relief of the poor and disadvantaged.

But the Christian past, in both its cheerily positive and its darkly negative aspects, places a question mark over Christian thinking and acting in the present. Every generation in the Church is sensitive to certain themes in the gospel, while remaining insensitive to others. In its attempt to understand and do the will of God in the present generation, the Church needs to listen to the voices of obedient hearers of the Word in other generations, if only in order to learn from them what the Church can no longer teach itself.

Most of the essays in this book are not, strictly speaking, purely historical studies. They are theological essays that attempt to apply historical insights to specific problems in the life and mission of the contemporary Church. They are, in other words, attempts to jog the memory of modern Christians, to remind them where they have been as they attempt to determine where they ought to go.

Some of the essays were delivered as lectures at the University of Chicago, the University of North Carolina, and Yale University. Others were given as the Stob Lectures at Calvin College and the McDonald Lectures at Emory University. Still others were published in journals and magazines like the *Christian Century*, *Christianity Today*, and *Theology Today*, Some had their origin in newspapers like the *Orlando Sentinel* and the *Raleigh News and Observer*. I am grateful to everyone who read these essays in their original form (or heard them as lectures) and made valuable, if sometimes unsettling, suggestions for their improvement.

Finally, I would like to dedicate this book to my students at five institutions: Harvard Divinity School, Lancaster Theological Seminary, Emory University, the University of Notre Dame, and, especially, Duke University. It is hard for me to imagine my life as a productive historian and theologian apart from continued engagement with these bright young men and women. It has been a privilege.

Taking the Long View

I

The Superiority of Pre-Critical Exegesis

In 1859 Benjamin Jowett, then Regius Professor of Greek at the University of Oxford, published a justly famous essay on the interpretation of scripture.[1] Jowett argued that "Scripture has one meaning—the meaning which it had in the mind of the Prophet or Evangelist who first uttered or wrote, to the hearers or readers who first received it."[2] Scripture should be interpreted like any other book, and the later accretions and venerated traditions surrounding its interpretation should, for the most part, either be brushed aside or severely discounted. "The true use of interpretation is to get rid of interpretation, and leave us alone in company with the author."[3]

Jowett did not foresee great difficulties in the way of the recovery of the original meaning of the text. Proper interpretation requires imagination, the ability to put oneself into an alien cultural situation, and knowledge of the language and history of the ancient people whose literature one sets out to interpret. In the case of the Bible, one has also to bear in mind the progressive nature of revelation and the superiority of certain later religious insights to certain earlier ones. But the interpreter, armed with the proper linguistic tools, will find that "universal truth easily breaks through the accidents of time and place"[4] and that such truth still speaks to the condition of the unchanging human heart.

Of course, critical biblical studies have made enormous strides since Jowett's time. No reputable biblical scholar would agree today with Jowett's reconstruction of the Gospels in which Jesus appears as a "teacher...speaking to a group of serious, but not highly educated, working men, attempting to inculcate in them a loftier and sweeter morality."[5] Still, the quarrel between modern biblical scholarship and Benjamin Jowett is less a quarrel over hermeneutical theory than a disagreement with him over the application of the theory in his exegetical practice. Biblical scholarship still hopes to recover the original intention of the author of a biblical text and still regards the pre-critical exegetical tradition as an obstacle to the proper understanding of the true meaning of that text. The most primitive meaning of the text is its only valid meaning, and the historical-critical method is the only key that can unlock it.

But is that theory true?

I think it is demonstrably false. In what follows I want to examine the pre-critical exegetical tradition at exactly the point at which Jowett regarded it to be most vulnerable, namely, in its refusal to bind the meaning of any pericope to the intention, whether explicit or merely half-formed, of its human author. Medieval theologians defended the proposition, so alien to modern biblical studies, that the meaning of scripture in the mind of the prophet who first uttered it is only one of its possible meanings and may not, in certain circumstances, even be its primary or most important meaning. I want to show that this theory (in at least that respect) was superior to the theories that replaced it. When biblical scholarship shifted from the hermeneutical position of Origen to the hermeneutical position of Jowett, it gained something important and valuable. But it lost something as well, and it is the painful duty of critical scholarship to assess its losses as well as its gains.

I

Medieval hermeneutical theory took as its point of departure the words of Paul: "The letter kills, but the Spirit gives life" (2 Cor. 3:6, NIV). Augustine suggested that this text could be understood in either one of two ways. On the one hand, the distinction between letter and spirit could be a distinction between law and Gospel, between demand and grace. The letter kills because it demands an obedience of the sinner that the sinner is powerless to render. The Spirit makes alive because it infuses the forgiven sinner with the new power to meet the rigorous requirements of the law.

But Paul could also have had in mind a distinction between what William Tyndale later called the "story-book" or narrative level of the Bible and the deeper theological meaning or spiritual significance implicit within it. This distinction was important for at least three reasons. Origen stated the first reason with unforgettable clarity:

Now what man of intelligence will believe that the first and the second and the third day, and the evening and the morning existed without the sun and moon and stars? And that the first day, if we may so call it, was even without a heaven? And who is so silly as to believe that God, after the manner of a farmer, "planted a paradise eastward in Eden," and set in it a visible and palpable "tree of life," of such a sort that anyone who tasted its fruit with his bodily teeth would gain life; and again that one could partake of "good and evil" by masticating the fruit taken from the tree of that name? And when God is said to "walk in the paradise in the cool of the day" and Adam to hide himself behind a tree, I do not think anyone will doubt that these are figurative expressions which indicate certain mysteries through a semblance of history and not through actual events.[6]

Simply because a story purports to be a straightforward historical narrative does not mean that it is in fact what it claims to be. What appears to be history may be metaphor or figure instead, and the interpreter who confuses metaphor with literal fact is an interpreter who is simply incompetent. Every biblical story means something, even if the narrative taken at face value contains absurdities or contradictions. The interpreter must demythologize the text in order to grasp the sacred mystery cloaked in the language of actual events.

The second reason for distinguishing between letter and spirit was the thorny question of the relationship between Israel and the church, between the Greek Testament and the Hebrew Bible. The church regarded itself as both continuous and discontinuous with ancient Israel. Because it claimed to be continuous, it felt an unavoidable obligation to interpret the Torah, the Prophets, and the Writings. But it was precisely this claim of continuity, absolutely essential to Christian identity, that created fresh hermeneutical problems for the church.

How was a French parish priest in 1150 to understand Psalm 137, which bemoans captivity in Babylon, makes rude remarks about Edomites, expresses an ineradicable longing for a glimpse of Jerusalem, and pronounces a blessing on anyone who avenges the destruction of the temple by dashing Babylonian children against a rock? The priest lives in Concale, not Babylon; has no personal quarrel with Edomites; cherishes no ambitions to visit Jerusalem (though he might fancy a holiday in Paris); and is expressly forbidden by Jesus to avenge himself on his enemies. Unless Psalm 137 has more than one possible meaning, it cannot be used as a prayer by the church and must be rejected as a lament belonging exclusively to the piety of ancient Israel.

A third reason for distinguishing letter from spirit was the conviction, expressed by Augustine, that while all scripture was given for the edification of the church and the nurture of the three theological virtues of faith, hope, and love, not all stories in the Bible are edifying as they stand. What is the spiritual point of the story of the drunkenness of Noah, the murder of Sisera, or the oxgoad of Shamgar, son of Anath? If it cannot be found on the level of narrative, then it must be found on the level of allegory, metaphor, and type.

That is not to say that patristic and medieval interpreters approved of arbitrary and undisciplined exegesis, which gave free rein to the imagination of the exegete. Augustine argued, for example, that the more obscure parts of scripture should be interpreted in the light of its less difficult sections and that no allegorical interpretation could be accepted that was not approved by the "manifest testimonies" of other less ambiguous portions of the Bible. The literal sense of scripture is basic to the spiritual and limits the range of possible allegorical meanings in those instances in which the literal meaning of a particular passage is absurd, undercuts the living relationship of the church to the Old Testament, or is spiritually barren.

From the time of John Cassian, the church subscribed to a theory of the fourfold sense of scripture.[7] The literal sense of scripture could and usually did nourish the three theological virtues, but when it did not, the exegete could appeal to three additional senses, each sense corresponding to one of the virtues. The allegorical sense taught about the church and what it should believe, and so corresponded to the virtue of faith. The tropological sense taught about individuals and what they should do, so corresponded to the virtue of love. The analogical sense pointed to the future and awakened expectation, and so corresponded to the virtue of hope. In the fourteenth century Nicholas of Lyra summarized this hermeneutical theory in a much quoted little rhyme:

> Littera gesta docet,
> Quid credas allegoria,
> Moralis quid agas,
> Quo tendas anagogia.
>
> [The letter teaches stories,
> Allegory teaches what to believe,
> The moral sense what to do,
> Anagogy where to aim for.]

This hermeneutical device made it possible for the church to pray directly and without qualification even a troubling psalm like 137. After all, Jerusalem was not merely a city in the Middle East; it was, according to the allegorical sense, the church; according to the tropological sense, the faithful soul; and according to the anagogical sense, the center of God's new creation. The psalm became a lament of those who long for the establishment of God's future kingdom and who are trapped in this disordered and troubled world, which with all its delights is still not their home. They seek an abiding city elsewhere. The imprecations against the Edomites and the Babylonians are transmuted into condemnations of the world, the flesh, and the devil. If you grant the four-fold sense of scripture, David sings like a Christian.

Thomas Aquinas wanted to ground the spiritual sense of scripture even more securely in the literal sense than it had been grounded in patristic thought. Returning to the distinction between "things" and "signs" made by Augustine in *De doctrina christiana* (though Thomas preferred to use the Aristotelian terminology of "things" and "words"), Thomas argued that, while words are the signs of things, things designated by words can themselves be signs of still other things. In all merely human sciences, words alone have a sign-character. But in Holy Scripture, the things designated by words can themselves have the character of a sign. The literal sense of scripture has to do with the sign-character of words; the spiritual sense of scripture has to do with the sign-character of things. By arguing this way, Thomas was able to show that the spiritual sense of scripture is always based on the literal sense and derived from it.

Thomas also redefined the literal sense of scripture as "the meaning of the text which the author intends." Lest Thomas be confused with Jowett, I should hasten to point out that for Thomas the author was God, not a human prophet or apostle. In the fourteenth century, Nicholas of Lyra, a Franciscan exegete and one of the most impressive biblical scholars produced by the Christian church, built a new hermeneutical theory on the aphorism of Thomas. If the literal sense of scripture is the meaning that the author intended (presupposing that the author whose intention finally matters is God), then is it possible to argue that scripture contains a double literal sense? Is there a literal-historical sense (the original meaning of the words as spoken in their first historical setting) that includes and implies a literal-prophetic sense (the larger meaning of the words as perceived in later and changed circumstances)?

Nicholas not only embraced a theory of the double literal sense of scrip-ture, but was even willing to argue that in certain contexts the literal-prophetic sense takes precedence over the literal-historical. Commenting on Psalm 117, Lyra wrote: "The literal sense in the Psalm concerns Christ; for the literal sense is the sense primarily intended by the author." Of the promise to Solomon in 1 Chronicles 17:13, Lyra observed: "The aforementioned authority was literally fulfilled in Solomon; however, it was fulfilled less perfectly, because Solomon was a son of God only by grace; but it was fulfilled more perfectly in Christ, who is the Son of God by nature."

For most exegetes, the theory of Nicholas of Lyra bound the interpreter to the dual task of explaining the historical meaning of a text while elucidating its larger and later spiritual significance. The great French humanist Jacques Lefèvre d'Etaples, however, pushed the theory to absurd limits. He argued that the only possible meaning of a text was its literal-prophetic sense and that the literal-historical sense was a product of human fancy and idle imagination. The literal-historical sense is the "letter that kills." It is advocated as the true meaning of scripture only by carnal persons who have not been regenerated by the life-giving Spirit of God. The problem of the proper exegesis of scripture is, when all is said and done, the problem of the regeneration of its interpreters.

In this brief survey of medieval hermeneutical theory, there are certain dominant themes that recur with dogged persistence. Medieval exegetes admit that the words of scripture had a meaning in the historical situation in which they were first uttered or written, but they deny that the meaning of the words is restricted to what the human author thought he said or what his first audience thought they heard. The stories and sayings of scripture bear an implicit meaning understood only by a later audience. In some cases that implicit meaning is far more important than the restricted meaning intended by the author in his particular cultural setting.

Yet the text cannot mean anything a later audience wants it to mean. The language of the Bible opens up a field of possible meanings. Any interpretation that falls within that field is valid exegesis of the text, even though that interpretation was not intended by the author. Any interpretation that falls outside the limits of that field of possible meanings is probably eisegesis and should be rejected as unacceptable. Only by confessing the multiple sense of scripture is it possible for the church to make use of the Hebrew Bible at all or to recapture the various levels of significance in the unfolding story of creation and redemption. The notion that scripture has only one meaning is a fantastic idea and is certainly not advocated by the biblical writers themselves.

II

Having elucidated medieval hermeneutical theory, I should like to take some time to look at medieval exegetical practice. One could get the impression from Jowett that because medieval exegetes rejected the theory of the single meaning of scripture so dear to Jowett's heart, they let their exegetical imaginations run amok and exercised no discipline at all in clarifying the field of possible meanings opened by the biblical text. In fact, medieval interpreters, once you grant the presuppositions on which they operate, are as conservative and restrained in their approach to the Bible as any comparable group of modern scholars.

In order to test medieval exegetical practice I have chosen a terribly diffi-cult passage from the Gospel of Matthew, the parable of the good employer or, as it is more frequently known, the parable of the workers in the vineyard (Matt. 20:1–16). The story is a familiar one. An employer hired day laborers to work in his vineyard at dawn and promised them the standard wage of a denarius. Because he needed more workers, he returned to the marketplace at nine, noon, three, and five o'clock and hired any laborers he could find. He promised to pay the workers hired at nine, noon, and three what was fair. But the workers hired at the eleventh hour, or five o'clock, were sent into the vineyard without any particular promise concerning remuneration. The employer instructed his foreman to pay off the workers beginning with the laborers hired at five o'clock. These workers expected only one-twelfth of a denarius, but were given the full day's wage instead. Indeed, all the workers who had worked part of the day were given one denarius. The workers who had been in the vineyard since dawn accordingly expected a bonus beyond the denarius, but they were disap-pointed to receive the same wage that had been given to the other, less deserving workers. When they grumbled, they were told by the employer that they had not been defrauded but had been paid according to an agreed contract. If the employer chose to be generous to the workers who had only worked part of the day, that was, in effect, none of their business. They should collect the denarius that was due them and go home like good fellows.

Jesus said the Kingdom of God was like this story. What on earth could he have meant?

The church has puzzled over this parable ever since it was included in Matthew's Gospel. Thomas Aquinas in his *Lectura super evangelium Sancti Matthaei* offered two interpretations of the parable, one going back in its lineage to Irenaeus and the other to Origen. The "day" mentioned in the parable can refer to the life span of an individual (the tradition of Origen), in which case the parable is a comment on the various ages at which one may be converted to Christ, or it can refer to the history of salvation (the tradition of Irenaeus), in which case it is a comment on the relationship of Jew and Gentile.

If the story refers to the life span of a man or woman, then it is intended as an encouragement to people who are converted to Christ late in life. The workers in the story who begin at dawn are people who have served Christ and have devoted themselves to the love of God and neighbor since childhood. The other hours mentioned by Jesus refer to the various stages of human development from youth to old age. Whether one has served Christ for a long time or for a brief moment, one will still receive the gift of eternal life. Thomas qualifies this somewhat in order to allow for proportional rewards and a hierarchy in heaven. But he does not surrender the main point: eternal life is given to late converts with the same generosity it is given to early converts.

On the other hand, the story may refer to the history of salvation. Quite frankly, this is the interpretation that interests Thomas most. The hours mentioned in the parable are not stages in individual human development but epochs in the history of the world, from Adam to Noah, from Noah to Abraham, from Abraham to David, and David to Christ. The owner of the vineyard is the whole Trinity, the foreman is Christ, and the moment of reckoning is the resurrection from the dead. The workers who are hired at the eleventh hour are the Gentiles, whose complaint that no one has offered them work can be interpreted to mean that they had no prophets as the Jews had. The workers who have borne the heat of the day are the Jews, who grumble about the favoritism shown to latecomers but who are still given the denarius of eternal life. As a comment on the history of salvation, the parable means that the generosity of God undercuts any advantage that the Jews might have had with respect to participation in the gifts and graces of God.

Not everyone read the text as a gloss on Jewish-Christian relations or as a discussion of late conversion. In the fourteenth century, the anonymous author of *The Pearl*, an elegy on the death of a young girl, applied the parable to infancy rather than to old age. What is important about the parable is not the chronological age at which one enters the vineyard, but the fact that some workers are only in the vineyard for the briefest possible moment. A child who dies at the age of two years is, in a sense, a worker who arrives at the eleventh hour. The parable is intended as a consolation for bereaved parents. A parent who has lost a small child can be comforted by the knowledge that God, who does not despise the service of persons converted in extreme old age, does not withhold his mercy from boys and girls whose eleventh hour comes at dawn.

Probably the most original interpretation of the parable was offered by John Pupper of Goch, a Flemish theologian of the fifteenth century, who used the parable to attack the doctrine of proportionality, particularly as that doctrine had been stated and defended by Thomas Aquinas. No one had ever argued that God gives rewards that match in exact quantity the weight of the good works done by a Christian. That is arithmetic equality and is simply not applicable to a relationship in which people perform temporal acts and receive eternal rewards. But most theologians did hold to a doctrine of proportionality; while there is a disproportion between the good works Christians do and the rewards they receive, there is a proportion as well. The reward is always much larger than the work that is rewarded, but the greater the work, the greater the reward.

As far as Goch is concerned, that doctrine is sheer nonsense. No one can take the message of the parable of the vineyard seriously and still hold to the doctrine of proportionality. Indeed, the only people in the vineyard who hold to the doctrine of proportionality are the first workers in the vineyard. They argue that twelve times the work should receive twelve times the payment. All they receive for their argument is a rebuke and a curt dismissal.

Martin Luther, in an early sermon preached in 1517 before the Reformation, agreed with Goch that God gives equal reward for great and small works. It is not by the Herculean size of their exertions but by the goodness of God that believers receive any reward at all. Unfortunately, Luther spoiled this point by elaborating a thoroughly unconvincing argument in which he tried to show that the last workers in the vineyard were humbler than the first and therefore one hour of their service was worth twelve hours of the mercenary service of the grumblers.

The parable, however, seems to make exactly the opposite point. The workers who began early were not more slothful or more selfish than the workers who began later in the day. Indeed, they were fairly representative of the kind of worker to be found hanging around the marketplace at any hour. They were angry not because they had shirked their responsibilities, but because they had discharged them conscientiously.

In 1525 Luther offered a fresh interpretation of the parable, attacking it from a slightly different angle. The parable has essentially one point: to celebrate the goodness of God, which makes nonsense of a religion based on law-keeping and good works. God pays no attention to the proportionately greater efforts of the first workers in the vineyard; rather, to their consternation, God puts them on exactly the same level as the last and least productive workers. The parable shows that everyone in the vineyard is unworthy, though not always for the same reason. The workers who arrive after nine o'clock are unworthy because they are paid a salary incommensurate with their achievement in picking grapes. The workers who spent the entire day in the vineyard are unworthy because they are dissatisfied with what God has promised, think that their efforts deserve special consideration, and are jealous of their employer's goodness to workers who accomplish less than they did. The parable teaches that salvation is not grounded in human merit and that there is no system of bookkeeping that can keep track of the relationship between God and human beings. Salvation depends utterly and absolutely on the goodness of God.

The four medieval theologians I have mentioned—Thomas Aquinas, the author of *The Pearl*, the Flemish chaplain Goch, and the young Martin Luther— did not exhaust in their writings all the possible interpretations of the parable of the workers in the vineyard. But they did see with considerable clarity that the parable is an assertion of God's generosity and mercy to people who do not deserve it. It is only against the background of the generosity of God that one can understand the relationship of Jew and Gentile, the problem of late conversion, the meaning of the death of a young child, the question of proportional rewards, even the definition of grace itself. Every question is qualified by the severe mercy of God, by the strange generosity of the vineyard owner who pays the nonproductive latecomer the same wage as his oldest and most productive employees.

If you were to ask me which of these interpretations is valid, I should have to respond that they all are. They all fall within the field of possible meanings created by the story itself. How many of those meanings were in the conscious intention of Jesus or of the author of the Gospel of Matthew, I do not profess to know. I am inclined to agree with C. S. Lewis, who commented on his own book *Till We Have Faces*: "An author doesn't necessarily understand the meaning of his own story better than anyone else."[8] The act of creation confers no special privileges on authors when it comes to the distinctly different, if lesser, task of interpretation. William Wordsworth the critic is not in the same league with Wordsworth the poet, while Samuel Johnson the critic towers over Johnson the creative artist. Authors obviously have something in mind when they write, but a work of historical or theological or aesthetic imagination has a life of its own.

III

Which brings us back to Benjamin Jowett. Jowett rejected medieval exegesis and insisted that the Bible should be read like any other book.[9] I agree with Jowett that the Bible should be read like any other book. The question is, how does one read other books?

Take, for example, my own field of Reformation studies. Almost no historian I know would answer the question of the meaning of the writings of Martin Luther by focusing solely on Luther's explicit and conscious intention. Marxist interpreters of Luther from Friedrich Engels to Max Steinmetz have been interested in Luther's writings as an expression of class interests, while psychological interpreters from Hartmann Grisar to Erik Erikson have focused on the theological writings as clues to the inner psychic tensions in Luther's personality. Even historians who reject Marxist and psychological interpretations of Luther find themselves asking how Luther was understood in the free imperial cities, by the German knights, by the landed aristocracy, by the various subgroups of German peasants, by the Catholic hierarchy, by lawyers, by university faculties—to name only a few of the more obvious groups who responded to Luther and left a written record of their response. Meaning involves a listener as well as a speaker, and when one asks the question of the relationship of Luther to his various audiences in early modern Europe, it becomes clear that there was not one Luther in the sixteenth century, but a battalion of Luthers.

Nor can the question of the meaning of Luther's writings be answered by focusing solely on Luther's contemporaries. Luther's works were read and pondered in a variety of historical and cultural settings from his death in 1546 to the present. Those readings of Luther have had measurable historical effects on succeeding generations, whose particular situation in time and space could scarcely have been anticipated by Luther. Yet the social, political, economic, cultural, and religious history of those people belongs intrinsically and inseparably to the question of the meaning of the theology of Martin Luther. The meaning of historical texts cannot be separated from the complex problem of their reception, and the notion that a text means only what its author intends it to mean is historically naive. Even to talk of the original setting in which words were spoken and heard is to talk of meanings rather than meaning. To attempt to understand those original meanings is the first step in the exegetical process, not the last and final step.

Modern literary criticism has challenged the notion that a text means only what its author intends it to mean far more radically than medieval exegetes ever dreamed of doing. Indeed, contemporary debunking of the author and the author's explicit intentions has proceeded at such a pace that it seems at times as if literary criticism has become a jolly game of ripping out an author's shirt-tail and setting fire to it. The reader and the literary work to the exclusion of the author have become the central literary preoccupation of the literary critic. Literary relativists of a fairly moderate sort insist that every generation has its own Shakespeare and Milton, and extreme relativists loudly proclaim that no reader reads the same work twice. Every change in the reader, however slight, is a change in the meaning of a text. Imagine what Thomas Aquinas or Nicholas of Lyra would have made of the famous statement by Northrop Frye:

> It has been said of Boehme that his books are like a picnic to which
> the author brings the words and the reader the meaning. The remark
> may have been intended as a sneer at Boehme, but it is an exact
> description of all works of literary art without exception.[10]

Medieval exegetes held to the sober middle way, the position that the text (any literary text, but especially the Bible) contains both letter and spirit. The text is not all letter, as Jowett and others maintained, or all spirit, as the rather more enthusiastic literary critics in our own time are apt to argue. The original text as spoken and heard limits a field of possible meanings. Those possible meanings are not dragged by the hair, willy-nilly, into the text, but belong to the life of the Bible in the encounter between author and reader as they belong to the life of any act of the human imagination. Such a hermeneutical theory is capable of sober and disciplined application and avoids the Scylla of extreme subjectivism, on the one hand, and the Charybdis of historical positivism, on the other. To be sure, medieval exegetes made bad mistakes in the application of their theory, but they also scored notable and brilliant triumphs. Even at their worst they recognized that the intention of the author is only one element—and not always the most important element at that—in the complex phenomenon of the meaning of a text.

The defenders of the single-meaning theory usually concede that the medieval approach to the Bible met the religious needs of the Christian community, but that it did so at the unacceptable price of doing violence to the biblical text. The fact that the historical-critical method after two hundred years is still struggling for more than a precarious foothold in that same religious community is generally blamed on the ignorance and conservatism of the Christian laity and the sloth or moral cowardice of its pastors.

I should like to suggest an alternative hypothesis. The medieval theory of levels of meaning in the biblical text, with all its undoubted defects, flourished because it is true, while the modern theory of a single meaning, with all its demonstrable virtues, struggles because it is false. Until the historical-critical method becomes critical of its own theoretical foundations and develops a hermeneutical theory adequate to the nature of the text that it is interpreting, it will remain restricted, as it deserves to be, to the guild and the academy, where the question of truth can endlessly be deferred.

2

Miss Marple Reads the Bible

Detective Fiction and the Art of Biblical
Interpretation

An important difference between historical-critical interpretations of the Bible and the church's traditional exegesis rests on the difference between their valuation of the role and importance of a text's reception. Traditional exegesis is quite willing to read earlier parts of the Bible in the light of later developments, while historical criticism is very reluctant to do anything of the kind.

Historical criticism attempts to set texts in their own place and time. It can do this properly only if it avoids anachronism: that is, reading back into earlier texts the views and assumptions of texts from a much later period. Traditional exegesis, on the other hand, assumes that no one can properly understand earlier developments in the biblical story without reading them in the light of later ones. How the story ends makes a difference for the beginning and middle of the story as well as for its conclusion. From the perspective of historical criticism traditional exegesis seems hopelessly anachronistic, while from the perspective of traditional exegesis historical criticism seems needlessly disoriented and fragmentary.

I

Reading a story from its conclusion is not such a strange activity when one leaves the Bible to one side and considers other forms of literature. Mystery stories, a genre of literature to which I am particularly addicted, provide a useful analogy. The mystery story in its classical form is often an enormous puzzle that is put together slowly, bit by bit, until at the end all of the small parts fall together into an intelligible pattern.

This kind of mystery story has two narratives. The first is a sprawling ram-shackle narrative that does not seem to be leading anyplace in particular. It is filled with clues, false leads, imaginative hypotheses, and characters who frequently seem overmatched by what appear to be quite ordinary criminal minds. The authorities must sometimes contend with reckless behavior by potential victims who carry the seeds of their own destruction. No one knows for certain where this apparently rudderless ship is drifting, not even (for several chapters, at least) the persons charged with bringing the ship safely to harbor. The principal characters, like the readers of the story (of whom they are oblivious), are often in deep puzzlement. Of course, one must concede that Sherlock Holmes at his most baffled is never as confused as Dr. Watson.

There is a second narrative, invariably recited by the principal investigator in the last or nearly last chapter. This narrative is crisp and clear and explains in considerable detail what was really occurring while the larger narrative was unfolding. The cogency of this narrative is not in the least undermined by the fact that none of the characters except the perpetrator of the crime and, until the very end of the story. the principal investigator himself or herself had any clear notion what the story was really about. Almost invariably the final recitation of the second, shorter narrative is accompanied by a brief period of intellectual stump-removal in which Miss Marple or Inspector Dalgliesh answers the objections of the characters who have not committed the crime and are not yet completely persuaded by the cogency and finality of the second, concluding narrative.

It is important to understand that this second narrative is not a subplot, even though it is short. It is the disclosure of the architectonic structure of the whole story. Therefore the second narrative quickly overpowers the first in the mind of the reader, who can no longer read the story as though ignorant of its plot and form. The second narrative is identical in substance to the first and therefore replaces it, not as an extraneous addition superimposed on the story or read back into it, but as a compelling and persuasive disclosure of what the story was about all along.

This also means that alternative plots must be discarded. Both the characters in the story and readers attempting to understand the story have suggested alternative plots and endings with varying degrees of plausibility. Indeed, one of the pleasures of reading mystery stories is the pleasure of resolving its puzzles for oneself. In the end, however, all alternative explanations must be abandoned. Just as the final narrative is not subverted by alternative theories proposed at any earlier stage in the development of the story, so can no alternative theories reasonably be kept after the ending of the story is known. The final narrative corrects all earlier narratives. It does not adjust to fit them.

The effect of all this on the reader is, of course, enormous. Casual conversations between characters that seemed at the time to be of no very great significance now appear to be charged with unmistakable importance. How, the reader wonders, could I have overlooked the Irish wool cap in the closet, the old newspapers on the front steps, the half-smoked cigar in the ashtray, or the chipped vase on the side table? Why did I put so much faith in the clever theory of Inspector Morse and so little in the astute observations of Detective-Sergeant Lewis? The sprawling, ramshackle narrative of events as lived by the characters is sprawling and ramshackle no more. What appeared on first reading to have been an almost random succession of events now proves to have been nothing of the kind. If one reads the last chapter first, one discovers a complex and intelligible narrative guided unerringly to its destined end by the secret hand of its author. Under the circumstances, reading backward is not only a preferred reading strategy; it is the only sensible course of action for a reasonable person.

II

Traditional Christian exegesis reads the Bible very much in this way—not exactly in this way, of course, but close enough to provide useful points of comparison. Early Christians believed that what had occurred in the life, death, and resurrection of Jesus Christ was of such importance that it had transformed the entire story of Israel and, through Israel, of the world. The long ramshackle narrative of Israel, with its promising starts and unexpected twists, with its ecstasies and its betrayals, its laws, its learning, its wisdom, its martyred prophets—this long narrative is retold and reevaluated in the light of what early Christians regarded as the concluding chapter God had written in Jesus Christ.

The New Testament is full of what we might call second narrative moments, short retellings of Old Testament stories in the light of Christ.[1] These second narrative moments are not regarded as subplots or additions tacked on to an otherwise complete story. They are believed by the speaker to uncover the plot in a literature that seems to be insufficiently plotted. They disclose at the end the structure of the whole from the beginning. It is, in fact, failure to discern the plot so disclosed, failure to read backward from Christ to Abraham and Moses, that has left heretics in some difficulty—or at least so Irenaeus and Tertullian thought.

The developing patristic argument had three elements in it. Tertullian put the first point forcefully in his *De praescriptione hereticorum*: heretics ought not to be allowed to use the Bible because it is not their book.[2] Gnostics who wanted to talk about the origins of the world as a great, unintended cosmic accident or Marcionites who posited the existence of two Gods should write their own inspired books, since the Christian Bible teaches nothing of the kind. Heretics who use the Bible are like beggars who wear garments that do not fit them and in which they appear to the discerning observer more than a little ridiculous.

In the second place, heretics ought not to be allowed to use the Bible because they do not understand it.[3] A myriad of quotations from the Bible does not make the arguments of the theologian who quotes it biblical. Heretics are like witty guests who entertain at parties by spontaneously constructing new poems from old. They quote well-loved lines from the works of established poets. Every line in the new poem is from Virgil or Horace and yet Virgil and Horace did not write it. The words are from the original poet, but the architectonic structure is not. Heretics, lost in the sprawling narrative of the Bible and ignorant of the second narrative that ties it together, have constructed a second narrative of their own. The words are from the Bible, but what the words say is not biblical. Heretics have got the second narrative wrong and are therefore as clueless about the meaning of the Bible as the characters in an Agatha Christie mystery are about the significance of the events in which they find themselves embroiled.

The second narrative the early fathers had in mind was the expanded baptismal confession.[4] When Christians confessed that they believed in God the Father Almighty, maker of heaven and earth, they were reciting the second narrative that unlocked for them the meaning of the first and excluded all alternative narratives. One could not confess that God the Father is the maker of heaven and earth without relegating Marcion's narrative of two Gods to the exegetical dustbin. Like the second narrative of Hercule Poirot, the second narrative of the early fathers rendered all alternative narratives redundant. Their second narrative, like his, was believed by them to be identical in substance to the first and therefore replaced it, not as an extraneous addition superimposed on the story or read back into it, but as a compelling and persuasive disclosure of what the story was about all along.

But why were Irenaeus and Tertullian confident that they had the correct second narrative? The third element in the early Christian campaign against heresy was an appeal to a succession of bishops stretching back over two centuries—not a terribly long time in the great scheme of things—to the age of the apostles.[5] The current orthodox bishop had been taught by a bishop who had been taught by a bishop who had been taught by a bishop who had been taught by an apostle. There were lists of these bishops that could be produced on demand. In other words, the church in the third century believed it had not only received the Septuagint from Jewish translators and a New Testament from the circles of the apostles; it had also received a second narrative that unlocked the mysteries of both. To be sure, the bishops were not the only people who had transmitted this second narrative from generation to generation, but they served as the public guarantors that the correct narrative had been transmitted.

One does not have to agree with the account of ancient Christian history offered by the early fathers to appreciate the force of their argument. Nor should one focus on these three elements to the exclusion of other important themes in early Christian writings. I have pointed out elsewhere the importance of what the Jesuits call discernment, the kind of insight that comes from disciplined prayer and long formation in the practices and habits of thought important to Christianity. When Athanasius argued that anyone who wants to understand the minds of the saints must first imitate their lives, he was touching on a theme no less important to the early Christian understanding of the Bible than apostolic succession and what I have called the distinction of first from second narratives.[6]

III

It might be objected that, while the analogy I have drawn with a mystery story may cast some light on the mind-set of interpreters who wrote premodern exegesis, it casts very little light on historical method or on the kind of exegesis that should be written by commentators who wish to interpret the Bible historically. But first appearances may be deceiving. In 1951 a well-known mystery writer, Josephine Tey, wrote a novel entitled *The Daughter of Time*.[7] In her story the protagonist, Alan Grant of Scotland Yard, was convalescing from injuries in a London hospital when he became fascinated with the historical question of whether Richard III had actually murdered his nephews to secure his claim to the English throne. With the aid of his friend, the actress Marta Hallard, he conducted a full-scale criminal investigation from his sickbed. In the end he concluded that Richard was falsely accused, a verdict agreeable to the Richard III Society but contested by historians who believe they have unearthed additional evidence against Richard since 1951. What is important to note, however, is not whether the conclusion Grant reached was correct, but how closely the investigative methods he used resembled the methods used by professional historians. Both detectives and historians are charged with reconstructing a probable sequence of events on the basis of evidence that is frequently fragmentary and ambiguous.

For example, like detectives, historians have good reason to be suspicious of narratives in which too many coincidences occur. Too many coincidences, like too many clues, suggest that someone may have tampered with the evidence. Yet history is full of surprises, and too many coincidences do in fact sometimes occur. The French medievalist Marc Bloch pointed to one such set of circumstances in his book *The Historian's Craft*:

> As Father Delahaye writes, in substance, anyone reading that the
> Church observes a holiday for two of its servants both of whom died
> in Italy on the very same day, that the conversion of each was brought
> about by the reading of the Lives of the Saints, that each founded a
> religious order dedicated to the same patron, that both of these
> orders were suppressed by popes bearing the same name—anyone
> reading all this would be tempted to assert that a single individual,
> duplicated through error, had been entered in the martyrology under
> two different names. Nevertheless, it is quite true that, similarly
> converted to the religious life by the example of saintly biographies,
> St. John Colombini established the Order of the Jesuates and
> Ignatius Loyola that of the Jesuits; that both of them died on July 31,
> the former near Siena in 1367, the latter at Rome in 1556; that the
> Jesuates were dissolved by Pope Clement IX and the Jesuits by
> Clement XIV. If the example is stimulating, it is certainly not
> unique.[8]

The difficulty of the task of reconstruction is compounded when, as is sometimes the case in biblical studies, there is little or no corroborating evidence outside the literary evidence of the biblical documents themselves. In such cases scholars may be forced to rely on literary evidence alone to re-create the historical setting of the document they have chosen for study. But literary evidence alone can mislead investigators attempting to reconstruct the past.

The story of John Eck, the Catholic controversialist who taught at the University of Ingolstadt during the early years of the Reformation, may be taken as a case in point. Eck had debated with Luther and Carlstadt in a famous exchange at the University of Leipzig in 1519. In 1529 he published the *Enchiridion of Commonplaces against Luther and Other Enemies of the Church*, a fiercely polemical handbook that attacked early Protestant teaching and the biblical exegesis that underlay it.[9] By turns witty, acerbic, and informative, the book was enormously popular with Catholic readers and went through multiple editions. It was in its own way a masterpiece of partisan writing.

In 1542 Eck lectured for the last time at Ingolstadt on the First Book of the *Sentences* of Peter Lombard.[10] The lectures were not only not polemical but made no reference whatever to what Eck regarded as dangerous Lutheran theological errors, though Luther himself was still alive. Rather than attack heretics, Eck discussed placidly the nature and scope of theology, the doctrine of the Trinity, the problem of the divine ideas, and the issue of predestination. In form and content the lectures provide an excellent example of late scholastic discourse, which is almost by definition nonpolemical. Eck cited Thomas, Scotus, and Ockham, but not Luther, Zwingli, or Bucer. Had we no other evidence for the dating of the *Enchiridion* and the lectures than their literary form and content, we would have been wholly justified in assuming that the nonpolemical lectures were an early work and the fiercely polemical *Enchiridion* a late one. But, of course, we would have been wrong. Even a tough-minded controversialist can turn his mind to other things.

Historians and detectives are similar in one other respect not explicitly mentioned by Josephine Tey, though the similarity would not, I think, have surprised her. Both construct second narratives. Sooner or later, historians, like their fictional counterparts in Tey's novel, must sort out the relevant evidence from the great picaresque narrative of history and say as briefly and clearly as they can what they think the evidence means. Of course, historians are not usually participants in the events they describe, and in that important respect they differ from Hercule Poirot and Sherlock Holmes. In a good detective story the investigator often arrives on the scene before the plot has completely run its course. More victims may die. The narrative may take fresh twists and turns, baffling the reader and even furrowing the brows of the nearly omniscient Poirot and Holmes.

But historians who work, as I do, in late medieval and early modern sources always arrive on the scene too late, after all the actors are dead and all the trails are cold, to unravel a mystery for which there is too little evidence or far too much. Historians cannot sit quietly in the corner of a café and simply watch suspects as they go about their daily duties. In that respect criminal investigators have an advantage that historians can only approximate through a vigorous use of their imaginations.

However, historians have one advantage denied even to the most astute detective. They know from the very beginning how things will turn out. They know because they live on this side of the events. They may engage in a teleological suspension of this knowledge in order to write, say, a history of France after Napoleon's return from his first exile in Elba. Indeed, they must suppress their knowledge if they ever hope to re-create the unsettled and excited atmosphere in Paris prior to the battle of Waterloo. No one present at the time in Paris, London, or Berlin knew how things would turn out in the end, even if some predictions were correct.

But historians know. They cannot not know. Daniel Patrick Moynihan once observed that "everyone is entitled to his own opinion, but not to his own facts." Historians know that Wellington and Blücher defeated Napoleon and terminated his brief restoration to power. Napoleon's contemporaries may have been surprised by his defeat, but historians cannot be. They know what the results were before they pull their chairs up to their desks. They are therefore professionally obligated to write a second narrative that takes that inescapable and perhaps at times even personally disagreeable knowledge into account.

It would, of course, be anachronistic to ascribe to the characters in the original historical setting a knowledge that they did not have at the time or to assume too readily a necessary and inevitable connection between early events and their later resolution. But resolution there was. Because of Waterloo my great-grandfather, who emigrated from Düsseldorf in the late nineteenth century, cheerfully announced to my mother that he was Prussian. He was Prussian because of the French defeat at Waterloo and the victors' subsequent decision to give the Rhineland, in which Düsseldorf is located, to Prussia.

It is not the task of historians to re-create the entire narrative of the past, even if such a re-creation were possible. Telling everything that happened is the task of chroniclers, not historians. Nor is it, taken by itself, an anachronistic act to reassess the past in the light of its immediate and longer-term consequences. Historians write second, not first narratives, that make sense of the past by keeping in mind how things turned out. The old ideal of Benjamin Jowett, that "Scripture has one meaning—the meaning which it had in the mind of Prophet or Evangelist who first uttered or wrote, to the hearers or readers who first received it," is therefore insufficiently historical.[11] Aside from the absurdity of an argument that assumes the complete passivity of the first hearers and their amazing unanimity in discerning the mind of the Prophet or Evangelist (an illusion easily refuted by anyone who has ever lectured or preached), Jowett omits altogether from the historian's task the historian's knowledge how things ended. But just as the defeat of Napoleon had consequences that provide an indispensable framework for a historical evaluation of his life and times, so, too, does the prophesying of the prophets and the preaching of the apostles. Historians worry no less than the early Christian fathers did about how things turn out.

If Jowett were correct, the only thing that would matter in American constitutional history would be the original debates at the constitutional convention. All questions of meaning should be referred to the events of that time. But the

American Constitution was drafted against the background of centuries of English case and statutory law, to say nothing of the impact of English political history from King John to George III. Since then it has been the fundamental legal charter of an energetic society. It must therefore now be read by scholars in the light of two centuries of American judicial precedents and legislation. Equal protection under the law, for example, has taken on meanings that were assuredly not in the minds of the original drafters but are fully consonant with the principles they had embraced. Constitutional history is therefore not an exercise in the phenomenology of constitutional conventions, nor can history be reduced to the search for original intentions, important as that study may be. The history of the Constitution is the story of the origins, development, and consequences of the fundamental law of the United States. All of it, and not some part of it, belongs to the historian's task.

IV

I do not want to suggest that, by pointing out similarities in the work of criminal investigators and professional historians, I fail to see the differences between them. Mystery stories, after all, have one conclusion, whereas the Bible has two. A good mystery ends shortly after the principal investigator recites his or her second narrative, whereas the great ramshackle narrative of world history blundered on as though nothing much had been resolved, even after the apostles offered their second narrative. By then, of course, things had changed. Gentiles in large numbers were incorporated into the long narrative of Israel's history with its God. Unlike the second narrative of mystery writers, the second narrative of the early church was directed toward both the past and the future. It not only clarified what had happened but also cast light on the unfinished narrative. But the story itself did not stop, even though the apostles thought it would do so very shortly. It kept on as before, stretching into what appeared to be an indeterminate future.

Nor would I want to suggest that either the New Testament writers or the early Christian fathers were engaged in the writing of critical history. "The appeal of Christianity to history," as Father Georges Florovsky once remarked in my hearing, "is not necessarily an appeal to historians." Yet all three—investigators, historians, and theologians—are confronted from time to time with the task of taming into submission a large and sprawling narrative that seems to lack any unity or cohesion. Each will construct in such circumstances a second narrative that purports to explain briefly what has actually been going on in the larger story. This second narrative must take into account how things have turned out in the end as well as how they began and developed over time. If the second narrative is convincingly constructed, it displaces all rival narratives and provides the indispensable framework for understanding and evaluating all prior events.

But a second narrative, because it purports to make sense of things, must itself make sense. What makes a second narrative convincing, whether on the lips of detectives like Inspector Morse or historians like Eamon Duffy, is that it "saves the appearances;" that is, accounts for all the relevant phenomena. It is pointless to accuse the butler of poisoning the Founder's Reserve Port if at the time it was opened he was on holiday in Brighton. It may prove incorrect to suggest that J. R. R. Tolkien had the discovery of atomic energy in mind when he wrote the *Lord of the Rings* trilogy, if it is true that (as C. S. Lewis, who was in an especially good position to know, has pointed out) the plot of Tolkien's novels had been developed prior to the production of the first atomic bomb. Hypotheses, however plausible, can nevertheless be false. In the end explanations must really explain. Unless second narratives account for the big narrative that spawned them, they are useless.

V

No analogy is perfect, and I can well understand if some objections to the analogy I have used in this essay have already occurred in the minds of readers otherwise sympathetic with my line of argument. Mystery stories, however ramshackle their first narratives, are generally written by one author in a limited period of time, whereas the Bible was written over a long period of time by many authors, most of whom did not know each other. Furthermore, the relationship between first and second narratives, which I use to characterize the relationship between the Old and New Testament, is in fact internal to each as well. The prophets offer their own second narratives to make sense of the earlier traditions they inherited, and the apostles are not altogether certain what the coming of Christ means for the future of Israel. Reevaluating what happened earlier in the light of subsequent events is characteristic of the Bible as such and not merely of the relationship between the testaments.

In the end, all an analogy can do is compare an aspect of A with an aspect of B in order to clarify something about A that might not otherwise be noticed. A good analogy can stimulate readers to fresh thinking by showing that two things which are not usually thought of together may be in some respects surprisingly similar. The comparison is bound to break down once the reader moves past the limited point the analogy makes into other aspects of the relationship between the terms in the analogy. Analogy depends for its force on difference as well as similarity. A is to B as C is to D, but A and B are not C and D and never will be.

I have argued two simple propositions in this essay and want to conclude with a third. The first proposition is that the analogy with mystery stories provides a useful way for approaching premodern biblical exegesis. There is a similarity between the kerygmatic retelling of the larger biblical story in the New Testament and the crisp retelling of the mystery narrative by the principal investigator in a novel by P. D. James or Agatha Christie. The kerygmatic retelling is summarized in the early church in the rule of faith, an equally crisp second narrative that purports to be key to the larger whole. There are, of course, differences between them. The second narrative of the mystery novelist is the product of rational reflection on a wide range of evidence, a good deal of which was present in the beginning for anyone who had eyes to see it. The second narrative of the early Christian church was based primarily on later events—that is to say, on what early Christians thought had happened in the life, death, and resurrection of Jesus Christ. But once both second narratives are in place, it is impossible to understand earlier events apart from them. In the order of being, the second narrative comes last. In the order of knowing, it comes first. That is why both mystery stories and the biblical documents are best understood by reading the last chapter first.

My second proposition is that historians, too, are involved in the writing of second narratives in which the knowledge of the way things turned out plays a significant role. It would, of course, be anachronistic to ascribe to the characters in the story a knowledge of how things would turn out as the events themselves were unfolding. But it is not anachronistic for historians to write history in the light of their knowledge, not only of how it unfolded, but also of how it ended. Unlike detectives and apostles, historians rarely feel confident that their second narratives are definitive and incapable of further improvement. But it is also true that historians attempt to write their second narratives as though they were definitive, neglecting no relevant category of evidence. Sooner or later all historians, including biblical scholars, succumb to the almost irresistible urge to imitate Miss Marple or Inspector Morse. They will invite a circle of concerned friends into the drawing room (or, more likely, classroom or seminar) to hear the second narrative they have pieced together to make sense of the evidence they have discovered. Every historian, like every successful investigator, has a second narrative to offer. It is, after all, what the craft of history is about.

My third proposition is fairly modest. I am inclined to think that biblical scholars who are also Christian theologians should worry less about anachronism and more about the quality of the second narratives they have constructed. I can well understand why biblical scholars are wary of a traditional exegesis that ascribes to characters in the Bible, especially characters in the Old Testament, an explicit knowledge of the finer points of Christian theology. Such explicit knowledge would have been impossible for them at the time. But I do not have to believe that second Isaiah had an explicit knowledge of the crucifixion of Jesus of Nazareth to believe that he was part of a larger narrative that finds its final, though not its sole, meaning in Christ. Like many of the characters in a mystery novel, Isaiah had something else on his mind. But the meaning of his work cannot be limited to the narrow boundaries of his explicit intention. Viewed from the perspective of the way things turned out, his oracles were revealed to have added dimensions of significance that no one could have guessed at the time. It is not anachronistic to believe such added dimensions of meaning exist. It is only good exegesis.

3

Inclusive Language
and the Trinity

Some Christians have become concerned about the use of inclusive
language in public worship. The traditional reference to God as
Father, Son, and Holy Spirit, with its strongly patriarchal overtones,
has troubled Christians who feel that more neutral language should
be used in the church's confessions and acts of public worship.
Various solutions and remedies have been suggested. One of the less
radical proposals is embodied in a new version of the "Gloria Patri,"
which has been adopted by some congregations. The words run as
follows:

> Glory be to our Creator,
> Praise to our Redeemer, Lord
> Glory be to our Sustainer,
> Ever three and ever one,
> As it was in the beginning,
> Ever shall be, amen.

On the face of it, there seems to be nothing objectionable in
this formulation. It is certainly appropriate in every generation for
Christians to praise the activity of God as creator, redeemer, and
sustainer. It is also appropriate for Christian congregations to try
to find ways to use inclusive language in worship as long as the
substance of the Christian faith can be preserved. Women have
suffered from discrimination and repression in Western culture, not
least at the hands of Christian churches. The use of more inclusive

language is one way the church can repent of its sins and begin to lead a godly, righteous, and holy life.

The difficulty with this "Gloria" is that it is put forward as a trinitarian confession ("ever three and ever one"), when it is nothing of the kind. The doctrine of the Trinity is not merely the teaching that God is three in his historical self-revelation to us, while remaining one God, but that in the mystery of the unity of his inner life God is three to himself as well. It is an affirmation of the nature of unconditioned reality and not merely about the nature of revelation. Trinity is, like predestination, a doctrine that does not make complete sense in itself but does make luminous sense of other things.

"Creator," "redeemer," and "sustainer" refer to historical operations of God. To affirm that one God acted in these three roles is at best subtrinitarian and at worst a repetition of the old Sabellian heresy. Furthermore, if "creator" is looked upon as an exact replacement for "Father," "redeemer" for "Son," and "sustainer" for "Holy Spirit," then both too much and too little is claimed for each person of the Trinity. If the Father is only creator and not redeemer and sustainer, if the Son is only redeemer and not creator and sustainer, if the Holy Spirit is only sustainer and not creator and redeemer, then the Bible becomes unintelligible. What does John mean when he speaks of the Logos as the one through whom all things were made? What does Isaiah mean when he celebrates Yahweh as redeemer? What does the church have in mind when it prays, "Veni creator spiritus"? You can see rather quickly why the church adopted the theological principle that the works of God *ad extra*, that is, directed outside himself, are indivisible.

The last phrase, "as it was in the beginning, ever shall be, amen," is also confusing if it is posited of the historical operations of God. Do the authors of the revised "Gloria" intend to confess that God is eternally creator? If so, do they intend to affirm the eternity of creation as an indispensable companion of God, along the lines described by Tertullian in his controversy with Hermogenes? It is difficult to tell just what is meant when language whose reference is temporal is substituted for language whose reference is suprahistorical. Very probably the intention is to save the trinitarian formulation, while removing nothing more than the offending noninclusive language. Unfortunately, the results do not match the good intentions. It is clear, in other words, that if we are going to revise our language of worship, we have to pick up the debate where it left off and not proceed as though such a debate never took place.

What I propose to do in this essay is to take a look at the doctrine of the Trinity in historical perspective. Why did the church confess that God is both one and three, and what theological purposes did this doctrine serve? Obviously,

I cannot hope in such a brief chapter to say everything that could be said about this subject, but I want to suggest several main themes that need to be considered in any further debate about this issue.

I

The doctrine of the Trinity is not a biblical doctrine in the sense that it is directly taught in the New Testament. What one finds in the New Testament is the apostolic preaching of a God revealed as Father, Son, and Holy Spirit, together with the ancient confession of Israel that God is one. The doctrine of the Trinity is a product of the church's reflection on its own proclamation. How can it confess that God is one without obscuring or confusing the threeness of God's self-revelation? How can it confess that God is three without lapsing into polytheism? In accounting for its own proclamation and in avoiding the twin dangers of unitarianism and polytheism, the church found that the doctrine of the Trinity clarified not only the church's understanding of God but a number of other doctrinal problems as well.

Take, for example, the problem of the intelligibility of the Bible. Fairly early on, heretical movements in the church attempted to offer alternative readings of the Bible that interpreted salvation as a rescue of divine fragments embedded in the soul from the world of matter or that pitted the redeemer God of the New Testament against the creator God of the Old. These alternative readings were opposed by Irenaeus and Tertullian, among others, who argued that the mere possession of a violin did not make one a violinist. To understand the Bible correctly, one must understand its underlying structure.[1]

These theologians had in mind certain clever people in the late Roman world who liked to compose poems by taking lines from established poets and combining them in a new way. They would take lines from, say, the first, fourth, and fifth books of Virgil's *Aeneid*, add a few lines from his *Eclogues*, and create a new poem. If one were to ask whether every line in the poem had been written by Virgil, the answer would be yes. Not a single verse in the poem had been composed by the anonymous "poet"; every word was authentic Virgil. But if one were to ask whether Virgil had written the poem, the answer would be a resounding no. Every line was from Virgil, yet Virgil had not written the poem. What had changed was the underlying pattern, the architectonic structure of the whole.

Irenaeus and Tertullian compared the heretics to these clever drawing-room poets. Every word they cite in their writings is from the Bible, yet their teaching is not biblical. What has changed is the underlying pattern, the unifying structural principle, the *skopos* of the whole. Only if the Bible is cited and interpreted in accordance with its underlying structure will it speak once again with the authentic voice of the prophets and apostles.

What is the underlying pattern of the Bible? It is summarized in the expanded baptismal confession: "I believe in God the Father Almighty, maker of heaven and earth; and in Jesus Christ his only Son our Lord . . . [and] in the Holy Spirit." This confession is regarded as both the underlying structure of the whole Bible and the purest distillate of its teaching. The Bible is about God, Father, Son, and Holy Spirit. Not to interpret it from that perspective is to misinterpret it.

How can the church be certain that it has the right hermeneutical key to the Bible, that it is interpreting the Bible from the right perspective? Irenaeus answers that question by referring to lists of bishops the church has preserved to validate its teaching. The bishops in the present who teach their flocks to read the Bible as the self-revelation of God under the three names were taught by bishops who were in turn taught by the apostles themselves. Only two generations separated Irenaeus from Christ. The church, therefore, is not only the inheritor of documents from the apostolic age; it is the beneficiary of a living teaching tradition initiated by the apostles.

The conviction that the Bible was to be read in this way left the church face to face with the real trinitarian problem: How were the three names to be reconciled with the confession that God is one? A number of solutions were proposed and found wanting.

The Arians in the fourth century proposed to reconcile the names of God with traditional monotheism by arguing that the Son is metaphysically inferior to the Father, a divine being, to be sure, but not God in the same sense that the Father is God. The Son is the first creature of God, superior to all other creatures and the agent of their creation, but still subordinate to the Father from whom he derives. Objections to this view took many forms, not the least of which was the complaint that the Arian heresy did not adequately account for the biblical texts that ascribe deity to the Son. The Arians lost themselves in details of biblical exegesis but failed to provide an explanation large enough to account for all the biblical data.

Sabellius in the third century provided a rival explanation. He conceded that the Son was fully God but looked upon the names, Father, Son, and Spirit, as attributes rather than as persons. Or to put that differently, he argued that God played many roles in history and that the three names were masks that God wore in the performance of those roles. Like Sir Alec Guinness, who played an entire family in the 1949 British movie *Kind Hearts and Coronets*, God is capable of assuming different guises at different times in the course of his self-manifestation in history.

This view also created exegetical difficulties. The story of the baptism of Jesus forms a case in point. According to the Evangelist, when Jesus is baptized, the Father says that Jesus is his well-beloved Son, and the Spirit descends on him like a dove (Mark 1:9–11). While Sabellians can explain how God can play different roles at different times, they cannot explain how God can play three different roles at the same time. Nor can they account for the prayer life of Jesus, at least for his last agonizing prayers in Gethsemane and on the cross. Unless there are real relations between the Father and the Son and not merely imaginary relations, the prayers of Jesus seem a curious charade.

Problems such as these led the church to conclude that the Bible is unintelligible unless God is not only three to us but also three to himself. While there is one God, that God exists in society. Such society is reflected in the historical self-revelation of God and his activity as Father, Son, and Spirit, but is not exhausted by it. Trinity is not merely a doctrine of how God acts; it is a doctrine of who and what God is. Therefore it can only be described by language appropriate to the verb "is"; namely, the language of being.

The appropriation by the church of metaphysical language about God does not represent a Hellenistic corruption of the simple Hebraic gospel of Jesus and his love. The New Testament itself, with its proclamation of one God under the three names, compels the church to speak metaphysically of God. One has only to read the accounts of the baptism of Jesus (Mark 1:9–11; Matt. 3:16–17; Luke 3:21–22), the language of the great commission (Matt. 28:19; Acts 1:7–8), the last discourse of Christ with his disciples (John 15:1–27, 16:1–15), or the Pauline and deutero-Pauline references to the work of the Spirit, Christ, and God (Rom. 8:9–11; 1 Cor. 12:4–6; 2 Cor. 13:14; Gal. 4:4–7; 2 Thess. 2:13–14; Eph. 4:4–6) to realize how swiftly one is forced by the text to confront questions about the being as well as the activity of God. Without the ontological Trinity, the church cannot adequately account for such texts. The church is obliged to confess the Trinity because it is committed to the public interpretation of the Bible.

II

The doctrine of the Trinity has also had an immediate bearing on the church's understanding of the sacraments and their role in human salvation. That bearing is obvious in the case of baptism, since Christians are baptized in the name of the Father, Son, and Holy Spirit. It is less obvious, but no less important, in the case of the Eucharist. The early opponents of the Arians saw this point and pressed it hard.

To understand the Greek insistence that the doctrine of the Trinity is practical because it touches on the central acts of worship of the Christian community, one must bear in mind the understanding of the drama of redemption embraced by the fourth-century theologians. Modern Catholic and Protestant Christians tend to think of redemption as primarily a matter of sin and forgiveness. Human beings have sinned against God and other human beings, and need to be pardoned. Greek Christians, on the other hand, tended to think of redemption primarily as victory over death and human mortality.

As the Greeks saw it, the principal human predicament from which there is no escape is the brutal fact of death. Death is not a gentle release from the world of materiality in which we have been imprisoned, but the last great enemy that threatens to thwart the purposes of God and to deprive human existence of all meaning. We are branches on a dying tree called Adam, whose roots have been cut. Its trunk is still sending out fresh shoots, but the signs of life are deceptive; the fresh shoots are, to use the phrase of Dylan Thomas, "green and dying." Cut off from the source of life, the whole human race is given over to death.

Only God is his own autonomous and endless source of life. It is therefore necessary for the branches to be cut off from the dying tree called Adam and transplanted in God, the endless source of inexhaustible life. But how can such transplantation take place? It is here that the doctrines of Trinity and incarnation become crucial.

The dying branches of Adam are cut off by baptism and transplanted into Christ. Because Christ is the Son and therefore fully God, he can serve as the source of life for human beings united to him by faith and baptism. Because Christ is the offspring of Mary and therefore fully human, it is possible for human beings to be so united to him. If he were not human, such a union would be impossible. If he were not God, such a union would be pointless.

The Eucharist is the sacrament through which this union is nurtured and perfected. Through the Eucharist the Son is present in his divine nature (the doctrine of the Trinity) and his human natures (the doctrine of the incarnation). As baptism and faith communicated life to the human soul, so, too, the Eucharist by a kind of reverse metabolism communicates life to the human body. Other food is digested by Christian believers, but the Eucharist as a heavenly food digests its own communicants, making them immortal and giving them a share in resurrection life.

All of this realistic language is used to combat views of the sonship of Christ that can be accommodated to a moralistic view of human salvation. Adoptionists taught, for example, that Jesus was a human being who merited adoption as a Son of God by his exemplary moral behavior. The implication of this view was that ordinary human beings could merit becoming sons and daughters of God by imitating the life of Jesus and conforming their behavior to his. Recent research has uncovered a similar mind-set among the Arians.

The doctrine of the Trinity is articulated in opposition to the myth that human beings can redeem themselves by exemplary moral conduct or that the initiative for human redemption comes from below. The story of Jesus is not the story of a human being who achieves elevation to sonship by his meritorious obedience to the will of God, but of a divine Son who condescends to assume human flesh in order to set right a situation that could have been corrected in no other way. What is at stake in the doctrine of the Trinity is not merely an understanding of the nature of God, but a vision of the nature of human salvation.

III

Augustine attempted to make the doctrine of the Trinity rationally comprehensible by drawing on analogies from human experience. Just as a human being has understanding, memory, and will without ceasing to be a single human personality, so, too, God is Father, Son, and Spirit without ceasing to be one God. In fact, argued Augustine, one would expect human nature to reflect a certain threefoldness-in-unity, since human beings were made in the image of a triune God. The image of God is by definition an image of the Trinity.

Probably the most important analogy that Augustine drew was an analogy between the inner life of God and the act of love. The act of loving requires for its completion a lover, a beloved, and the bond of love. In the inner life of the Trinity, the Father is the lover, the Son is the beloved, and the Holy Spirit is the mutual bond of Love that binds them. The use of this analogy had an important consequence for Christian discourse about God.

It offered one of the clearest explanations ever conceived of the aseity of God, that is, of the independence of God from creation and of the perfection of God's life apart from anything outside itself. Just as lovers need nothing but each other and the love that binds them, so God was complete in himself prior to creation, requiring nothing outside himself for his perfection. If that is true, then both creation and redemption are graces, unmerited gifts of God, who needed neither to create nor to redeem. While God cannot will his own nonexistence and cannot exist otherwise than as a Trinity (since that is a matter of nature and not of will), God has an absolute right to create nothing outside himself.

It was precisely this point that the Greek theologian Origen was unwilling to grant. Since God is eternal and immutable, God must always have been what he is now. Since God is now known as creator, he must always have been creator. The idea of a God who was inactive and not therefore eternally creating was absurd to Origen. If God is an eternal creator, then the world is an eternal companion of God. To affirm the opposite is to affirm a potential in the being of God that has never been actualized. A contingent world implies a mutable God. Origen sees no other possible conclusion.

Athanasius recognized that Origen had failed to separate the problem of the generation of the Son by the Father from the problem of the creation of the world.[2] The absolute being of God and the contingent being of the world are two radically dissimilar modes of existence. The relationship between Father and Son is eternal and necessary; the relationship between God and the world is contingent and voluntary. The mystery of God is that he cannot not exist; the mystery of creation is that it need not have existed at all.

In the movie *Tin Men*, one of the salesman tells another that he was recently impressed at a salad bar by the sudden realization of the probable existence of God. "All those vegetables," he says, "coming out of the earth—and I hadn't even gotten to the fruits." This exchange leads to one of the great comic scenes in the movie, in which the salesman to whom he has spoken prays in front of a salad bar like a priest at an altar. While all of this is proposed in great good fun and without any intention of being serious, the screenwriter has actually touched on a central theme of trinitarian theology: the richness and diversity of creation as an illustration of the goodness of God, who created as a gift for others what he did not need for himself.

That insight is lost if we focus on the historical activity of God as creator and dismiss all talk of an ontological Trinity. It is, of course, a good thing to confess that God is creator; it is even better to confess with Augustine the aseity of God, who made the cosmos for the sheer joy of giving it to others. Nothing in the world is there by necessity; everything is there by choice. Nothing in the world exists because God could not live without it; everything—at least everything good—exists as a gift. I cannot properly enjoy an ear of corn or a walk in the cool evening breezes or conversation with old friends unless and until I know that it is the personal gift of a good God, who gave to me what he was under no compulsion to give. The Christian confession of one God eternally subsisting in three persons is a confession of the gratuitous goodness of all good things.

IV

This brief survey of trinitarian theology has given us, I think, some guidelines by which to test inclusive language reformulations of the doctrine of the Trinity.

Does the new language account in a more comprehensive or penetrating way for the biblical data than the old language did? Does it offer a vision of salvation compatible with Christian tradition? Does it protect the transcendence of God and the goodness of the created order? If it does, it ought to be gladly embraced by all. If it does not, it ought to be rejected.

I have already indicated why I feel that the triad "creator, redeemer, and sustainer" will not do as a substitute for the older language of "Father, Son, and Holy Spirit." This does not mean that such language cannot be used in Christian worship, but only that it cannot be used in such a way as to give the impression that it is trinitarian language. Not all names of God are trinitarian names; some are names of operations. "Creator," "redeemer," "sustainer" are operational or economic names. But trinitarian language is ontological language. It is the language of God's being, not of God's doing.

As the language of God's being, it is more primitive, more foundational, more inescapable than the language of God's doing. God was Father before he was creator (I am speaking logically rather than temporally). He would have been Father even if he had never created. "Father" represents God's relationship to God and only in a later and subordinate sense God's relationship to creatures. "Creator" never represents God's relationship to God, but solely God's relationship to creatures. God is Father by nature and creator by choice.

The commitment of the church to the ontological Trinity does not forbid it from using other names in the liturgy, such as the Good Shepherd, the True Vine, the Bread from Heaven, or even the Mother from whom we have been born and by whom we are comforted (Deut. 32:11; Ps. 131:2; Job 38:29; Isa. 42:14, 49:14–15, 66:13; Matt. 23:37; Luke 15:8–10; John 1:13, 3:5–8). Since there are no more Christians by natural birth but only by conversion, and since "born-again" Christian is a tautology, the Johannine image of the Holy Spirit as the mother who brings us to spiritual birth is a metaphor that ought to have played more of a role in Christian worship than it has. However, what is not permitted to the church is to abandon the use of trinitarian language for God or to substitute other names for the ontological names of Father, Son, and Spirit. To keep silence in a time of conflict over the doctrine of the Trinity is to commit what Karl Rahner calls "virtual heresy." To baptize or ordain in the economic names of creator, redeemer, and sustainer is to leave catholic Christianity for an enthusiastic sect.

Someone may object that no human language can capture the reality of God. That is, of course, true. The mystery of God always exceeds our intellectual grasp. God is beyond sexuality, beyond male and female, and the names of God have an analogical rather than a univocal signification. Christian theology has always insisted that apophatic theology, which proceeds by denial of what God is not, is higher than kataphatic theology, which proceeds by affirmation.

The implied counterproposition, however, is not true: namely, that because our affirmations cannot capture the mystery of God's being, it does not matter very much what we call God. I have spent a good deal of time in this chapter trying to show exactly how much was at stake in the use of trinitarian language by the church. Trinitarian theology influenced how Christians interpreted the Bible, how they understood the drama of redemption and their role in it, even how they valued the created world around them. Other, more inclusive ways of talking about God may serve to achieve the same ends, though the burden of proof in this as in all reconsiderations of Christian tradition rests on the aspiring reformers.

4

Creator God

The Debate on Intelligent Design

"Intelligent design" is the theory that the universe is too complex a place to be accounted for by an appeal to natural selection and the random processes of evolution—that some kind of overarching intellect must have been at work in the design of the natural order.

In principle, intelligent design is religion-neutral. The intelligent designer is not named, and no claim is made that the designer is the Christian God. But in fact, intelligent design is mainly advocated in America by conservative Christians, who regard the account of creation in the opening chapters of Genesis as a scientific description of the origin of the world.

When the members of the conservative school board of Dover, Pennsylvania, a small community near Harrisburg, required students to read a short statement concerning intelligent design before studying ninth-grade biology, they met stiff resistance from some parents and teachers. The result was a court case in Harrisburg that was eventually settled against the school board.

It is easy to understand why intelligent design appeals to conservative Christians. As long as all Christians, conservative and liberal alike, confess that their God is the "maker of heaven and earth" and the "creator of all things, visible and invisible," they are on record as supporters of what looks for all the world like intelligent design. Christians have always brushed aside the notion that the world is self-generating, a random concatenation of miscellaneous atoms accidentally thrown together by no one in particular and serving no larger purpose than their own survival. The first article of the Christian creed could not be clearer: the world exists by the will of God. No intelligent designer, no world.

What less conservative Christians are not committed to is the idea that intelligent design excludes the possibility of evolution. For example, the Roman Catholic Church has taken the informal position that evolution is one of the tools God used in the creation of the world. Christoph Cardinal Schönborn has even argued that a scientist who uses evolution as the grounds for atheism is speaking as an amateur theologian, not as a professional scientist. Science has no answer to the question of whether there is a God.

Nonfundamentalists are similarly skeptical of the idea that the biblical story of creation is a scientific account that should be read as literally as possible. As long ago as the third century the great biblical scholar Origen raised substantial doubts about whether a literal reading of the story made good theological sense. In his view, readers should distinguish stories that are both true and factual (like the story of the crucifixion of Jesus) from stories that are true, but not factual (like the parables of the Good Samaritan or the Prodigal Son). Was there actually a good Samaritan, who helped a Jew wounded by thieves, or a prodigal son, who wasted his father's substance in riotous living? Who knows and, even more importantly, who ultimately cares? The power of the stories is independent of the question of whether they actually happened in space and time.

The same is true for the account of creation. Origen could not believe that light and darkness existed before there were sun, moon, and stars. Or that the invisible and transcendent God took a daily stroll in the Garden of Eden to enjoy the evening breezes like a squire surveying his estates. Or that the maker of heaven and earth could not locate Adam and Eve when they hid from him, and had to ask them to show themselves.

These "absurdities" (as Origen labeled them) were unsubtle hints from God that he wanted the account of creation read in an altogether different way, not as history but as truth "in the semblance of history." Truth embedded in "the semblance of history" is truth conveyed through fiction. But truth conveyed through fiction is still God's truth. No one has an excuse not to pay attention to it.

After all, Origen was aware that it is possible to devote oneself to the study of the world and conclude that it was not made by God. Aristotle thought the world was eternal and had no beginning, while the Gnostics thought it was the result of an unplanned and unfortunate accident. Moreover, there are random cruelties in nature—tornadoes, hurricanes, tidal waves, disease—that seem easier to bear if no good God is posited.

But for Origen the truth embedded in the "semblance of history" was the teaching that God is the ultimate source of everything that exists. The details of how creation happened were unclear to him (though he had some ideas), but the fact that it occurred seemed to him beyond any doubt. Belief in a Creator was therefore for Origen a conclusion of faith grounded in a proper reading of scripture. It was intelligible, even rationally persuasive, to believers, but did not rest on reason alone.

Of course, there are always readers of the Bible—then as now—who miss even the broadest hints and insist on reading the creation story as straightforward history. Reading literally a text that God intended to be read nonliterally was regarded by Origen as a mark of spiritual immaturity, the consequences of which were never good.

But even if one were to set aside an overly literal reading of the creation story and reject the assumption that intelligent design and evolution are always mutually exclusive, other questions would still remain. Can an intelligent designer be known from the intelligent design of the world? And, if so, to what extent and by whom? Or, to put it somewhat differently, is knowledge of an intelligent designer public knowledge, equally accessible to all?

St. Thomas Aquinas thought that some things could be known by philosophers about God on the basis of reason alone. Rational reflection on the world could lead intelligent people with no religious commitments to the conclusion that there was a First Cause or Unmoved Mover responsible for the existence of this world and its progress toward its own natural ends. One could even call this First Cause "God." What one could not do on the basis of reason alone was conclude that the First Cause had created the world from nothing or redeemed it through Jesus Christ.

Thomas suggested that whatever philosophers learned about God from a study of the world was always fragmentary and mixed with errors. Even a lifetime study of the honeybee, one of God's smaller creatures, left philosophers with as many questions as answers. How much less could unaided human reason learn from nature about nature's God! Which is why Thomas argued for a supernatural self-revelation of God that corrected reason's errors and gave it a more complete and intellectually satisfying account of the world as God's creation.

John Calvin went further than Thomas by arguing that human reason had been damaged by sin. It was not merely reason's limitations that had to be overcome (as Thomas had argued), but reason's inescapable disorientation. Something had gone fundamentally wrong with the noetic machinery of the human mind.

In order to understand Calvin's argument, it may be useful to distinguish three terms: (a) the natural knowledge of God, (b) natural theology, and (c) a theology of nature. Calvin asked whether human beings have a natural knowledge of God (to which he answered yes); whether they can arrange what they know from nature into an intelligible pattern known as natural theology (to which he answered no); and whether redeemed—and only redeemed—human beings can construct a legitimate theology of nature by reclaiming nature as a useful source of the true knowledge of God (to which he again answered yes).

Part of Calvin's argument sounds like the current argument for intelligent design. God is a great craftsman (*opifex*) who has left the marks of his craftmanship on the world (*opificium*). While the world is never part of God (as pantheists mistakenly assume) and God remains transcendent at every point of contact with the universe, the world is nevertheless the theater of God's glory. When the psalmist wrote that "the heavens declare the glory of God and the firmament shows forth God's handiwork," he was describing a ceaseless activity that has never diminished, much less been terminated. Marks of God's glory—or, if you prefer, marks of God's intelligent design—are everywhere.

To which Calvin adds an idea from Cicero's *De natura deorum*. All human beings have what Cicero called a *sensus divinitatis*, an unshakable intuitive knowledge that there is a God, a feeling that back of the mystery of the being of the world lies the even greater mystery of the being of God. No one knows intuitively who this God may be or what this God may be like. But everyone knows intuitively that this God simply is.

The dramatic proof for Calvin that Cicero was right is the fact that even human beings who are not particularly religious turn instinctively to this unknown God in moments of crisis. Flood, pestilence, and war can drive otherwise irreligious men and women to prayer. This phenomenon of "foxhole religion" can be summarized in the old ditty "And bos'n Bill was an atheist still, except sometimes in the dark."

Less dramatic proof for Calvin lay in the spread of world religions. Wherever human beings can be found, there can also be found some form of religion. Calvin did not think that all human beings instinctively worshipped the true God. But in his view even the worship of lesser gods was valid evidence of a universal "sense of divinity."

All of which left Calvin with a difficult question: if the marks of God's intelligent design are ubiquitous, and if human beings know intuitively God exists, why are they so unresponsive to the world as the theater of God's glory?

The question brought Calvin back to St. Augustine's account of original sin. The doctrine of original sin is not the teaching that human beings have problems (though all human beings do). Original sin is the teaching that human beings are themselves the problem. Something has gone wrong with the human race at a level too deep for therapy. Did this so-called original sin have noetic consequences? Did it affect human knowing?

Theologians in Calvin's day who thought it did tended to argue that such impairment was in the use of what was known rather than in the faculty of knowing itself. Human beings could undoubtedly learn some truths about God from a study of nature. But as sinners they were sure to misuse what they knew.

Calvin was dissatisfied with this explanation. He was convinced that sin showed itself not only in the misuse of what was known but in the faculty of knowing itself. Human knowing had been skewed by human sin, though human beings had not been blinded by it. Blindness might have reduced human culpability for chronic misconduct. Something lesser, but no less dangerous, was at work.

Calvin used three images to describe what he had in mind. The first image compared what fallen human beings can learn about God from nature to the scattered sparks that dot the ground around a dying campfire. The sparks give neither heat nor light unless they are raked together. So, too, the sparklike moments of discernment of which fallen humanity is capable kindle neither affection nor insight unless they are drawn together into an intelligible pattern.

The second image presupposes the darkness of a lonely countryside as a storm is brewing. The moon and the stars are covered by thick clouds, and the only light available to the traveler crossing a meadow is provided by sudden flashes of lightening. Momentary flashes of light are better than no light at all, but they serve more as a warning of the traveler's predicament than as a useful guide out of it.

The third image is probably the most effective. Calvin compared sinners with an old man whose eyesight had been dimmed by age. To be sure, the old man can see a book that is handed to him, but he cannot read it. He can read it only if he is given his spectacles. So, too, fallen human beings cannot read the book of nature and learn about God without the assistance of the spectacles of scripture. The self-revelation of God in nature is only barely visible to eyes blurred by sin.

What fallen human beings can see are scattered sparks of truth, momentary flashes of illumination, and blurred pages from the book of nature. When sinners nevertheless try to construct out of these fragments a sound natural theology that points to the true God, they succeed only in assembling a picture of what Calvin called an idol, a deity who is not really God, only a cheap substitute for the real thing.

Nevertheless, Calvin remained optimistic about the recovery of nature as a reliable source of the knowledge of God for believers. In his view nature was only too willing to reveal its theological secrets to minds renewed by the Holy Spirit and eyes corrected by the spectacles of scripture. Unfortunately, there was for Calvin no public access to the knowledge of God through nature, absent the presence of grace.

"No public access to the knowledge of God through nature" brings us back to the current argument over intelligent design. Some issues in the debate are so modern that older Christian tradition has no wisdom to offer. Calvin never heard of Darwin, though he did know Lucretius and the Epicureans and would not have been entirely astonished by the arguments of some Darwinians. One can only say that he believed the development of nature was never random or ever outside the control of God.

Origen, however, enters the debate early when he warns against reading the creation account in Genesis as a scientific description of the world's beginnings. Not all advocates of intelligent design read the Bible this way, but some clearly do. Origen's suggestion that the creation story is true like the parables but not true like the Norman invasion of England seems eerily relevant. In his view, Genesis answers the question why the world exists, but not how it came to be.

The debate moves to familiar ground when advocates of intelligent design argue that one can proceed from an observation of what appear to be elements of design in nature to the affirmation of the existence of an intelligent designer. Advocates of this position claim that their argument is religiously neutral and does not violate the nonestablishment clause of the U.S. Constitution. After all, their argument for intelligent design does not identify the intelligent designer as the God of any particular religion. As they see it, their argument is a conclusion of reason alone based on empirical observation.

But the advocates of intelligent design cannot escape theology so easily. Whether they like it or not, what they have offered is a form of natural theology. Leaving God unnamed does not make their argument any less theological, especially when they claim that the elements of complex design they have observed in nature are present because of the activity of their unnamed intelligent designer.

Thomas Aquinas accepted a similar claim that reason unaided by faith could move from a consideration of causes and effects in nature to a consideration of the existence of an unnamed First Cause or Unmoved Mover. But Thomas knew that talk about "First Causes" and "Unmoved Movers" was nevertheless talk about God and belonged to natural theology. Natural theology was, for him, theology grounded in reason alone.

Calvin rejected out of hand the possibility (which Thomas allowed) of a successful natural theology. On his principles, advocates of intelligent design had reversed the proper order of knowing. People do not believe in an intelligent designer because they observe in nature the marks of intelligent design. Indeed, the opposite is true. People find intelligent design in the natural order, because they believe on other grounds in the existence of an intelligent designer.

On the one hand, Thomas offers an approach to intelligent design that leaves an opening for intellectuals like the columnist Charles Krauthammer, who admits he believes in some kind of intelligent design, but finds himself unable to identify the intelligent designer with any of the Gods currently on offer. He is also firmly convinced that intelligent design should not be confused with natural science.

On the other hand, Calvin offers what is probably a better account of the role actually played by intelligent design among its conservative advocates. Conservative advocates of intelligent design claim that anyone can be led to belief in an intelligent designer by a scientific study of nature. But that is unlikely to have been the path they themselves followed. As Christians they assumed the existence of an intelligent designer and read the evidence drawn from the natural order through the spectacles of their Christian faith. The results were not hard to predict.

But inadequate theology should not be allowed to discourage better. The good news is that mainline churches are not going to join the fundamentalist jihad against evolution. But that does not mean they can be indifferent to the doctrine of creation.

The world is, as Calvin correctly argued, the theater of God's glory. The heavens do declare the glory of God and the firmament does show forth God's handiwork. Christians have no excuse not to celebrate that fact. The more intelligently, the better.

5

Mary Reconsidered

Protestants have, on the whole, been extremely reluctant to talk about Mary, the mother of Jesus. Any Protestant theologian who suggested that Mary's role in the history of salvation might be an important theological issue would likely be informed that there are theological matters of more pressing concern to Protestant clergy and laity. Even the early fundamentalists who insisted on the Virgin Birth as one of the key fundamentals of the faith were less interested in Mary than in her virginity.

One can argue, of course, that the traditional Protestant reluctance to talk about Mary reflects the New Testament's reluctance to offer much information about her. The Bible really has little to say about Mary, and much of what it does say is not highly complimentary to her. She cannot seem to comprehend what her son is about and tries to interfere. Indeed, the blood relationship between Jesus and Mary appears to stand in the way of her faith relationship. When a woman says to Jesus (Luke 11:27), "Blessed is the womb that bore you and the breasts that you sucked," he responds, "Blessed rather are those who hear the word of God and keep it!" And when Jesus is notified (Mark 3:32) that "your mother and your brothers are outside, asking for you," he replies, "Whoever does the will of God is my brother, and sister, and mother." According to the witness of the New Testament, there is a distance between Jesus and his mother that can be bridged only by faith.

Luke's portrayal of Mary as humbly obedient when she learns she is to be mother of the Messiah and John's picture of her role at the cross are the high points of the New Testament witness to Mary. She is not at the center of the New Testament but at its periphery. At the time of the birth of Jesus and at the cross, Mary is not the initiator; she is the humble recipient and observer of the mysterious action of God. When Mary tries to intervene in the course of events, she is very much like Peter. She misunderstands what is happening and by her action stands in the way of the fulfillment of God's will.

But while the New Testament does not focus on Mary, it does have a number of impressive things to say about her. In the Gospel of Luke, Mary represents the remnant of Israel. When she breaks into song in the presence of her cousin Elizabeth, she sings the New Testament reformulation of the song of Hannah (1 Sam. 2:4–7): "The feeble gird on strength....Those who were hungry have ceased to hunger. The barren has borne seven.... The Lord ... brings low, he also exalts."

The virginity of Mary is a sign of the divine initiative. As God brought forth a son from Sarah, who was too old to bear a child, so he brings forth a son from Mary, who as yet has no husband. In establishing the covenant with Abraham, God acted by creating a possibility where no human possibility existed. In fulfilling the covenant with Abraham, God once again created a new possibility for men and women where no natural possibility could be found. Sarah was the recipient of a covenantal blessing: "And God said to Abraham, 'As for Sarai your wife...I will bless her, and...she shall be a mother of nations; kings of peoples shall come from her'" (Gen. 17:15, 16). This covenantal blessing is echoed in the words of Luke 1:28 ("Hail, O favored one, the Lord is with you!") and Luke 1:42 ("Blessed are you among women, and blessed is the fruit of your womb!").[1] Mary is a sign of the continuity of the people of God, of Israel and the church.

Of course, even very low-church Protestants do not wholly neglect Mary. The Apostles' Creed confesses that Jesus was born of the Virgin Mary, and thus, by the back door, Mary enters into Protestant worship. There is little in the New Testament about the Virgin Birth itself. Matthew and Luke speak of it; possibly John also, though that is open to question. Paul makes no mention of it.

Contemporary men and women, who have difficulty believing in any kind of miraculous birth, stumble in the creed over the word "virgin." The ancient church, though it knew perfectly well how babies are made, stumbled, not over the noun "virgin" but over the verb "born." Early Christians believed that God had intervened in human history, taken humanity upon himself, and become a Jewish child, though without surrendering his deity. The early Greeks who heard this message found such an action improper. It was improper that an uncreated God should link himself with something created in this way. What could a transcendent God have to do with human clay? The word "born" as applied to God was a terrible stumbling block for ancient non-Christians. It was extremely difficult for them to believe that Mary was a sign that God had decisively intervened in human history by taking flesh in Jesus of Nazareth. But the early church persisted with its awkward claims. In the end, early Christians were interested in Mary not for her own sake but as a sign, a guarantee of the reality of the incarnation. Although Mary was seen as the last of a covenantal line that began with Sarah and continued through Hannah and Elizabeth, affirmations about Mary were not so much about her as about her son. Mary was understood as a signpost pointing to Jesus Christ and to the reality of the intervention of God in human history.

The unbiblical reluctance of Protestants to deal with the figure of Mary may be understood as a reaction to certain later developments in the life of the church. In the Middle Ages as well as in the earlier age of the fathers, Mary increasingly became an object of interest in herself. I will not attempt to summarize all the ways in which Mary claimed the attention of medieval theologians, but only mention a few:

1. *Immaculate conception.* It is not really made clear in the New Testament why Mary should be the mother of Jesus Christ without the aid of a human father—unless, as John intimates in his description of regeneration as a kind of virgin birth, this marvelous act was intended to show that the advent of Jesus was not a human possibility but solely a divine one. If one can apply the text of John 1:13 to Jesus rather than the church, Jesus was born not by any human will and not through human cooperation but by the will of God alone.[2] And the sign for this is the virginity of Mary at the time of the birth of Jesus. Or perhaps, as Luke suggests, the Virgin Birth shows the extreme humility of Mary, who, precisely because she had no husband, occupied the bottom rung of Jewish society.

But this is speculation. The fact is, no theory is put forward to explain why Mary should be a virgin. Matthew stresses the idea that virgin birth fulfills the ancient prophecy of Isaiah 7:14, which only pushes the unanswered question further back in time: why was such a prophetic utterance made in the first place, and why was it applied to Jesus? Luke feels that the virgin birth is further vindication of the principle that "with God nothing will be impossible," though the primary vindication of that principle is the conception of John the Baptist in the barren womb of his mother Elizabeth (Luke 1:37).

In the absence of any clear explanation for the necessity of the Virgin Birth, the church began to devise theories. It connected procreation with lust and sin, and exalted virginity as a higher state of moral purity, as if a virgin could not be impure and as if procreation within marriage were not the will of God!

Furthermore, the transmission of original sin was believed to take place in procreation, though the sexual act itself was not looked upon as evil. Lust is sinful, and fallen humanity conceives in lust. At the moment of conception, sin is mysteriously transmitted to the child by means of the perverted self-regard that accompanies the biological act. By doing away with birth through procreation, so the theory ran, Jesus was preserved from the human predicament in which all find themselves. He is not involved in original sin. Therefore he is Emmanuel and can save his people from their sins.

But what about Mary? Isn't it fitting for the mother of Jesus also to be preserved from original sin? Wouldn't that contribute to the guarantee that her son could not be involved in hereditary sinfulness? If there is no sinful procreation and if the mother herself is preserved from original sin, then surely the Savior is free from all taint of sin.

The medieval church did not, of course, affirm that Mary was also born of a virgin (since there was no biblical evidence to support such a theory); rather, they argued that she was sanctified and preserved from sin through an immaculate conception. When some theologians (such as Thomas Aquinas) argued that to exempt Mary from sin would undercut the centrality of Jesus Christ as Redeemer,[3] they were told (by Duns Scotus, among others) that one gives greater honor to Jesus Christ by saying that he preserved the Virgin Mary from sin than by holding that he waited to save her only after she had fallen.

Modern Catholic theologians argue that the immaculate conception should not be divorced from the saving work of Christ. Mary was preserved from original sin, not apart from Christ, but as a pre-effect of his death and resurrection. Mary, like every other Christian, is "a lamb of Christ's redeeming." The immaculate conception does not undercut that reality.

Similarly, the dogma of the bodily assumption should not be seen in isolation from the church or its eschatological future. As God transformed Mary in body and soul, so God will transform all the redeemed. Mary is, in this sense, a sign of the completion of human redemption at the end of time.

2. *The maternity of Mary.* Mary is not simply a virgin; she is also a mother. And the medieval church rang the changes on that theme. God chose Mary to be the mother of Jesus Christ, as he once chose Abraham to be the father of his people, Israel. According to the Genesis account, when God made Adam he took the dust of the earth. But redemption begins, not with dust, but with the body of Mary. It is from her flesh that the Messiah comes. Mary is the second Eve, the fulfillment of Genesis 3:15.

God chose Mary. But Mary, according to medieval Catholic thought, merited that choice. She cooperates with God in becoming the mother of Jesus Christ. God does not use her as a potter uses clay or as he once used the dust of the earth from which he formed Adam. Mary has freedom of choice. She chooses to cooperate with God; she accepts the message of the angel in Luke's narrative; she gives her assent. That choice, that assent, that cooperation, is meritorious.

Mary is thus a type of the church. Like Mary, the church has freedom of choice, the ability to decide. God respects the human reality of the church. He does not deal with it as if it were inert clay. And the church's choice to cooperate with God is meritorious. God respects the creation he has made. He deals with it as a responsible covenant partner. And he graciously rewards the good works of that partner. God does not destroy human freedom but works with it.

Mary is also an example for the church. She obediently and humbly accepted the role God offered her, even though it brought her suffering. There is no obedience to God that does not involve some personal cost to oneself. The church is called to imitate Mary, her obedience and selfless love.

3. *Cooperation in redemption.* Mary is more than mother and virgin; she is also a covenant partner. At the cross Mary does not stand above or below her son; she stands beside him, sharing in his sorrows and suffering as only a mother can suffer. But for the good of the church and its redemption, Mary takes the suffering of her son upon herself. She offers him to God the Father for the sake of the church, even at the cost of her own spiritual torment. At the cross she is the bride of Christ. Through the sufferings of Mary and her son, the church is born. Jesus came from Mary's womb, but the church comes from her broken heart. All forsake Jesus and flee, all except Mary. She belongs to the faithful remnant of God's covenant people. It is not the case that all humanity has been faithless to God and that God finds a faithful covenant partner only in Jesus Christ. Mary, too, is faithful. She is the elect remnant. And from her faithfulness and the faithfulness of Jesus Christ, the redemption of the world is effected. As Mary consents to the Incarnation, so she consents to the cross, and by her consent and self-sacrifice she cooperates in the work of the redemption.

At this juncture one must not forget the analogy between Mary and the church. The church, like Mary, is also the mother of the faithful. A Christian is born in the womb of the church, nourished by its sacraments and teaching. Like Mary the church also stands by a cross, not the cross on Calvary but the cross over the altar. Like Mary the church offers Christ to the Father, in this case as a re-presentation of the body and blood of Christ for the sins of the people in the unbloody sacrifice of the Mass.

4. *Intercessor.* Mary is not only mother, virgin, and bride. She is also intercessor.[4] In the Middle Ages it became increasingly difficult for ordinary Christians to believe that Jesus Christ was really a man. People tended to think of him solely as divine, whatever orthodox teaching might say. Consequently,

he receded farther and farther into heaven and became more and more remote and inaccessible. Increasingly, it was Mary to whom people looked for compassion. Jesus Christ was a judge who spent his time scrutinizing Christians to make sure that they were using to best advantage the means of grace he had provided for them in the church and the sacraments.

A second development was closely related to this. Medieval Christians believed that Jesus Christ was the God-man and, as such, perfectly obedient to the will of God. But in this obedience he had an advantage over ordinary men and women. He could be obedient in the power of his divine nature. Ordinary mortals do not have this advantage. When they are tempted, they have no divine nature to give them the power to obey. How can Jesus, therefore, really understand the temptations that befall ordinary men and women? How can he have compassion on them? Mary, on the other hand, is wholly human. Originally to call Mary pure was simply to call attention to her freedom from the taint of sin. But this began to take on a new meaning. To call Mary a "pure" human being was to call her a *real* human being. She obeyed and pleased God without a divine nature. As a real human being Mary can have pity on people in their sins and temptations. One should therefore pray to the compassionate Mary; she will pray to her son; and her son cannot really deny his mother's requests. This medieval vision of the role of Mary is a vision that early Protestants were unable to affirm or could only affirm in part. Mary as one who cooperates with God or who participates in the redemption of the world was an alien theological point of view for them. Protestants have always felt that human beings do not cooperate with God in the sense of earning merits. As Luther argued, good works are given, not to God, who does not need them, but to the neighbor, who clearly does. Any view in which Mary or the church offers something to God reverses the direction of both the original sacrifice of Jesus and the eucharistic sacrifice. The church does not offer a sacrifice to God to procure his benefits; the movement is all the other way. God offers himself to sinners in the suffering love of the cross. God nourishes the church through the benefits of Word and sacrament. The church does not offer anything to God, except perhaps gratitude and praise. God offers everything to believers, which they then gladly share with their neighbors. Mary as co-worker and Mary as co-offerer are images traditional Protestants think unbiblical.

Moreover, Protestants agree with Thomas Aquinas in opposing any Marian theology that seems to them to undercut the centrality of Jesus Christ. God found a faithful covenant partner only in his son.

1. On the other hand, Mary is a sign that God has really intervened in human history, really involved himself in human clay, human suffering, and human temptations. If there is a reason to reject a theology that is interested in

Mary in herself, there is no reason to reject one that makes affirmations about Mary as a signpost pointing away from her to God's mysterious activity in Jesus Christ. Mary is humble. She stands at the periphery of the New Testament, and there is where she should be. She is a sign pointing to Jesus Christ. Truly biblical Mariology is only another term for sound Christology.

2. Mary is also a sign that God's new act in Christ stands in historical continuity with his saving acts in the Old Testament. To be sure, Christian theologians are correct when they say that Jesus as Messiah undercuts many of the expectations of the Old Testament. In a very real sense the Messiah who came is not the Messiah who was expected. But Mary is a sign that the promise is fulfilled as well as transformed. With Simeon, Anna, Zechariah, Elizabeth, and John the Baptist, Mary belongs to the Old Testament people of God who stand on the threshold of fulfillment. A church that takes Mary seriously may say no not only to denials of Christ's humanity but also to denials of the authority of the Old Testament.

3. Furthermore, the image of Mary as a type or analogue of the church is not a bad one, so long as the whole biblical witness is taken. Mary is not only the obedient maiden, she is not only the sorrowing mother; she is also one who does not understand what God's purposes are, who intervenes when she ought to keep silent, who interferes and tries to thwart the purpose of God, who pleads the ties of filial affection when she should learn faith. And that is what the church is like. It is not only faithful; it is faithless. It is not only a custodian of God's truth; it falsifies the Word of God as well. The church, like Mary, is just and sinful alike, obedient and interfering, perceptive and opaque, faithful and faithless. It is false theology to say that Mary, because she is feminine, adds an element of compassion that is somehow missing in God. On the contrary, there are no bounds to the compassion of God, of which the compassion of Mary is a finite and limited reflection. Like the rest of the church, Mary loves because she was first beloved.Mary confesses that she is not worthy to be chosen by God. That is not false humility. It is the truth of every human being's situation before God. The words of Luther on his deathbed are applicable to Mary as well as to the church of which she is the type: "We are beggars; this is true." To recognize this fact is to give Mary her true honor, to recognize her rightful place in the history of salvation. Mary is the sign of the continuity and reality of God's saving activity. To understand this is to hear in the salutation the echo of the blessing of Sarah; to find in her song the strains of Hannah's; to say with Luke: "Hail, O favored one, the Lord is with you!... Blessed are you among women, and blessed is the fruit of your womb!"

6

The Catholic Luther

A Critical Reappraisal

That the theology of Martin Luther might in certain respects be
continuous with ancient and medieval Catholic tradition was not the
first proposition the sixteenth-century Catholic opponents of Luther
were keen to demonstrate. On the contrary, they were eager to prove
that Luther was the originator of a series of dangerous new ideas that
clashed with orthodox Catholic thought on almost every topic. After
all, Luther had rejected the authority of the pope, encouraged the
closure of monasteries, ridiculed Catholic princes, and married a
renegade nun. He had questioned the doctrine of transubstantiation
(though not the real presence of Christ in the Eucharist), denied the
possibility of human merit, and even suggested that sinners were
justified by faith alone.

Of course, there was a limited sense in which justification by
faith alone was a sound Catholic teaching. Any Catholic theologian
in the sixteenth century could freely admit that the thief on the cross
was justified solely by his faith, since a life of virtue informed by
charity was no longer possible for him to pursue. However, the
unique example of the dying thief was the exception that proved the
general rule. Ordinary sinners were justified, not by faith alone (as if
mere belief were ever enough), but by the faith that works by love—
that is, by the habit of charity that transforms sinners and sets them
in motion to serve God and do good works for the benefit of their
neighbors. When Luther was excommunicated by Pope Leo X and
condemned as an outlaw by the Catholic emperor Charles V, there

were plenty of Catholic theologians in Louvain, Paris, and Rome, to say nothing of Oxford and Cologne, who thought that Luther had gotten exactly what he deserved.

I

The first considered Catholic judgment about Luther (rendered while Luther was still a priest in good standing and an influential member of the Reformed Congregation of the Hermits of St. Augustine) was that he had fallen into heresy—or rather that he had fallen into a great dismal swamp of heresies and had induced other unsuspecting Christians to wade into the bog of false teaching after him. Luther was an archheretic, one who had attacked the doctrine of the Catholic Church at its heart and had encouraged others to do the same. Indeed, Luther's rebellion against the church had unwittingly spawned fresh heresies (like the rejection of infant baptism and the reduction of the eucharistic elements of bread and wine to the status of mere signs), errors of which even Luther himself disapproved.[1]

By heresy Luther's contemporaries did not mean a simple error in theological judgment. All theologians make mistakes. Some mistakes can be avoided, but others are attendant on the fact that human beings are asked to talk about transcendent divine realities in fallible human language. There is always an unavoidable gap between God's knowledge of God and any derivative human knowledge of God, a gap that Duns Scotus acknowledged when he distinguished between *theologia in se* (theology in itself) and *theologia in nobis* (theology in us). Heresy is therefore less a failure of knowledge than a problem of will. According to the sixteenth-century definition, a heretic is someone who persists in error after the church has patiently instructed him or her in correct Catholic teaching. Heretics stubbornly insist on their own way. As a matter of principle they will not be corrected by any external authority, however lofty. Although heretics frequently claimed for themselves the moral high ground and asserted the claims of conscience against repressive power, their orthodox opponents often suspected that they would not be corrected because of a defect in their character. Heretics were not in their judgment good people, and arch-heretics were even worse. Only a morally reprehensible person would voluntarily assume the role of a murderer of souls or remain so heedless of consequences.

Such a view of heresy may help to explain why so much of the early Catholic reaction to Luther took the form of character assassination. Of course, the sixteenth century was not a polite age. Indeed, it was, if anything, a golden age of invective in which the phrase "polite disagreement" was regarded as an oxymoron. Still, the attempt to discredit Luther's teaching not by refuting it but by discrediting his character seems to have rested on the conviction that only a morally flawed human being could have attacked the church so ferociously.

Johannes Cochlaeus, one of Luther's early Catholic opponents, published in 1549, three years after Luther's death, a widely read and deeply influential book, *Commentary on the Acts and Writings of Dr. Martin Luther.*[2] Cochlaeus (whom Luther had once labeled Dr. Rotzlöffel—that is, Dr. Snot-spoon) assembled a large collection of scurrilous back-fence gossip about Luther and anecdotes of doubtful provenance. It was Cochlaeus who was the source of the rumor, later picked up by Erik Erikson in *Young Man Luther*, that Luther had suffered a severe cataleptic fit in the Augustinian friary at Erfurt. It was also Cochlaeus who suggested in a parody of the Gospel account of the birth of Jesus that Luther's mother was a woman of loose sexual morals who worked as an attendant in a public bathhouse, where she was seduced by a demon. Cochlaeus charged that it was this demon, and not Hans Luther, who was Martin's true father.

Perhaps the most famous story is the account by Cochlaeus of the origin of the Reformation. According to this account Luther needed a new cowl, since his old cowl was worn and threadbare. He was, after all, a district vicar in the Augustinian Order in charge of ten priories and a professor *in Biblia* on the theological faculty at the University of Wittenberg. He needed to look reasonably well attired for his public duties. When his colleagues in the Augustinian house in Wittenberg dared him to attack the preaching of indulgences in the neighboring territories controlled by Duke George of Saxony, Luther obliged them by accepting the bet in an amount sufficient to buy a new cowl. The Ninety-five Theses were written not because Luther was serious about the theological questions at stake or even cared about them at all, but because he needed forty-two guilders to replenish his shabby wardrobe.

Lack of theological seriousness was the least of Luther's moral failings. He was a drunkard, a lecher, and a glutton, who rebelled against Rome, apostatized from his vows, and defiled a nun. Cochlaeus could find nothing whatever to praise in Luther's moral character. In the end the Protestant Reformation was for Cochlaeus a tangle of discredited heresies that found their origin in the dangerously flawed moral character of the principal architect of the Protestant Revolt, the former Observant Augustinian friar, Dr. Martin Luther.

According to the Catholic historian Adolf Herte the picture of Luther drawn by Cochlaeus captured the ordinary Catholic imagination and dominated Catholic discourse until the end of the nineteenth century. The critical Catholic reassessment of Luther began in the twentieth century with the publication in 1904 of a careful study entitled *Luther und Luthertum in der ersten*

Entwicklung by the German Dominican historian Heinrich Denifle.[3] As the Vatican archivist Denifle had access to a student copy of Luther's unpublished "Lectures on Romans" delivered in Wittenberg in 1515–16. Using these unpublished lectures and other writings Denifle undertook a detailed reassessment of Luther's theology from Luther's own writings. "My only source for Luther," claimed Denifle, "was Luther himself."

In the preface to the Latin edition of his collected works published in 1545 Luther confessed that he had been troubled as a young theologian by the single word *iustitia*, a word variously translated in English as "justice" or "righteousness." In Romans 1:16–17 St. Paul had announced to his readers that the *iustitia Dei*, "the righteousness or justice of God," had been revealed in the Gospel. Luther reported that all his teachers at Erfurt and Wittenberg had taught him that this passage referred to what Luther called the active righteousness of God. It referred, in other words, to what God is and does: namely, that God is righteous and will punish wicked sinners justly. Whereas Luther was not inclined to dispute the claim that God was a righteous judge, he was unable to see how such an announcement by Paul was good news for sinners, especially for sinners like Luther who were troubled in their consciences about their own failings. However, after meditating on this passage for an extended period of time, Luther reported that he had had a sudden insight into its meaning that revolutionized his thinking. He realized that Paul was referring not to the active righteousness of God, but to what Luther called God's passive righteousness. Passive righteousness is not what God is, but what God gives to sinners. In other words, Paul was announcing not that God was a righteous judge who punishes sinners (however true that may be), but that God is a merciful Father who gives unworthy sinners the righteousness they otherwise lack. *Iustitia passiva* is the righteousness with which God makes unjust sinners just. Such an announcement was indeed good news for sinners, and it no longer astonished Luther that St. Paul wished to celebrate it.

Denifle, who was a distinguished medievalist in his own right, searched medieval commentators to see whether Luther's claim about the Catholic interpretation of Romans 1:16–17 could be substantiated. Contrary to Luther's claim, Denifle could find no medieval commentator who thought Romans 1:16–17 referred to the active righteousness of God. On the contrary, the overwhelming consensus among medieval commentators was that St. Paul was speaking about the passive righteousness with which a merciful God makes undeserving sinners righteous. That Luther thought otherwise and thereby misrepresented the medieval Catholic tradition on St. Paul provided for Denifle compelling evidence, if any evidence were still needed by the faithful, that Luther was theologically incompetent.

Such a judgment may not seem to the casual reader like a great step forward in the Catholic reevaluation of Luther, but it represents an important shift from an exclusive focus on Luther's moral character to an active engagement with Luther's theology. Not that Denifle abandoned entirely the Cochlaeus tradition of character assassination! On the contrary, Denifle repeated several moral charges against Luther (including, among others, the clearly false charge that Luther, like Henry VIII and Francis I, was syphilitic). He underscored these charges with a zest and passion that belied his reputation as a dispassionate reader of complex texts from the past. "Luther," cried Denifle, "there is nothing divine in you!" Be that as it may, Denifle nevertheless thought it worth his while to argue with Luther theologically.

In 1911–12 Hartmann Grisar, a Jesuit historian, published a multivolume psychological study of Luther.[4] Unlike Cochlaeus, who argued that the Reformation had its origin in Luther's flawed moral character, or Denifle, who added the charge of Luther's theological incompetence to the older charge of his moral turpitude, Grisar posited that the Reformation found its real origin in Luther's disturbed psyche. Luther demonstrated again and again throughout his career that he had a pathological hatred of good works. His coping mechanism for dealing with this irrational hatred, argued Grisar, was his construction of an unbiblical and uncatholic doctrine of justification by faith alone, a doctrine completely without precedent in the antecedent Christian tradition. Had Luther not been disturbed psychologically, he might never have constructed the doctrine of justification by faith alone or misled thousands of the Catholic faithful into heresy and schism. Of course, even Grisar, with his psychological theory of the origin of the Reformation, could not bring himself to abandon entirely an attack on Luther's moral character, though he did soften it to some degree. He suggested, for example, rather than asserted, that Luther might have been syphilitic. Still, by introducing the question of what he regarded as Luther's psychological imbalance, Grisar had unwittingly introduced the question of diminished responsibility. If Luther suffered from a form of mental illness, he should not be portrayed any longer by Catholic theologians as the malevolent genius who voluntarily rebelled against Rome and engineered the most successful attack on the Catholic Church in its long history. Either he was desperately wicked or he was desperately ill, but he could not reasonably be regarded as both.

The most important breakthrough in the Catholic reassessment of Luther was the publication in 1939–40 of the two-volume study *Die Reformation in Deutschland,* by the German Catholic historian Joseph Lortz.[5] Lortz rejected entirely the Cochlaeus tradition of Luther scholarship and dismantled the ancient and by now antiquated Catholic myth of Luther's moral turpitude.

Luther had always claimed to have been a good monk, if somewhat overscrupulous, and Lortz found no evidence whatever to doubt his claim. Moreover, Lortz argued against Denifle and other Catholic theological detractors that Luther's theology was filled with profound insights into the Gospel, which Catholics could and should read to their own theological and spiritual benefit. No one had spoken more movingly or reflected more deeply than Luther on the theology of the cross. To be sure, Lortz did not believe that Catholics could embrace the whole of Luther's teaching, since on some issues he was clearly in error. But heresy on some issues did not mean heresy on all. For Catholic theologians and historians not to recognize Luther's theological genius was to miss a shining and obvious fact that they should have long since recognized and acknowledged.

Lortz attributed what he regarded as the tragedy of the Reformation to theological causes. It was Luther's misfortune to have been trained at Erfurt in the theology and philosophy of William Ockham, the fourteenth-century English Franciscan. Lortz regarded Ockhamism (or nominalism, as it is also called) as "fundamentally uncatholic." For Lortz the best intellectual expression of Catholicism was the theology and philosophy of the thirteenth-century Dominican Thomas Aquinas, the first scholastic doctor to have been declared a saint. Had Luther been educated at Cologne in Thomistic theology rather than at Erfurt in Ockhamism, he would have found in the Catholic scholastic tradition the theological resources to combat the Pelagianizing tendencies— that is, the overemphasis on human achievement at the expense of grace—in late medieval Ockhamism. Unfortunately, Luther read Gabriel Biel and Pierre d'Ailly, two of the more important late medieval interpreters of Ockham, rather than Thomas Aquinas. As a result Luther made what can only be regarded as a legitimate Catholic protest against the uncatholic theology in which he had been trained. Thomas Aquinas would undoubtedly have made a similar protest. But since Luther lacked the theological stability and balance the study of the theology of Thomas Aquinas would have given him, he overshouted himself into heresy. Had Luther only enrolled at Cologne, had he only been formed like John Capreolus and Ignatius Loyola in the theology of Thomas Aquinas, his story might have had a different and happier ending. The tragedy of the Reformation might very well have been averted and Europe spared its painful religious divisions and wars.

Some Catholic historians were willing to go even further than Lortz in their positive reassessment of Luther. Otto Pesch, while he was still a Dominican, wrote a massive comparison of the doctrine of justification in Thomas Aquinas and Martin Luther and concluded that their differences were more a matter of theological style than of theological substance. Thomas wrote sapiential theology and Luther existential, but their views on grace and justification were remarkably similar.[6]

Other historians, such as the Franciscan Reinoud Weijenborg, were drawn back to earlier modes of Luther interpretation.[7] Weijenborg was particularly attracted to the method of psychological analysis first attempted by Hartmann Grisar. Weijenborg began with the well-known fact that Luther's father opposed bitterly his son's ambition to become an Augustinian friar and only reluctantly agreed to his son's wishes. In order to elicit (or, perhaps more accurately, extort) his father's permission, Luther had concocted what Weijenborg regarded as a wholly fictitious miracle. He told his father, who leased a copper smelter in Mansfeld and who wanted desperately for his clever son to advance beyond his father and become a lawyer like his maternal uncles, that God had intervened miraculously in his life. He reported that he had made a spontaneous but nonetheless binding vow to St. Anne, the patron saint of copper miners, when he was nearly struck by lightening on the road from Mansfeld to Erfurt. Just outside the village of Stotternheim God had stopped Martin Luther in his tracks with a violent storm. "Help, St. Anne," Luther allegedly cried out in mortal terror, "I will become a monk!" Actually, argued Weijenborg, no such event occurred. The entire incident was a fabrication designed to deceive his father and wrest from him the permission he would never otherwise have given. Once safely ensconced in the Augustinian cloister Luther could not face up to the guilt of what he had done and so constructed the doctrine of justification by faith alone as a way to rationalize his lie to his father and his even more serious blasphemy of God.

Weijenborg's return to an older and essentially negative view of Luther was unable to derail the movement of Catholic historians through the door Lortz had opened. Historians did not have to agree with Lortz's assessment of the causes of the Reformation (Theophilus Böhner, for one, did not) to agree with him that the Reformation—especially the Reformation as embodied in the life and work of Martin Luther—was a theological event in the history of Western Christendom that could no longer be dismissed by Catholic historians as mere heresy. Furthermore, the reassessment at the Second Vatican Council of the Catholic Church's relationship to other Christian churches, Orthodox and Protestant, added a strong ecumenical impulse to the growing Catholic fascination with Luther. A series of important monographs on Luther were written during this period by Catholic authors—scholars such as Peter Manns, Erwin Iserloh, Stephan Pfürtner, Harry McSorley, Otto Pesch, and Jared Wicks. Their studies did not completely rehabilitate Luther as a Catholic theologian, though Manns and Pesch leaned in that direction. Most Catholic theologians, however sympathetic to Luther, had to admit that there were, after all, serious issues still remaining between Luther and Rome. But the new Catholic Luther research took Luther seriously as a profound, if problematic, theologian and attempted to understand his mind from the inside. By doing so, Catholic historians exorcised once and for all the spirit of Cochlaeus.

II

The Protestant assessment of Luther had always been more or less positive, even among Luther's Protestant opponents, many of whom deeply resented the fact that they had been roughly handled by Luther at one time or another. The Zurich theologians—to cite a famous example—once suggested to John Calvin that he was able to maintain his strongly positive view of Luther because unlike them he did not understand German. But even the German-speaking Swiss were willing to accept the general notion that Luther had been a prophet, sent from God, to inaugurate a new evangelical age.

The Lutherans wanted more. They were not satisfied to claim Luther as a prophet but wanted to emphasize his role as a teacher of true doctrine. Luther had decisively reformed Christian teaching not only on issues like justification that separated Catholics from Protestants but also on issues like the presence of Christ in the Eucharist that separated Lutherans from other Protestants. The late sixteenth-century Lutheran motto "Gottes Wort und Luthers Lehr vergehen nun und nimmermehr [God's Word and Luther's teaching will never pass away]" encapsulated the Lutheran determination to explain and defend Luther's teaching against all rival conceptions of the Gospel, Protestant or Catholic.

The Pietists in the late sixteenth and seventeenth centuries were a good deal less interested than the orthodox Lutherans in Luther as a teacher of true doctrine. They stressed instead Luther's role as a model of faith. Luther was for them the archetypal Christian believer. The Pietists were struck by Luther's report that he had suffered from various anxieties and temptations to despair (what he called his *Anfechtungen*, or "trials") before he broke through to a sudden assurance of faith. The Pietists took Luther's struggles as a universal pattern for all sinners struggling to break through the dark night of despair into the bright sunlight of faith. Just as Luther struggled for faith so, too, should all believers. What was most important for the Pietists was therefore not Luther's correct teaching (although they affirmed it) but his experience of faith.

Later Protestant interpreters painted a wide variety of changing images of Luther. Some saw Luther as a kind of German Thomas Jefferson, a champion of civil liberties who had defended the freedom and rights of the human conscience against the repressive power of church and Empire. Still others saw him as a symbol of German nationalism, a patriot who had warned his "dear Germans" against foreign manipulation. Wilhelm Dilthey at the beginning of the twentieth century hailed Luther's Reformation as an expression of the spirit of the modern age, while Ernst Troeltsch condemned it as an unfortunate regression into the Middle Ages. Luther has been claimed throughout the twentieth century as a patron for a dizzying array of Protestant theological positions, from Ritschlian liberalism and Bultmannian existentialism to confessional Lutheranism. If the Catholic tendency had once been to offer a single negative image of Luther, the Protestant tendency has been to offer a confusing array of positive ones, not all of which are entirely compatible with each other.[8]

The issue that dominated Protestant Luther research in the early and mid-twentieth century was the problem of Luther's *Turmerlebnis*, or "tower experience." Denifle had debunked this so-called tower experience or sudden insight into the meaning of Romans 1:16–17 as evidence of Luther's abysmal ignorance of the medieval theological tradition. Protestants, especially Protestant eager to show that something genuinely new had occurred in the theology of Martin Luther, attempted to define the exact nature of this experience and to date it more precisely. Scholars argued whether Luther had understood the *iustitia Dei* in a new Reformation sense as early as 1508 or as late as 1519. Heinrich Boehmer thought that Luther experienced his breakthrough in April or May 1513, while preparing his lecture on Psalm 30. Emanuel Hirsch argued that Luther was lecturing on Psalm 31:2 when his insight occurred, while Erich Vogelsang emphasized Luther's lecture on Psalm 70:2.[9] The emphasis in this intra-Protestant debate was on what historians regarded as Luther's new evangelical insight and not on his continuity, real or imagined, with the past. Ernst Bizer believed that Luther's sudden insight had liberated him from the monastic "humility-theology" of the middle ages, while Uuras Saarnivaara suggested it had delivered him from the mere Augustinianism espoused by most medieval theologians.[10]

In recent years the focus of discussion has shifted from a heavy, almost exclusive, emphasis on Luther's discontinuity with the past to a new fascination with his continuity. Ecumenically minded theologians interested in achieving renewed progress in Catholic-Protestant relations have again posed the question of Luther's relationship to his Catholic past. These theologians point to the Catholic elements in Luther's theology from his commitment to orthodox understandings of the doctrine of the Trinity and the two natures of Christ to his fierce defense of the real presence of Christ in the Eucharist. They underscore the indisputable fact that Luther did not intend to found a new church but only to renew the one, holy, catholic, and apostolic church in which he had been baptized. Does the charge of heresy against Luther, even in its watered-down modern form, rest on a tragic misunderstanding? Is it simply a question badly posed?

Many of Luther's Protestant contemporaries would have thought so at the time, since they were themselves engaged in a thorough redefinition of heresy. This redefinition rested in part on a new vision of the unfolding of church history and in part on older assumptions commonly held. Christians in the sixteenth century, Protestant and Catholic alike, shared with their ancestors a deep suspicion of anything that appeared to be a theological innovation. In his *Reply to Sadoleto*, John Calvin observed that he had been offended, while still a Catholic, by what he had regarded as the novelty of Protestant teaching and resisted it for an extended period out of reverence for the Catholic Church. Only when he had persuaded himself that Protestant teaching was in fact a restoration of the ancient Gospel rather than a theological novelty did he at last embrace it. Calvin did not dispute for a moment Cardinal Sadoleto's contention that theological novelty should at all costs be avoided. On that point Calvin and Sadoleto were in absolute agreement. Where they differed was in their definition of what constituted theological novelty.[11]

Sadoleto was convinced that heresy and schism had been introduced into the Catholic Church by the early Protestants. In his view dissidents like Calvin and Farel had preferred something new—namely, Luther's eccentric understanding of justification by faith alone—to something old—namely, the settled and ancient traditions of the Catholic Church on grace and penance. Sadoleto was serenely confident that the Catholic Church had preserved the ancient faith of the apostles in an unbroken tradition from the first century to the sixteenth and that any deviation from that living tradition as taught by Catholic bishops betrayed a heretical passion for novelty.

Calvin was no less confident that the Catholic Church had in fact deviated from ancient tradition during the Middle Ages, when through theological inattention and laxity it had embraced views not found in the New Testament or the writings of the early fathers. The early Protestants, all of whom shared Calvin's conviction that the Catholic Church had fallen from its original fidelity to apostolic teaching, not only subjected Catholic teaching to a searching critique that was both exegetical and patristic, but even compiled anthologies of quotations from the fathers to support their claims for the antiquity of Protestant teaching. The Protestant assault on Catholic teaching stimulated Catholic theologians to compile their own anthologies of quotations from the fathers to support their claim that the Catholic Church stood in unbroken continuity with the church of the early ecumenical councils. By 1566 more than eighty anthologies of patristic writings had been compiled by Catholics and Protestants alike. Melanchthon, for example, compiled an anthology on eucharistic theology, while Robert Barnes, Anton Corvinus, Erasmus Sarcerius, Guy de Brès, and Andreas Musculus offered anthologies on the subject of justification by faith.[12] Calvin, who prepared no such anthology, nevertheless laced his *Institutes of the Christian Religion* with citations from the early fathers. In short, the controversy between Protestant and Catholic was conceived less as a clash between a new theology and an old one than as a contest between two competing theological visions, each claiming (and each with a certain right to do so) to be more ancient than its rival. What remained unchallenged in this debate was the medieval assumption that what is older, in theology as in life generally, is superior to what is new.

If the question of Luther's catholicity is raised within the context of the sixteenth-century Protestant redefinition of heresy, the answer is a resounding yes. In the view of his evangelical allies Luther has acted as any authentically Catholic reformer should have acted. He has reformed the Catholic Church according to principles embedded in its oldest and therefore most authentic traditions. He has resisted ferociously theological innovations introduced into the faith and life of the church during the Middle Ages, from the sale of indulgences to the philosophical description of the real presence of Christ in the Eucharist as transubstantiation. In the clash between Luther and his critics, Luther could claim that he was "more ancient than thou" and that his opponents were mired in later theological innovation masquerading as ancient tradition. Luther's opponents thought that he was teaching novelty, because what he said was new to them. In fact, what Luther was doing—at least as Luther and his Protestant contemporaries understood it—was offering to the church a rich feast of its earliest traditions. That such ancient traditions struck his critics as novelty was in itself a sad commentary on the theological crisis in the sixteenth-century Catholic Church.

III

Of course, just as Catholic theologians have backed away from a far too simple reading of Luther as a dangerous heretic, so, too, have Protestant theologians retreated from what now seems a much too easy use of the adjective "catholic." Critical studies of the early church have forced both Catholic and Protestant scholars to admit that the question of continuity and discontinuity with ancient Christianity is a good deal more complex than it appeared in the sixteenth century, when Catholics and Protestants cheerfully compiled competing anthologies of quotations from the fathers on disputed issues, confident that the fathers, or at the very least a solid majority of the "sounder fathers," were safely in their corner.[13] Still, the questions posed in the sixteenth century remain relevant for ecumenical theology even if Protestants and Catholics might wish to answer them somewhat differently from their ancestors. How can one determine the extent of Luther's catholicity without first defining the norms according to which one would render judgment? If "catholic" means "whole" and "complete" as well as "universal," how many ingredients are needed to make a "whole" and "complete" Christian theologian? To put it crudely, is Luther complete enough? Or is he, if no longer the wildly dangerous heretic Catholics once feared, nevertheless an incomplete theologian, Christian but not Catholic, profound but not altogether trustworthy?

David Yeago wrote a much-quoted essay, "The Catholic Luther," that underscores the problem.[14] Yeago was writing against certain Protestants, especially Lutherans (even more especially Norwegian-American Lutherans), who wanted to see Luther as offering the church a decisive break with its Catholic past and proposing an entirely new approach to Christian thought and practice. "Behold, I am doing a new thing," cried the prophet Isaiah, "have you no eyes for it?" Against such Protestants Yeago argued that Luther's turn to reformation was also a turn to the sacraments and that the Protestant Luther showed distinct signs of being more Catholic in his regard for the sacraments than the observant Catholic friar he replaced. Catholic laity who are familiar with such sayings as "lost as a Jesuit in Lent" will not have difficulty believing that a member of a religious order in the Catholic Church might be liturgically challenged or that a member of a preaching order might reflect more on the preached Word than on the sacraments. However, what Yeago did not mention was that what he regarded as Luther's renewed and revitalized interest in the sacraments was an interest in three sacraments—baptism, keys, and Eucharist—and not seven; that he rejected the doctrine of transubstantiation (though not the doctrine of the real presence of Christ); and that his view of the priesthood of all believers undercut the special role of the hierarchical priesthood in the sacrament of penance. Are we to conclude that some Catholic tendencies are enough to qualify Luther as a Catholic theologian, when on other issues he defended positions that flatly contradicted the teaching of the Roman Catholic Church in the later canons and decrees of the Council of Trent?

Perhaps it is clear by now that the debate about Luther as a Catholic theologian is really, in the end, a debate about the catholicity of the churches that trace their origin to his reforming work. John Calvin introduced in the sixteenth century a phrase that was picked up in the twentieth century by the Second Vatican Council. The phrase is *vestigia ecclesiae*, traces of the church. When asked whether the Roman Catholic Church was still a true church of Jesus Christ, Calvin replied that he could see "traces of the church" in it. To understand what Calvin had in mind, imagine an attic stuffed with items that family members could not bring themselves to throw out: photo albums, 78 rpm records, an ancient sewing machine, magazines from the early twentieth century, boxes of letters from relatives who fought in the Civil War, a steamer trunk filled with programs and invitations from commencements, bar mitzvahs, first communions, and weddings, a dressmaker's dummy, collections of costume jewelry and perfume of doubtful ancestry, a Kaypro computer that still works, lithographs from deservedly unknown artists, disks containing antiquated software, a collection of baseball cards from the 1940s and 1950s, and unopened cartons containing goodness knows what. For Calvin, the Catholic Church was like this overstuffed attic. It had schlepped everything along from century to century—good traditions, bad traditions, bright ideas, bad ideas—until it could barely move under the weight of what it could not bring itself to discard. But in that great clutter there remained items that were precious and that did in fact belong to any true church of Christ—scripture, the preaching of the Gospel, baptism, genuine saints and martyrs, the ancient creeds, and the theological writings of great teachers, especially the early Christian fathers. Is the Catholic Church genuinely Catholic? On Calvin's reading he could not simply admit that it was; what he preferred to say was that he could see, among the unnecessary clutter of its traditions, teachings and practices that were genuine traces of a truly catholic church.

When the Second Vatican Council took over the language of Calvin to describe the Protestant churches, it had something else in mind. Imagine a remodeled Soldier Field on a raw February evening. Huddled at the fifty-yard line around a small fire there is a group of shivering Protestants. A cold breeze from the Illinois plain blows across the field and adds to the misery of this little group. They have excluded themselves from the fullness and warmth of the Catholic church, but they have managed to save some traces of authentic Catholicism before they departed—scripture, the preaching of the Gospel, baptism, genuine saints and martyrs, the ancient creeds, and the theological writings of great teachers, especially the early Christian fathers. Catholic Christians can only celebrate these traces of the church in the various Protestant churches, but they are left with the haunting question: why are the Protestants satisfied with so little?

In the two uses of this single phrase we have a clash between two competing visions of catholicity. The sharp disagreement since the sixteenth century between Catholics and Protestants over catholicity has been not so much a disagreement between a church that affirms the importance of catholicity and one that denies it as an argument between two Christian communities that understand catholicity in radically different ways.

In this disagreement the Catholic report on Martin Luther remains mixed. There are issues on which Luther is orthodox by any traditional standard of Catholic theology. Obvious examples are Luther's commitment to the doctrine of the Trinity and the two natures of Christ. Luther indicates at the beginning of the Smalcald Articles that he has no quarrel with either dogma, and theologians do well to take him as his word. Whatever disagreements may have existed between Luther and normative Catholic thought, they cannot be found in the Nicene Creed.

There are other issues on which Luther displays what one might call Catholic tendencies but does so without embracing Catholic teaching. Perhaps the clearest example of this phenomenon is Luther's understanding of the Eucharist. No one insists more firmly than Luther on the bodily presence of Christ in the Eucharist or attacks more vigorously any attempts to portray the Eucharist as a mere memorial of Christ's passion. The bread and wine do not merely signify Christ's body and blood; the consecrated bread and wine *are* Christ's body and blood. The operative verb for Luther is the verb *est* and not *significat*. At the same time, Luther rejects the doctrine of transubstantiation and offers the cup to the laity.

Finally, there are still other issues on which Luther differed so sharply with traditional Catholic thought that it was not possible in the sixteenth century, and still is not, to regard him as Catholic in the sense of adhering to accepted norms of Roman Catholic teaching. A prime example is Luther's studied indifference to the office of bishop and his rejection of the hierarchical priesthood. For Luther, all Christians by virtue of their baptism have the right to preach and preside at the sacraments. Or to translate that judgment into sharper Catholic language, even a simple Christian may in principle confect a valid Eucharist or hear confession and absolve from sin. For the sake of good order in the church, lay Christians cede to the properly called and ordained pastor the right to do in public what all laypersons (including women) have the inherent right to do, namely preach and preside.

Luther remains in this respect a stand-in for the churches he represents— partly agreeing with the Catholic Church, partly demonstrating laudable Catholic tendencies, and partly remaining stubbornly, even bafflingly, committed to positions that seem alien to any Catholic way of being Christian in the world. At the same time, Catholics and Protestant have learned not only to recognize in each other *vestigia ecclesiae* (by which they mean very different things) but also to learn from each other's differences. In a way that was not true in the sixteenth century—or at least never true to the same extent—each community can be richer for the existence of the other without abandoning the hope of eventual reunion. In the case of Luther this mutual enrichment might mean that even if Catholics are not quite able to embrace the old bomb-thrower (as Sir Geoffrey Elton once described him) as a wandering sheep of their own fold, they are at least able to recognize him as a sheep belonging to the same Shepherd. Unlike Denifle, modern Catholic theologians can find in Luther's writings an authentically Christian voice whose witness to a common Gospel can edify as well as irritate his Catholic readers. Considering that the story of the Catholic Luther started with an entirely unsympathetic Catholic account of a morally reprehensible archheretic, the modern Catholic narrative has already reached a happier, if not yet final, chapter.

7

Starting Over

Reformation and Conversion

The Reformation began, almost accidentally, as a debate over the meaning of the word "penitence." I say "accidentally" because the controversy over indulgences that set in motion the first stirrings of the Protestant Reformation seemed at the time far too limited and restrictive an issue on which to hang an entire program for the reform of the church. Only the year before, in 1516, Luther had composed a probing series of propositions on the hopeless condition of the human will without grace. He had followed it up in 1517 with a stinging barrage of ninety-seven theses against scholastic theology, theses that questioned with inescapable directness the church's use of the philosophy of Aristotle. But when the reform began, it was not Luther's attack on the method and conclusions of German academic theology but his criticism of the medieval theory of penance that captured the imagination of Europe.

Luther may only have intended to attack the extravagant claims that were being advanced by the Dominican John Tetzel, who was selling indulgences across the river in the part of Saxony under the jurisdiction of Duke George. But when Luther sat down at his desk to draw up his theses for debate, he found that he could not direct his criticisms against the narrower issue of indulgences without discussing the far broader question of the meaning of penitence.

The first thesis touches the central issue. Jesus Christ announced the imminent coming of the Kingdom of God and invited his listeners to repent. What exactly, Luther asked, did he have in mind? Did he mean to urge submission to the sacrament of penance? The Latin text of the New Testament, with its translation of the words of Jesus as *penitentiam agite* ("do penance"), certainly could give that impression. Underneath the Latin formula of the Vulgate, however, was the original Greek verb with its Hebrew antecedents. What was demanded by the preaching of Jesus was a "conversion," a "return," a "change of mind or intention," a fundamental turning of one's life to God, which begins but does not end with the first assent of the will to the Gospel.

Debate over the meaning of repentance is basic to Protestantism. From the early and formative decades of the Protestant Reformation through the Evangelical Awakening of the eighteenth century to the Bangkok Assembly in 1973 and the Lausanne Covenant of 1974, Protestants have returned again and again to the theme of penitence and conversion.

American Protestants are, of course, familiar with the tradition of the Evangelical Awakening, which has left its mark on American churches from the time of Edwards and Asbury to the present. Less well known, but no less important, are the reflections of the Protestant Reformers on the subject of repentance. While John Cotton was accustomed to "sweeten his mouth" with a passage from John Calvin before retiring, most American Christians are more familiar with Calvinism than with Calvin. American evangelism has been molded more by Edwards, Finney, Moody, Sunday, and Graham than by the theology of the sixteenth-century Reformers.

I

Common to almost all early Protestant discussions of repentance is a barely disguised hostility to every theory of conversion that stresses proper preparation for the reception of grace. Opposition to the notion of preparation for grace led Protestants inevitably to reject all medieval theologies of penance, the most Augustinian and restrained as well as the most Pelagian and careless. Nevertheless, it is fair to state that the form in which Luther first encountered a theory of preparation for grace was the form in which it was elaborated by Gabriel Biel in his *Collectorium* on the *Sentences* of Peter Lombard.

Biel was the first professor of theology at the University of Tübingen, a university founded in the last quarter of the fifteenth century. Biel was balanced, judicious, immensely learned, and deeply spiritual. He was famous not only inside Germany but outside it as well; his works appeared in French as well as in German editions. But his understanding of repentance, about which he wrote learnedly and at great length, was fundamentally defective, from Luther's point of view.

It was not that Biel failed to ground his arguments in the Bible or in the Augustinian tradition of the Western church. Indeed, Biel's ruminations on penitence are laced with frequent quotations from the Bible: James 4:8; Luke 11:9; Jeremiah 29:13; and, above all, Zechariah 1:3: "Turn to me, says the Lord of Hosts, and I will turn unto you." The text from Zechariah summed up in the briefest possible scope the essence of Biel's theology of penance.

As Biel saw matters, God had established a covenant with the church, the terms of which are proclaimed in the Gospel. God promises to give saving grace to everyone who meets the conditions of his covenant. What God demands of sinners under the terms of the covenant is, quite simply, that they love God above everything else and their neighbors as themselves. Sinners can do this, of course, because the demand of God is matched to human ability. Although sin has damaged the human natural capacity for loving God, it has not obliterated it. To put it in its crassest form, grace is a reward for exemplary moral virtue, a virtue that Biel, like Kant, thought lay in the power of the unconverted will.

Luther rejected categorically this understanding of preparation for grace. Morally good acts do not have a claim on the favor of God. The real preparation for grace, if one can use this language at all without occasioning misunderstanding, is the preparation that God has made by his election, calling, and gifts. Luther agreed with Biel that God has established a covenant, but it is a covenant whose basis is diametrically opposed to the covenant recommended by Biel.

Against Biel, Luther held that God promises to give his grace to "real sinners." "Real sinners" are people who are not merely sinners in fact (everyone, after all, is a sinner in that sense), but who ruefully acknowledge that they are sinners. "Real sinners" conform their own judgment of themselves to the unsettling judgment of God over them and by doing so justify God in his Word of merited condemnation and unmerited grace. Paradoxically, it is the "real sinner" who is justified by God and who knows both theoretically and experientially what repentance offers and demands. The Gospel as Luther conceived it is both easier and harder than the Gospel Biel offered. Being a real sinner is a condition that, on the face of it, anyone can meet; but it is harder because it demands rigorous honesty in the face of inconvenient truth. Penitents cannot prepare themselves for grace because they must be crucified by the Word of God's judgment and die. Repentance has to do with death and life and not merely with the resolute decision of an already good person like Biel to improve his frankly unimpeachable character.

Luther's objection to Biel's theory is not merely that it harbors a thoroughly unrealistic view of human nature, though that is part of his objection. Even more important for Luther than the fact that no one can live up to Biel's theory of repentance is the fact that no one is expected to. The Gospel does not demand moral virtue as the preparatory stage of conversion. Biel's view of the matter is not only unworkable; it is irrelevant. The sole precondition for authentic conversion is real sin; the sole preparation that matters is the preparation that God has made in the Gospel. In the end, it is not merely human vices that need forgiveness, but also human virtues.

The saying of Jesus that the whole have no need of a physician is a saying that the church has always had great difficulty in assimilating. It seems so much more reasonable to believe that God will be merciful to those people who meet certain prior expectations: the right ideology, the right sex or race, the right degree of devotion to the causes currently supported by the right elements in society. "But when we were right," Luther observed in one of his earliest writings, "God laughed at us in our rightness."[1] God's quarrel is with the whole human race and not merely with certain factions in it. Judgment falls not only on the theologically heterodox but also on the theologically pure. The one absolutely indispensable precondition for the reception of grace is not to be right— not even in the sense of theological orthodoxy—but to be sick. The Gospel is for real sinners.

II

The church provides the context within which authentic repentance can take place. It may seem surprising to lay so much stress on the church in early Protestant thought, since Protestants have often been regarded as religious individualists who affirmed the right of private judgment against the corporate power of the late medieval church. But in point of fact the late medieval church was the home of a private and individualistic piety, while Protestantism has been hopelessly social from the beginning. Whether talking of ordination or of eucharistic theory, Protestants have focused on the congregation rather than the individual as the fundamental reality from which theological reflection must proceed. Critics may accuse Protestants of talking about the church too much or of talking about it in the wrong way, but not of neglecting it.

The church can, of course, stand in the way of authentic conversion, and in his *Reply to Sadoleto*, Calvin accused the late medieval church of doing precisely that. In a lengthy bill of particulars Calvin charged the late medieval church with keeping people from repentance by the disunity of its life and the disorder of its teaching. In particular, the church had urged upon the faithful a duty of implicit faith in its own teaching authority, while, to use Calvin's vivid language, the "leaders of faith neither understood [the] Word nor greatly cared for it" but taught "doctrines sprung from the human brain." Not surprisingly, this "supine state of the pastors" led swiftly to the "stupidity of the people," who thought that the "highest veneration paid to [the] Word was to revere it at a distance, as a thing inaccessible, and abstain from all investigation of it."[2] Reverence for the church—any church—in its unreformed state can only impede progress toward the radical change of direction that is demanded by Jesus in the Gospels.

Even in the worst of times the church is, to use Calvin's favorite imagery, a mother and school, which nurtures and instructs men and women in the Christian faith. When confronted by the Augustine quotation "I would not have believed the Gospel if the authority of the Church had not moved me," Calvin agreed with it, much to the surprise of his conservative critics. The important thing, however, is not to quote Augustine—anyone armed with the *Milleloquium* can do that—but to know what he meant.

It is obvious what he did not mean. Augustine did not intend to teach that the authority of the church is so great, so metaphysically higher in the scale of being, that the Gospel derives its authority in a secondary fashion from the prior and more encompassing authority of the church. Augustine said that he would not have believed the Gospel if the authority of the church had not moved him; he did not say, or mean to imply, that he would not have believed the Gospel if a committee of bishops had not approved it. The authority of the Gospel is primary, and the authority of the church is secondary and derivative.

The authority of the church to which Augustine alluded is the authority of the holiness of its life and the faithfulness of its witness. In a word, Augustine was moved to trust the Gospel because he first trusted the people who told him about it. The Gospel is better than the church, but it is never found except in the human and therefore touching witness of the church. The church, like the Samaritan woman, tugs at the sleeve of the unbeliever and says: "Come, see a man, which told me all the things which ever I did: is not this the Christ?" That is the authority of the church, the authority of a faithful and self-effacing witness.

To this church has been committed the power of the keys, the power to bind and to loose the penitent from their sins. Yet it is a power that the church does and does not have. It does not have it in the sense that it is not a power that inheres in the community as a group, as color, weight, and texture are qualities of an object. But it does have it in the sense that as a community it proclaims by word and deed the authority of the Gospel. The Gospel, not the church, binds and looses from sins, and yet it does not do so apart from the church that bears it and bears witness to it.

Repentance—at least repentance in the sense in which it is recommended in the New Testament—is not a spontaneous religious emotion that springs up in the human heart without prior sufficient cause. It is a response to the message of God's judgment and grace, a message proclaimed by the church, the community established by God in which faith is formed. While the Gospel can and does reach outside the church, and while God is never limited in achieving his purposes to any instrumental means, nevertheless, the church is the principal sphere and context for authentic conversion. Repentance is, if you will not misunderstand me, a churchly function. Indeed, it is the perpetual activity of a church reformed by the Word of God.

III

The repentance to which a Christian is called is a continuous and lifelong process. While conversion begins, as everything in history does, at some point in time, the process of conversion is not completed until every aspect of the human personality is driven out into the light of God's severe mercy, judged and renewed. Conversion proceeds layer by layer, relationship by relationship, here a little, there a little, until the whole personality and not merely one side of it has been re-created by God. Conversion refers not only to the initial movement of faith, no matter how dramatic or revolutionary it may seem, but to the whole life of the believer and the network of relationships in which that life is entangled: personal, familial, social, economic, and political.

That is why the church is called a school. Faith is not only something we have; it is something we are learning. Mastery of the Greek alphabet is not the same thing as mastery of the *Odyssey*, yet mastery of the one proceeds from mastery of the other. The first moment of penitence initiates one into the school of faith, but the lessons to be learned can be grasped only by long and patient experience. To change the metaphor, conversion is not only the little wicket gate through which John Bunyan's pilgrim quickly passes as he abandons the City of Destruction; it is the entire pilgrimage to the Celestial City.

No aspect of Reformation teaching on penitence is more foreign to the American evangelical experience of the past two centuries than the stress on conversion as a process rather than as a crisis in human life. Evangelicals have always emphasized the initial moment of faith in which one passes from death to life, from darkness to light. This is a moment celebrated, recalled, and, when the experience fades, recaptured. While sanctification may be a process, conversion is the work of a moment.

The Protestant reformers did not agree, but that was not because they despised the first stirrings of faith or the resolute convictions of people who bore witness to what they had seen and heard. They did not agree because they had a somewhat different doctrine of sin and were convinced that sin was such a complex phenomenon and so intricately embedded in human thinking and willing that only a thousand conversions would root it out.

Or maybe I have put that too negatively. The Reformers were convinced that only those who love God can hate sin. A thoroughly unconverted sinner is a perfect child in his knowledge of sin. Only a saint knows what sin is, and therefore only a person who has progressed in the love of God can see with sufficient clarity the exact character of the sin that is distorting his life. It requires some growth in grace to repent properly. The more one grows in the love of God, the more perfect one's repentance. Mourners sitting on the anxious bench or filing into an inquirer's room have, unfortunately, only a child's-eye view of their own sin. Real repentance, real conversion of life, is an activity of the spiritually mature.

Repentance is consistently portrayed by the Reformers as a return to baptism, a return to the foundation of God's gifts and promises, which are generous enough to sustain us throughout our whole life. They must be reappropriated and reaffirmed; they cannot be superseded. By the process of repentance, of continuous conversion, we appropriate the mercy and gifts of God at a deeper level than we have ever experienced them before.

Perhaps the most striking image of baptism in early Protestant literature is the one offered by Huldrych Zwingli. Baptism is like the cowl or uniform that is given to a novice in a mendicant order. The young boy of twelve in a Franciscan or a Dominican priory is a member of his order from the very moment he accepts its uniform and the obligations that wearing it entails. But he is not a Franciscan in the same sense as an older brother of eighty-two, who has worn the brown robe of St. Francis all his long and varied life. The young novice must grow up into the uniform he has been given. So, too, baptism is our uniform; we must grow up into it. It is cut for a far more generously proportioned figure than ours. But we will grow up into it as we are continuously converted at ever deeper levels of our personality by means of the Word of God. Conversion does not bypass baptism; it fits us to it, so that we take all that is offered and become all we profess.

IV

Every conversion has a price. Something is gained, but something is lost as well, and the loss may prove to be painful. There is a tendency in certain circles of American evangelicalism to offer the Gospel as the solution for pressing human problems without mentioning that there is another side to the question. The Gospel not only resolves problems that trouble us; it creates problems that we never had before and that we would gladly avoid.

Sometimes the problems are vocational. In the preface to his *Commentary on the Psalms*, published in 1557, Calvin, who was generally reluctant to offer any information about himself in his published works, broke his silence to talk about his sudden and unexpected conversion to Protestantism. In a brief passage of unusual candor Calvin confessed that his principal ambition both before and after his conversion was to lead the quiet life of a humanist scholar, alone with his books, his commentaries, and his grammars. Against his own personal preferences he was driven by God to assume a role in shaping history.

Sometimes life itself is at stake. It makes sober reading to examine the pages of the *Martyrs' Mirror* and to realize that almost none of the first generation of leaders of the Anabaptist moment lived to see that movement reach its tenth anniversary. Not all of the martyrs were Anabaptist; certainly not all were Protestant. From William Tyndale to Edmund Campion, from Robert Barnes to Thomas More, from Hugh Latimer to John Fisher, conversion to Christ in the sixteenth century could entail the loss of one's own life. The age could, and frequently did, exact a grisly price for heeding the radical call of Jesus to turn about in one's tracks and head in a diametrically opposite direction.

Yet most frequently the problems are what one might loosely call moral problems. Every human decision has its moral aspects, and since every human decision is qualified by obedience to the Gospel's demand for repentance and conversion, human life is somewhat more complicated than it was before. It is no longer possible simply to adopt the customary attitudes toward war or race or business or marriage or abortion or any other question that affects individual or corporate life. Every decision stands under the question posed by the words of Jesus: "Repent, for the Kingdom of God is at hand!"

Calvin describes the life of the converted by two ponderous phrases: mortification of the flesh and vivification of the Spirit. The first phrase is clear enough; it means death to the old way of thinking and acting. But the second phrase is the one not to be lost sight of. The death of the old is for the sake of the birth of a new reality.

Luther was fond of talking about the strange and proper work of God. The "strange work" refers to God's work of wrath and judgment; the "proper work" designates the work of mercy and renewal. Both were spoken of in the Bible, but they were not given equal emphasis. Their relationship is dialectical. God does the strange work of judgment and destruction for the sake of the proper work of mercy and love. The old, unrepentant, faithless, unconverted reality must be destroyed, but not as an end in itself. God destroys the old decadent self in order to create in its place a new reality almost too glorious to be imagined. Suffering is for the sake of joy.

V

These four themes from early Protestant thought—the denial of the possibility of preparation for the reception of grace, the insistence on the church as the context in which genuine repentance takes place, the description of conversion as a continuous and lifelong process, and the warning that there is no conversion that does not exact a price from the penitent—are certainly not the only themes that need to be considered by the church in the present as it ponders its own evangelistic mission. Indeed, they may even need to be corrected by insights derived from the Bible or other voices in the Christian tradition. But they are insights that cannot be lightly set aside. As Calvin observed, when we deal with repentance and the forgiveness of sins, we are dealing with "the sum of the gospel."[3]

8

Forgiving the Unforgivable Wrong

I thought I had lost the capacity to be shocked. After all, the slaughter of the innocents is nothing new. My wife and I have a dark memento of gratuitous cruelty to children: a poster from the Holocaust Museum that shows a group of Jewish children, already separated from their parents and waiting quietly for the freight trains that will take them to Auschwitz or Buchenwald, where—if they are lucky—they will suffer a swift death. After a while, news of fresh acts of violence against children loses its power to shock, even when it still dismays.

But the recent murder of young Amish girls in a one-room schoolhouse in Nickel Mines, Pennsylvania, slipped past the defenses I thought I had safely in place. The act seemed so unexpected, so random, so senselessly cruel, so out of place with the tranquil setting of the school or the peaceful ideals of the Amish themselves, that it was difficult to take in, much less to understand.

The shooter, Charles Carl Roberts, knew the Amish girls would not resist, though he brought restraints with him, just to be safe, especially since (as it appears) he intended to abuse them sexually before he murdered them. But the Amish schoolteacher, alarmed by his behavior, slipped out the back door, ran to a neighbor's house, and did what must have seemed to Roberts the un-Amish act of calling the police. Their unanticipated arrival upset his timetable and saved the girls from rape, if not from his angry gunfire.

Nonviolence is a way of life among the Amish, who, like the Mennonites, are descendants of a sixteenth-century radical Christian group called Anabaptists. Anabaptists were particularly impressed by Jesus' teaching on the subject of nonviolence. They read the commandments of Jesus to turn the other cheek, to renounce the sword, to return good for evil and to forgive one's enemies, as rules binding on all Christians and not just on some subgroup of the especially pious.

In their view Christians could not be soldiers, because soldiers are required to take human life in time of war, or magistrates, because magistrates are duty bound to order violence done in the name of justice. The command to use no violence against another human being and to forgive unjust wrongs was absolute and admitted of no exceptions. As the Lord's Prayer made perfectly clear to the Anabaptists (and to their Amish descendants), forgiveness is not extended to the unforgiving. "Forgive us as we forgive" is the intractable rule.

And so the Amish forgave Roberts for imprisoning their children, for maiming and murdering them, and even for intending to molest them while they were helplessly in his power. They forgave him, not because he had been driven by private demons or because his act was anything but heinous. They forgave him because they thought Jesus had told them to and they were not clever enough to think he didn't mean it.

Forgiveness is tough work, and forgiving the unforgivable unimaginably hard. Most of us, whatever our faith commitments or lack of them, would have to whisper a prayer—at least to "the close and holy darkness"—for the grace of a bad memory, before struggling to forgive such wrongs, or even wrongs much smaller.

But the Amish matched their words with deeds. They invited Roberts' widow to the funerals of their children, insisted that some of the money raised to help them be used to help her, and even attended the graveside service of the man who had so cruelly wrested their children from them.

By doing so, the unworldly but morally substantial Amish gave their worldly but morally less substantial fellow citizens a brief glimpse of a peaceable kingdom, where the lion lies down with the lamb, where swords will be beaten into plowshares, where violence ceases and a gentle magnanimity reigns. You can't say it is impossible or hopelessly utopian, because you have just seen it done.

9

The Domestication of Prophecy in the Early Reformation

Martin Luther was sometimes hailed as a prophet by his admirers in the sixteenth century.[1] By identifying Luther as a prophet, no one meant to suggest he was a visionary whose predictions of future events had proven uncannily accurate. If accurate predictions were the final test of a true prophet, Luther would have been something of a disappointment. The unanticipated twists and turns of his improbable life often took Luther by surprise and would have confounded any seer. Even his prediction that the world would soon end—since he could not imagine how the world could grow any worse or be more ripe for a last judgment—proved in the end to be false. Luther died in Eisleben in 1546, and the world continued on its merry way into an indeterminate future.

When Luther's allies called him a prophet, they were not calling attention to his ability to foretell the future. They knew perfectly well Luther claimed no private revelations from God. Their definition of prophecy was somewhat more mundane. A prophet for them was primarily a messenger from God, someone who like the ancient prophets of Israel carried an important and authoritative Word. In Luther's case, he was regarded as a prophet whose message had inaugurated a new evangelical age in the history of Christianity. Even if one differed with Luther over details—and many of his admirers did—no one could deny that his message had made a crucial difference. Had Luther remained silent, European history might very well have taken a different turn.[2]

Prophecy as a Transforming Word

There were, of course, a number of would-be reformers in the early years of the Reformation who claimed direct inspiration from God. Three of the most famous of these charismatic figures were the so-called Zwickau Prophets: Nicholas Storch, a weaver and lay preacher; Thomas Drechsel, a blacksmith of good character; and Markus Thomae (known more commonly as Stuebner), a sometime student at Wittenberg whose father owned a bathhouse. The leading figure of the three was clearly Storch, the weaver, who claimed to be instructed by the Holy Spirit (or by an inner Word) to oppose a religion that relied too much on such externals as sacraments and images of the saints. True Christianity is inward, argued Storch, and the truly devout rely on the inner voice of God.[3]

Luther, who thought himself second to none in his admiration for the work of the Holy Spirit in human life, nevertheless asserted that the inner activity of the Spirit is mediated by external signs, symbols, sacraments, and words.[4] The Word that God speaks to the human heart is always a mediated Word. It is invariably external before it is internal. The external Word provides a check on the tendency of human beings to confuse their inmost feelings with the voice of God.

Luther said as much in his polemical treatise *Wider die himmlischen Propheten*.[5] He ridiculed the prophets of inwardness, who pitted a fresh but untrustworthy inner Word against the ancient but reliable external Word of scripture. Nor was Luther convinced by Storch's constant appeal to the Holy Spirit. Indeed, in Luther's view the Zwickau Prophets had so frequently claimed to have heard the voice of the Holy Spirit that a disinterested observer might easily get the impression that "they had swallowed the Holy Spirit, feathers and all."

More important than Storch, Drechsel, and Stuebner was their radical pastor at St. Katherine's Church in Zwickau, Father Thomas Muentzer.[6] Muentzer was no admirer of Luther and called him such unflattering names as Doktor Lügner and Doktor Leisetritt (Dr. Liar and Dr. Pussyfoot). Muentzer differed sharply with Luther over nearly every issue. He could see no reason to think that God had ceased to make his will clear to believers by dreams, visions, and prophetic ecstasy. There were too many examples in the Old and New Testaments for Muentzer to concede that direct revelation by the Holy Spirit was impossible. He was therefore willing to defend in principle the proposition that fresh revelations from God do occur, even in Zwickau, and to offer in support his own claim that he had heard on more than one occasion the inner voice of God.

In actual practice, however, Muentzer was a good deal more conservative than his rhetoric implied. His extant works are full of biblical exegesis and notably devoid of fresh oracles from God. To be sure, Muentzer's exegesis is anything but standard, and his interpretation of some texts must have left his congregations breathless. But imaginative exegesis, however unconventional, is not the same thing as a direct vision from God. In the end, Muentzer in Zwickau was no Daniel in Babylon. He was an interpreter, offering fresh insight, rather than a seer, delivering fresh oracles.

Luther and Muentzer agreed about one thing, however. They agreed that Christianity was not a scribal religion. For Luther this meant that Christianity was ultimately about realities that stood outside the biblical text. These realities were inaccessible apart from the Bible, but the Bible was always a means to an end and never the end itself. In an unforgettable image Luther called scripture the "swaddling clothes" in which the Christ child was wrapped.[7] Luther saw no way to gain access to Christ apart from the biblical stories in which Christ was presented, but he warned that no one should confuse the wrapping with the priceless gift it contained. To master the biblical text and to miss its chief point was what Luther regarded as a fool's bargain.

What both Muentzer and Luther were listening for was the voice of the living God. To the extent they were intent on hearing that voice, they considered themselves less as scribes, custodians of a Word once spoken in the past, than as prophets, servants of a Word freshly spoken to their own generation. The principal issue between them was whether the voice of God was mediated by something external to the self. For Muentzer God spoke (or, at the very least, could speak) in a still small voice within. For Luther the Word God spoke afresh to the human heart had first been spoken by ancient prophets and apostles.

Which meant, of course, that Luther could not escape the scribal work he tended to regard as secondary. Even though careful work with texts was never more than a means to a larger end for Luther, it was nevertheless an essential means to that end. Accordingly, Luther's days were devoted to writing lectures and commentaries on the Bible, preaching on biblical texts, and even translating the Bible from Greek and Hebrew into Latin (the language of the classroom) and German (the language of the streets).

Luther observed that the Bible distinguished two kinds of words: *Heisselwörter*, or words that simply name and classify already existing things, and *Thettelwörter*, or words that effect whatever they signify.[8] When Adam named the creatures found in the Garden of Eden, he used *Heisselwörter*, language as a symbolic system that orders a reality it did not create. But when God created the world, he used *Thettelwörter*, language that is indistinguishable from reality-transforming deeds. "Let there be light," said God, according to the book of Genesis. "And there was light." As Psalm 33 put it in a gloss on Genesis, "God spoke and it was done."

What made the Bible such an extraordinary book from Luther's perspective was that it is about words that alter reality and do not merely describe it. The ancient prophets of Israel seemed to Luther to bear a reality-altering Word from God. Like God, who "spoke and it was done," prophets spoke a *Thettelwort* from God that changed whoever heard it—sometimes for the better, other times for the worse, but was never in vain, never without some effect. As with the prophets, so, too, with the later apostles and evangelists. Luther recommended that whoever wanted to hear the authentic voice of God should abandon reliance on what Luther regarded as an ill-defined and untrustworthy Inner Word and listen instead to the voices of the prophets and apostles recorded in scripture.

When Luther described the transforming Word of God as a *Thettelwort*, he was using language more commonly associated in medieval Christianity with the sacraments. Medieval Christians believed a sacrament is a sign that effects what it signifies. Baptism, for example, does not in their view merely signify a ritual cleansing from sin. It effects what it signifies by washing away the guilt and punishment of original sin, including, for adults, the guilt and punishment of any actual sins committed prior to baptism.

Preaching, however, was never accorded by medieval theologians the status of a sacrament. Sermons could—and should—instruct parishioners about the nature of the church's sacraments and even warn them about the dangers of neglecting their use. But sins were forgiven in medieval Christianity by attending to baptism and penance, not by listening to sermons, however eloquent or orthodox. Medieval preachers prepared their congregations to receive the grace offered through sacraments, but saving grace was offered through sacraments and not through preaching. The prophetic task of the preacher in medieval Christianity was subordinated to the sacramental role of the priest. Good preaching benefited the church, but sacraments were essential to its life.

Luther saw matters differently. The Word of God was a *Thettelwort*, not a *Heisselwort*. It was Word as deed, not Word as adjective. The Word first spoken directly by God, then indirectly through prophets and apostles, was a powerful sign that effected what it signified. The same God who said "Let there be light" also declared, "Your sins are forgiven you." Luther concluded that this Deed-Word of God is the fundamental sacrament and that baptism, Eucharist, and preaching are the three forms in which this fundamental sacrament is expressed in the practices of the church.

Baptism, as Luther pointed out in the *Small Catechism*, is not merely water; it is water joined to the transforming Word of God. Similarly, the Eucharist is not merely bread and wine; it is bread and wine joined to the same transforming Word. Even preaching is not merely human language; it is human language joined to and taken into the service of the Word of God. So far from subordinating the prophetic work of the church to its priestly functions, Luther redefined the priestly functions of the church in the light of its prophetic task. Priests, like prophets, bear the lively and life-giving Word of God to new generations.

Which meant, from Luther's perspective, that Muentzer and the Zwickau prophets had it all wrong. Storch thought sacraments were a distraction that made it more difficult to hear the voice of God. Like the other Zwickau Prophets, Storch advocated inwardness over external practice. God, in his view, spoke directly to the human heart without external signs and symbols. But it was precisely the external signs and symbols Storch denigrated that offered Luther what he regarded as the only possibility for men and women to hear again the voice of God.

Luther was therefore happy to be called a prophet as long as everyone understood that modern prophets were bearers of a Word that did not arise from their own inward spirituality or prophetic visions but was mediated to them through scripture. Unlike the ancient prophets of Israel, modern prophets were not the recipients of fresh oracles—Thomas Muentzer and the Zwickau Prophets to the contrary notwithstanding. But the fact that their prophetic proclamation was derived from scripture did not make it any less a lively and transforming Word from God.

As Luther's career makes plain, early Protestants were interested not only in a renewal of the study of the Bible in its original languages, but also in a renewal of its oral proclamation to the church. Preaching became such a central focus of the early Protestant movement that it overshadowed the celebration of the Eucharist, which had been the central focus of medieval worship for more than a millennium. Even sacraments were redefined as visible words of God. Heinrich Bullinger summed up the consensus of the early Protestants on their prophetic task when he wrote in the Second Helvetic Confession, "Praedicatio verbi dei est verbum dei [The preaching of the Word of God is the Word of God]." Luther could not have put it better.

Prophecy as a Craft

While Protestants supported the renewal of preaching, they arrived somewhat late on the scene. Already in the fifteenth century many of the so-called imperial free cities in the Holy Roman Empire had taken matters into their own hands. Weary of uninspired preaching, they had invited gifted preachers to serve as

Leutpriester (or people's priests) in their major churches. Unlike other parish clergy, the new class of skilled preachers was paid out of public funds rather than from church treasuries. They were excused from many of the pastoral duties other clergy were required to discharge in order to devote themselves to preparing sermons for Sundays and feast days.

The most famous of these *Leutpriester* was undoubtedly John Geiler of Kaysersberg, an Alsatian who preached in Strasbourg on the eve of the Reformation. Books of his sermons were immensely popular and circulated widely throughout German-speaking Europe. Geiler normally preached two sermons back to back on Sundays, each an hour long. One sermon was on the assigned pericopal lesson for the day and the other on a theme of Geiler's own choosing. Geiler once preached a famous thematic series on Sebastian Brant's *Ship of Fools*. His style could be fairly crisp. Commenting on war and peace, he observed: "Peace makes wealth, wealth makes one cocky, cockiness brings war, war brings poverty, poverty makes one humble, and humility establishes peace again."[9]

Geiler wanted to stress the importance of the prophetic task of preaching over the priestly task of presiding at the Eucharist. He did so by underlining the close link between preaching and the sacrament of penance. Preaching frequently casts the cold light of God's judgment on the failings and foibles of erring humanity, motivating the wayward members of Christ's flock to confess their sins to a priest. Penance, when correctly administered, is a powerful remedy for sin. It absolves sinners from mortal sins, that is, serious infractions of God's law. The Eucharist, on the other hand, can only cleanse sinners from minor faults known as venial sins.

The conclusion seemed clear to Geiler. As mortal sin is more important than venial sin, so penance, which dissolves mortal sin, is more important than the Eucharist, which cleanses from venial. Therefore the preacher who calls men and women to penance is more important than the priest who presides at Mass. It was an ingenious argument, but, on basis of Catholic principles, a theological nonstarter. Everyone knew that Eucharist was more important than penance because it was the one sacrament in which Christ himself was substantially present. There was no way to top that. In medieval Christendom the priest at the altar was always more important than the prophet in the pulpit.

Although early Protestants had to provide their own ideology of preaching, they could admire the skill exercised by the late medieval masters of the craft. Even the young Philip Melanchthon, who had never heard Geiler preach in person, nevertheless wrote a Latin elegy to mark the occasion of his death. After hearing a sermon by Huldrych Zwingli, who was at the time a *Leutpriester* in Einsiedeln (and not yet a Protestant), Caspar Hedio remarked that his preaching was "elegant, learned, weighty, rich, penetrating, and evangelical, clearly such as to return to the effect of the ancient theologians."[10] Without a doubt there was much to admire in the work of *Leutpriester* like Geiler and Zwingli, not least their learning and skill. Preaching, after all, is a craft and not merely a charism.

Preparation for preaching required a different, more demanding, education than preparation to preside over sacraments. Most medieval clergy, especially parish priests, were not university-trained. Clergy who studied at universities were often siphoned off for important posts in dioceses, religious orders, and government service. Protestants, however, wanted a preaching clergy who could read the Bible in Greek and Hebrew as well as in Latin translation and had studied rhetoric, philology, and the early Christian fathers. When Calvin preached—which he did as often as seven times a week—he took the Greek and Hebrew Bible with him into the pulpit and translated the text into French as he spoke. It was a model for what the leadership of the movement hoped would happen on the smaller parish level as well.

What the Protestants had in mind became particularly clear in Zurich, where Huldrych Zwingli, formerly of Einsiedeln, now a *Leutpriester* in the Grossmünster (and an increasingly influential Protestant reformer), established a regular seminar called *Prophezei*. Later Puritans called similar seminars in England, modeled on the Zurich archetype, "Prophesyings." The seminar combined in one event the continuing education of clergy, religious instruction for schoolboys, and theological education for the laity.

The clergy of the city and canton of Zurich, together with boys from the Latin school, gathered early in the morning in the choir of the Grossmünster. If the biblical passage under consideration were taken, say, from the book of Genesis, it would be read first in Hebrew, then in the Greek translation of the Septuagint, and finally in Latin. One minister had been assigned to give a thorough exposition of the text. A second had been delegated to respond briefly to the first exposition and to offer corrections and suggestions of his own. A third minister discussed how the text might best be preached to the laity—at which point the doors of the church were opened and a fourth minister shared with the local congregation the results of the morning's studies in an extempore homily.

Prophesying in Zurich required hard exegetical work on the part of the would-be prophet. While Storch was correct to think that prophets should be devout, he neglected to mention they should be learned as well. The medieval church had not required parish priests to master Greek and Hebrew and demanded only enough Latin to get by. But the early Protestants, who redefined pastoral ministry as a prophetic office, set the educational bar much higher. By inducting all Protestant ministers into what an earlier generation would have regarded as a preaching order, the early reformers increased the prestige of parish clergy, while excluding from their ranks worthy candidates who could not meet the new educational standards. It is a nice question whether St. Augustine, who could never get his mind around Greek, would have qualified for ordination in one of the new Protestant churches.

Christ as Prophet

The model prophet was, of course, Jesus Christ. The early church had already identified him as a greater prophet than Moses. In the view of early Christians, he had been anointed by the Holy Spirit to bear witness to the truth, even at the cost of his own life. According to the Gospel of Luke, his public ministry began with the reading of Isaiah 61 in the synagogue at Nazareth, a passage descriptive of a prophetic calling: "The Spirit of the Lord God is upon me, because the Lord has anointed me to bring good tidings to the afflicted; he has sent me to bind up the brokenhearted, to proclaim liberty to the captives, and the opening of the prison to those who are bound." The account of the baptism of Jesus by John in the Gospel of Matthew alludes to a similar anointing, when it mentions a descent of the Spirit "like a dove alighting on him." The book of Acts also identified Jesus as a prophet when it summarized a sermon of Peter in the Second Temple. According to Peter, Jesus was the prophet whom God had promised to raise up in the latter days. Although the Christology of the New Testament could hardly be summarized in the words of a liberal Protestant hymn, "O young and fearless Prophet of ancient Galilee, thy life is still a summons to serve humanity," it is nevertheless clear that the role of Jesus as a prophet was essential to the church's understanding of his identity.

Parish clergy in the later Middle Ages had not identified their work so much with Christ's role as prophet as with his role as priest. According to the book of Hebrews, Christ, who admittedly did not belong to the priestly tribe of Levi, was nevertheless described as a priest forever after the order of Melchizedek. Whenever Catholic priests were ordained, they believed they were inducted into that same nonlevitical order. Indeed, Christ shared his priesthood with them. It was not a common priesthood shared with the laity. Only a validly ordained priest could consecrate bread and wine in the confidence that God would transform the consecrated elements into Christ's body and blood. Every time parish clergy presided at the Eucharist, heard confession of sins, baptized the newly born, or anointed the dying, they were performing services of which Christ was the priestly source and archetype.

Protestants, on the other hand, identified with Christ as prophet, both because they regarded his priestly office as unique and unrepeatable and because they had redefined the priestly functions of the parish clergy as largely prophetic.

Just as preaching was the spoken Word of God, so, too, were the sacraments the Word of God in visible form. In order for preaching to be a transforming Word of God, it must, of course, be derived from scripture and conform to its central teaching. Christ as prophet—namely, as a teacher of saving truth—provided the norms according to which scripture could be properly understood and apart from which it would inevitably be misinterpreted.

The fact that Christ was the final and definitive teacher of saving truth put an end for early Protestants to all free prophecy, including the new oracles touted by the Zwickau Prophets. No one wanted to deny that fresh insight was always possible, even from Storch and Muentzer. What Luther and Zwingli rejected was the claim of all radical visionaries to fresh revelation. Christ's prophetic office had put an end to free prophecy. True prophets were now governed by the rule of faith, understood not as an addition to scripture but as its distillate.

In his classic treatment of the threefold office of Christ as prophet, priest, and king, John Calvin observed that Christ was anointed by the Holy Spirit as a prophet, not only in his own person, but also as the head of his body, the church.[11] The anointing of Christ was the act that authorized the preaching and teaching of the Gospel by Christians. Sometimes the prophetic office of the church was discharged informally, as laypeople spoke God's Word of judgment and grace to each other in private conversation. Sometimes it was discharged formally by clergy, who proclaimed the Gospel publicly through sermons and the administration of the sacraments. But however it was discharged, it was an extension of the work of Christ as prophet.

It is difficult to overstate the importance of Christ's prophetic office for the early Protestant movement. Just as medieval priests considered themselves authorized to preside at the sacraments through their participation in the priesthood of Christ, so Protestant pastors considered themselves authorized to preach and teach the Word of God through their participation in the anointing of Christ as prophet. The sermon, which had played a subordinate role in the medieval church, became the central act of Protestant worship. Laity, who had come to church under the old order to pray and adore the consecrated host, were now told to be quiet and listen to the sermons that had once been optional. No wonder Calvin characterized the rightly ordered church as a school and not merely as a nurturing mother.

Conclusion

Which brings us, finally, to the title of this chapter. Early Protestants domesticated prophecy by rejecting the dreams and visions of radicals like Storch and

Muentzer, on the one hand, and by institutionalizing prophecy as a mediated and derivative activity, on the other. But while the Protestant reformers domesticated prophecy, they did not tame it. They were aware that the Word of God, understood as Luther had understood it, was a *Thettelwort Gottes*. It was a transforming Word that was never wholly under the control of the interpreter. God used human language to achieve God's purposes, which might—or might not—be identical with the aspirations of the would-be prophets who proclaimed them.

Set in this context, the claim that Martin Luther was a prophet seems a good deal less radical than it first appeared. He was, in the end, only one prophet among many, understood as the recipient not of fresh revelations but of fresh insights into an ancient and settled revelation. Indeed, viewed from one angle, the Protestant Reformation could be described as a prophetic movement in the late medieval Catholic church. It transformed what had been a sacramental fellowship in which preaching had been regarded as beneficial but not essential into a worshipping assembly in which the public preaching of the Word became the central defining act. If Catholic priests were authorized to preside at sacraments by an appeal to Christ as a priest forever after the order of Melchizedek, Protestants were authorized to preach and teach by an appeal to Christ as a prophet and teacher of saving truth. The shift from sacrament to sermon had fateful consequences for both Protestants and Catholics. But that is the subject of another essay.

10

The Learned Ministry Revisited

When I first started teaching, I read a symposium on the meaning of ordination in a religious periodical. One of the contributors, a theological student from a seminary in the eastern United States, described ordination as setting out on a quest. The minister did not have all the answers to the questions that his people would raise, but together with his people, as co-learner, he would seek answers to the meaning of life.

Humility is usually a virtue, but it is possible for humility to be misplaced. G. K. Chesterton posited a mythical people too humble to believe the multiplication table. It is humility for ministers to disavow that they have all the answers; but it is not humility to claim that they have no answers at all. The church has received answers to the great questions of life that it did not cook up and that it has a responsibility to transmit. Ministers are ordained as bearers of the church's Gospel of a crucified Lord, however much their communication of that Gospel may bear their own individual stamp. Fundamental to the original Protestant conception of the ministry is the conviction that the minister is a teacher in a church which is, to quote John Calvin, both mother and school.

School, however, is not the image that springs to mind when one attends a typical Protestant congregation on Sunday. To be sure, there are classes of instruction for adults as well as children, usually taught by lay volunteers. But the sermon itself is, more often than not, structured to inspire, move, warn, exhort, and entertain, rather than to instruct. The late Halford Luccock of Yale once characterized the preaching of his day as "a string of nursery stories tied together with baby ribbon." The preaching of our day, evangelical as well as mainline, may be described as formal exercises in "theology lite," low in intellectual nourishment and rarely filling.

Of course, ministers are not ordained simply as teachers. Some Protestant traditions emphasize other aspects of ministry more than the teaching office. Nevertheless, the teaching office is an indispensable function of the ordained ministry, even in the most charismatic traditions. Implicit in the structure and curriculum of almost any Protestant divinity school, liberal or conservative, is a doctrine—however loosely framed—of the minister as teacher. What that implies and how the office of teacher is related to the other functions of the ministry form the subject of this essay.

I

The ordained ministry was regarded by the early church as a gift of God to the congregation and not simply as representative laity chosen by the congregation to perform certain special functions. The church recognized, of course, that individual charismatic gifts were granted to all members of the Body of Christ and not simply to a select few. Every Christian received the Spirit at baptism, and the Spirit equipped each Christian for service in the world. By the gifts granted through baptism, each Christian shared in the unified ministry of Jesus Christ.

But the Spirit that grants differing gifts to each Christian in the Body of Christ also establishes the order that regulates that body. The charismatic ministry of the church is not an unstructured ministry, even though that structure may appear at times to be rather loose. Offices are regarded as a gift of the Holy Spirit to the church, and there are important elements of church order in the New Testament that are of a quite primitive origin. That does not mean, however, that the actual development of church polity is simply the working out of a blueprint found in the New Testament or that there is no tension between the Pauline view of the church and its later embodiment. But the principle at least seems to be clear: offices and order in the church are regarded as gifts of the Holy Spirit.

Very early in the history of the church the doctrine of the monarchical bishop developed. The bishop was the teacher of authentic Christian doctrine. Unity with the Catholic church and membership in it were dependent on unity with a Catholic bishop by obedience to him. From a Catholic perspective the hierarchy is essential to the continued existence of the church. The Catholic formula might be summarized as no bishop, no church, or at least no church in the full and proper sense of the term.

The Protestant Reformers rejected the idea that the Roman Catholic hierarchy is essential to the existence of the church. But they did not reject the idea that offices and structure belong by divine ordination to the nature of the church. Indeed, it is impossible to understand the origin of the Protestant Reformation without understanding Luther's high view of the office of a theological doctor. Luther was a medieval theological professor who had taken a vow in 1512 to defend the church against false doctrine. Because of that vow and that office Luther claimed that, he bore a responsibility to speak out when he believed the Gospel was being distorted. As a private individual, he might well have kept his peace and allowed himself to be meekly instructed by others. But as a teacher in the church, he felt that he dare not keep silent. It was the medieval understanding of the office of a doctor and not the modern understanding of freedom of conscience that lay behind Luther's thinking. Indeed, from Luther's perspective the crisis of the Reformation may be understood as a crisis of confidence in the teaching office of the church.

There is, however, an unresolved tension in Luther's doctrine of ministry that Luther himself does very little to clarify. On the one hand, a Christian congregation has the right, divinely granted, to select its own pastor. In a sense the congregation antedates the ordained ministry and bestows on it the authority to perform certain functions on behalf of the church and in its name. On the other hand, the pastor is the bearer of the very Word that antedates the Christian congregation and calls it into existence. There is, therefore, a sense in which the ordained ministry has received its authority to preach the Gospel directly from God and prior to the creation of the congregation. Nevertheless, though ambiguities in Luther's doctrine of the ordained ministry exist, it is possible to conclude that Luther regards the office of the minister of Word and sacraments (including the teaching office) as essential to the life of the church and not as an alien imposition on the life of the self-sufficient congregation that can get along well without the public proclamation of the Word and the administration of the sacraments.

The Congregationalists resolved Luther's dilemma by emphasizing the priority of the congregation. For Congregationalists, as for Presbyterians, the pastor is a bishop or teaching elder. However, unlike Catholics, who argue, "No bishop, no church," the Congregationalists argued, "No church, no bishop." The church exists as a covenant community before a pastor is called. And a pastor can only be a pastor as pastor of some local congregation. For Catholics there cannot be a church, at least over the long haul, unless there is a hierarchy.

For the Congregationalists there cannot be an ordained ministry unless there is first a local church. The visible congregation is the fundamental reality. The pastor lives from that reality and is dependent for his office on it.

Even in this view of the church, however, the congregation is incomplete—or, as the early Congregationalists would say, not "organical"—until it had called and ordained a pastor. Furthermore, the pastor, when he had been ordained, was not simply regarded as a functionary of the congregation. God, acting through the congregation, had bestowed on the minister the authority to proclaim the judgment and mercy of God to the congregation and, if necessary, in the face of its opposition. The proclamation of the Word of God and the teaching of authentic doctrine were not subject to the approval and ratification of the congregation. The minister in the exercise of his office was endowed with an authority that had been entrusted to the congregation for only a brief time, so that the congregation in turn might delegate it to a called and ordained ministry.

There is, in other words, a motif in church history that, however various its forms, recurs with remarkable persistence: although the whole people of God shares in the ministry of the church in virtue of baptism, offices in the church are to be regarded as gifts of the Holy Spirit. A church that lacks an ordained ministry is incomplete, precisely because it lacks one of the gifts of the Spirit. Though there are differences of opinion as to what offices are essential to the church, there is at least agreement that the ministry of Word and sacrament belongs to that essential minimum.

II

While baptism is the ordination of all Christians for ministry in the world, ordination is the act of setting aside some Christians for public ministry to the church. That does not mean that ordained clergy do not have a ministry to the world; they share in that ministry, as do all other Christians in virtue of their baptism. That also does not mean that service to the church may not involve the clergy in pioneering adventures outside the walls of the local parish. But it does mean that ordination is concerned principally with inner-churchly functions. The parish minister is, to use one of the titles associated by long tradition with the office of the pope, the *servus servorum dei*, the servant of the servants of God. The minister's function is to assist in equipping the people of God for their ministry to the world.

It would be an exaggeration to say that the laity have no inner-churchly functions to perform. There is a common priesthood of all of the faithful in which all Christians participate. This common priesthood has many aspects. When the

Reformers, however, spoke of the priesthood of all believers, they referred principally to the right of all Christians to hear the confession of sin. Luther was not opposed to confession; he was opposed to making it a clerical monopoly. All Christians may hear confession and be bearers to one another of God's Word of judgment and grace. To be such a priest is to be Christ to the neighbor.

What all Christians may do privately, the ordained ministry has been set apart to do publicly. Ordained ministers do not differ from their parishioners in essence (as Roman Catholics maintain) but solely in function. The principal task of the layperson is mission to the world; the principal task of the clergy is mission to the church.

III

The function of the ordained ministry is the public proclamation of the Word of God in its manifold forms to the congregation. Ordination is for the purpose of preaching, teaching, and administering the sacraments. Anyone who has been ordained to the ministry of the church but who no longer is occupied with the public service of Word and sacraments is no longer performing the function for which he or she was ordained. Ordination is not a general commissioning for the service of God; that is the purpose of baptism. Ordination is so indissolubly linked to the service of Word and sacraments that it is meaningless apart from them.

In the Roman Catholic tradition ordination is directed specifically toward the sacrament of the Eucharist. Preaching has not been regarded as the principal function of the ordained ministry, and theology is less central to the life of the local Catholic parish than it is to Protestants. Grace is given to the faithful through sacraments rather than through homilies, though homilies perform an important task of theological and moral instruction.

The Protestant Reformers, however, redefined the role of the ministry in terms of the proclamation and teaching of the Word of God. The sermon is not merely doctrinal instruction or moral exhortation. It is a means of grace. From a Catholic perspective the sermon has now become a sacrament. God speaks through human language and uses human words to effect those changes in the human condition that Catholic theology restricts to the power of the sacraments.

IV

The offices of preaching, teaching, and discipline are inseparable from the single office of the ministry of the Word of God. The Reformed tradition made the most elaborate attempt to separate the ministry of the Word into four distinct offices: teacher, pastor, elder, and deacon. According to Reformed theology the teacher was responsible for explaining the meaning of scripture and its theological and ethical implications, though without resorting to exhortation or rhetorical appeals for decision (a description that badly characterizes the work of any decent teacher, regardless of the discipline). A pastor also teaches, but differs from the teacher with respect to the mode or manner of his teaching. Unlike the teacher, the preacher is expected to use rhetorical arts to move his listeners to decision or action. Discipline is exercised by the pastor together with a group of lay elders. The poor are cared for by the lay deacons of the congregation. The division of labor is logical, admirable, but also artificial.

Everything in Protestant theology comes back to the multifaceted character of the Word of God. The Word teaches, nurtures, moves to decision, judges, disciplines, and encourages. It must find expression in works of charity or it remains only the letter that kills. Wherever the Word of God is proclaimed, it fills all four offices: teaches, exhorts, disciplines, and moves to acts of charity. Even the Sunday school, which ostensibly separates the office of preaching at 11:00 a.m. from the office of teaching at 9:30 a.m., combines teaching with lay preaching, worship, and discipline. The Word of God cannot be compartmentalized, even though one may for a brief period of time emphasize one aspect of the Word more than another. Teaching is a legitimate activity of the church, but one can never rule out in advance the possibility that the taught may be converted to the teaching, may assimilate the teaching in worship and prayer, or may respond to the teaching by an act of compassion for another in distress. The ministry of the Word of God is finally indivisible.

V

The Reformers understood the discharge of the office of minister as the faithful transmission of the Word entrusted to the ordinand. Christian ministers are not freelance religious prophets, however much the work of the ministry may involve the concrete proclamation of God's judgment and grace. Nor are they *homines religiosi*, people more sensitive than their fellows to religious values, more quickly overcome than they with the mystery and wonder of existence. The work of the minister is rather prosaic in comparison with these more romantic notions of the meaning of ministry. To be a minister is, to put it bluntly, to be a servant, and the virtue most highly prized in a servant is not originality, but fidelity. Ministers have been ordained to transmit a message that they did not compose and that they dare not alter. They have been called, not to improvise their assignment, but to fulfill a role prescribed for them by someone else.

Fidelity in their calling does not mean, of course, that ministers pass on everything they receive. Ministers are not curators of outdated techniques. They are not echo chambers in which every voice that claims the attention of the church may resonate unhindered. Fidelity does not exclude discrimination. The faithful minister is not one who passes on unchallenged everything that he or she receives in the church. The faithful minister is the one who hears the voice of the Shepherd through the cacophonous clamor of all the voices speaking to and for the church. "He who hears the Word of God," said Thomas à Kempis, "is freed from a multitude of opinions." Not everything we receive should be passed on. True fidelity is fidelity to Christ, not to the past per se.

Furthermore, faithful transmission does not do away with the necessity of interpretation. If ministers pass on what they receive without further interpretation, they may pass on something quite different from what they received. Theological formulations require interpretation if their intention is to be preserved.

It is a principle of Protestant theology that God comes to men and women as they are and not as God would like them to be. That means that God is revealed before men and women are ready to receive him. Not only the moral life of men and women but also their intellectual life is unprepared for the divine self-manifestation. God takes the human race by surprise; he comes when men and women are least ready for him.

This means that theologies have a mixed character. They are partly true and partly false. Talk about God is a human enterprise and, like every other human enterprise, is marked by finitude, error, and sin. That does not mean that the church's talk about God is so relative that it has no authority at all or that the church is so humble that it no longer believes that it is witnessing about a matter that makes the difference between life and death. It does not mean that the church surrenders its age-old claim to be led by the Spirit. But the presence of the Holy Spirit in the church does not mean that the church is infallible any more than it guarantees that the church is without sin. The Holy Spirit is a pledge, a down payment. The Spirit guarantees that the church will some day be without error as it will someday be without sin. But at the moment the church stands under the sign of "not yet." It has and it does not have. It is a deceiver, yet true.

The church makes mistakes, but it also tells the truth. In spite of its finitude, sin, narrow-mindedness, and error, God works through it in the world, calling men and women into fellowship with himself. The church's witness, its theology, its testimony are all human. It has its treasure in earthen vessels; it knows only in part. But the fact that the church sins does not cancel out the reality of its claim to be the people of God; and the fact that the church errs does not cancel out the truth of its proclamation that Jesus Christ is Lord and Redeemer. The treasure is in an earthen vessel, but it is real treasure.

VI

In witnessing to the truth the church dares not simply repeat without interpretation the formulas of the past. Robert Chiles, in his book *Theological Transition in American Methodism, 1790–1935,* gives a striking example of the way in which theological affirmations can have a markedly different meaning in different historical circumstances. Wesley protested against the eighteenth-century Calvinist doctrine of predestination in the name of the freedom and sovereignty of divine grace. He argued that God was not the prisoner of a divine decree but was free to be gracious to whomever he would be gracious. In other words, God was free to be gracious to the whole human race. Wesley stressed the freedom and sovereignty of God's merciful activity.

In the nineteenth century, however, there was a subtle shift of emphasis in Methodist theology. Wesley stressed the freedom of God's grace. Later Methodists, while citing Wesley copiously, stressed the freedom of the human will. What was a theological point for Wesley became an anthropological point for his followers. Wesley argued that God can be gracious to any penitent but that men and women cannot come to God until moved by divine grace. His followers argued that human beings are free moral agents and that God's grace cannot overcome the sovereign freedom of the human will. The formulas are much the same, but the point is fundamentally different.

Fidelity to one's calling as an ordained minister of Word and sacraments means that one must free oneself from the disposition to take every theological affirmation from the past literally. Some can, and should, be taken literally, but not all. The Latin and Greek fathers worked with metaphysical categories and with philosophical assumptions that we do not share. If we take literally many of the things they said, we would be forced to reject them. But rejection is a sign of failure of nerve; it is a sign of the inability or unwillingness to penetrate beneath the culturally conditioned statement of a doctrine to its intention. Repeating a formula from the past without translation is very much like repeating a statement from a foreign language without translation. Its meaning has been lost, not because it is meaningless in itself, but because its meaning has not been translated into terms that are meaningful to us.

Many times the past speaks to us directly, without the aid of a conscious act of interpretation. But many times it does not. If we repeat what we have received without making its meaning clear, we have failed to discharge our office responsibly. We are to deliver what we also received. But that act of delivery involves us in interpretation. Repetition without interpretation may be a sign, not of fidelity, but of incompetence.

The difficulty with the image of the minister as a messenger is that the minister is not merely a messenger. Every minister is also a witness. Ministers are claimed by the very message that they proclaim. There is in all Christian proclamation the Wesleyan note: "What we have seen and heard with confidence we tell." There is in preaching always the note of witness: "Come, see a man who told me all that I ever did. Can this be the Christ?"

In a sense this aspect of Christian proclamation is the most embarrassing. People who are honest with themselves would not want the credibility of the Gospel to be measured solely by the impact of that Gospel on their own lives. Yet there is no way to escape from the element of witness by compartmentalizing life. The Gospel that is preached lays claim to the whole of life, and something is fundamentally wrong with a proclamation of the good news that is untouched by it. The preacher is a witness who claims to know the reality of which he or she speaks otherwise than by hearsay. Ministers are not simply messengers and teachers. They are witnesses, people grasped by the power of what they proclaim.

Yet the original image is still valid. Christian ministers are not merely witnesses; they are also messengers. They have been commissioned by the church, not to give their own testimony, but to carry its message. And that message is valid, whether or not Protestant ministers believe it, whether or not they profit from it, whether or not they enjoy it. The power and truth of the message are quite independent of the personal faith of the messenger who delivers it. It is God's counsel and promise that ministers declare, not their own, and God is truthful, though every human being be false.

The late Carl Michalson of Drew used to suggest to his classes that they ought to preach the faith of the church even if they could not claim the whole of that faith for themselves. The church, he said, lives from the Word of God; it cannot live from heresy. Though what Michalson recommended sounded like theological novelty to his students, he was actually doing nothing more than reaffirming the position of the church against the Donatists. The Word and sacraments of the church are not the minister's personal property. Ministers have no right to deny them to their parishioners simply because they find no life in them for themselves, nor does their unfaith invalidate that Word and those sacraments.

We were horrified, as I recall, by Michalson's suggestion. It seemed to us like hypocrisy to speak a Word that we had not made our own, perhaps could not.

In the American tradition we equated preaching with the affirmation of personal religious experience. We grasped the witness element of preaching; we understood it subjectively. But we did not grasp the *extra nos* dimension; we did not grasp the objectivity of God's Word and work outside us. God is doing his work in the world whether we participate in it or not, whether we understand it or not, whether we feel it or not. It is not through our religious experience that God brings life and healing to the world, though our experience may confirm for us the objectivity of God's working. It is by his Word and sacraments that God brings men and women into fellowship with himself, apart from our religious experience and even, perhaps, in spite of it.

VII

Responsibility for the faithful transmission of the Gospel is corporate. Among the radical reformers, that responsibility was characteristically exercised by the local congregation of believers. Pilgram Marpeck, for example, makes it clear that deviant interpretations of the Bible are best corrected in a group discussion with other laypeople who have met the moral demands of the New Testament and paid the cost of discipleship. The Lutheran and Reformed traditions, on the other hand, have generally appealed to synods and councils as the place to reconcile conflicts over the meaning of the Bible. The controversy in Holland, for example, between the Reformed Orthodox and the followers of James Arminius was settled by the Reformed equivalent of an ecumenical council held at Dordrecht in 1618. Even the United Methodists, who have bishops, rely not on bishops but on the elders of an annual conference to certify new ordinands and to provide for the orderly transmission of the Gospel from one generation to another. It could be argued that one of the chief differences between Protestants and Roman Catholics is that Catholics assign principal responsibility for the faithful transmission of the Gospel to bishops, while Protestants assign it either to presbyters in synod (the magisterial Reformation) or to the local congregation of the laity (the radical Reformation).

VIII

The faithful transmission of the Word of God commits the church to the provision of a learned ministry. The Reformers did not affirm the right of private judgment. There were, to be sure, radical reformers who believed that the Bible in the hands of a plowboy instructed by the Holy Spirit was better and more to be trusted than what a learned pastor or teacher taught them. But this was a minority position.

The Reformers envisioned a learned ministry, gifted persons set apart by the church for the study of Holy Scripture, for the study of theology, for the study of the fathers. This learned ministry not only preached to the laity but also produced confessions that were meant to be guides for young Christians and for those less learned, to lead them by clear paths into the meaning of Holy Scripture. The Reformers did not believe that any person's opinion was as good as anyone else's or that it made no difference what one believed as long as one was sincere. The meaning of Holy Scripture was too important for the church to treat it so casually. Pastors and teachers were given to the church for its edification.

What the Reformers did reject was the doctrine of implicit faith. There is a sense, of course, in which the Reformation retained a doctrine of implicit faith. To be committed to the Christian faith does not mean that one understands every mystery of that faith. There is a sense in which one believes implicitly what one does not understand. What the Reformers rejected was the idea that the laity, because they were instructed by pastors and teachers, had no theological responsibility of their own. One cannot simply say, "I believe what the church teaches," and assume that one has thereby discharged one's responsibility to understand the Christian faith. On the contrary, every layperson has the responsibility to understand his or her faith. That does not mean that every layperson is a teacher of others, though the gift of teaching may be given to a layperson as well as to a pastor. But it does imply that laypeople should seek to understand what it means to be Christian, what demands are laid upon them by God, and what is given to them in the Gospel. Not private judgment but the theological responsibility of the whole people of God is the thrust of the Protestant movement.

IX

To sum up, then, one may say that there are certain elements in the Protestant tradition concerning the teaching office of the church that are still important for our consideration: (1) although the whole people of God shares in the ministry of the church by virtue of baptism, officers in the church are to be regarded as a gift of the Holy Spirit; (2) while baptism is the ordination of all Christians for ministry in the world, ordination is the act of setting aside some Christians for public ministry to the church; (3) the function of the ordained ministry is the public proclamation of the Word of God in its manifold forms to the congregation; (4) the offices of preaching, teaching, and discipline are inseparable from the single office of the ministry of the Word of God; (5) the discharge of the office of a minister is the faithful transmission of the Word that has been entrusted to the church; (6) the minister in transmitting this Word is both a messenger and a witness; (7) responsibility for the faithful transmission of the Word is corporate; and (8) the faithful transmission of the Word of God commits the church to the provision of a learned ministry.

II

Marriage, Celibacy, and Ordination

The acute shortage of Roman Catholic priests worldwide made the question of whether to allow priests to marry a pressing issue for the synod of Catholic bishops that met in Rome in 2006. Of course, some Catholic priests are already married. Anglican priests who convert to Catholicism while married are almost routinely accepted by Rome for reordination as Catholic priests. They are not alone. Priests in Eastern Rite Catholic churches—at least outside the United States—may also marry prior to ordination. Roughly half of the Catholic priests of the Maronite Church of Lebanon elect to marry.

Eastern Rite Catholics such as the Maronites and Melkites are following rules that would be familiar to any Greek Orthodox Christian. Priests may marry prior to ordination, but not after. If their spouse should die, they may not remarry. Furthermore, bishops are chosen from the ranks of celibate clergy. However, the vast majority of Roman Catholics follow the Western or Latin Rite. These Western Rite Catholics have not been served by married clergy—except for Anglican converts—for a very long time.

It was not always so. Priests in Anglo-Saxon England were allowed to marry, though the practice was stopped after the Norman invasion of 1066. The Norman ban on clerical marriage was reinforced in 1139, when the Second Lateran Council declared priestly marriage invalid throughout the entire Catholic Church.

Of course, there were people, then as now, who broke the rule of celibacy—some of them quite spectacularly. But the rule itself was clear: no celibacy, no priestly ordination. Catholic bishops understand this rule. It is a constant theme of their lives as priests. But they also know that celibacy is not an unchangeable theological dogma. Patriarch Gregorios III Laham of the Melkite Catholics put it bluntly at an early session of the 2006 synod: "Celibacy has no theological foundation." It is a long-standing discipline that could be modified by Pope Benedict XVI, if he deemed it appropriate to do so.

Working against the possibility of change is the fact that the practice of celibacy is deeply rooted in the ascetic impulses of Christianity. Catholics are not alone in thinking that self-denial is an important step in the human quest for a closer relationship with God. Self-denial may, in fact, be particularly important in a Western culture that denies itself nothing.

But celibacy also has a more pragmatic root. Priests who are single can be moved from Boston to Los Angeles within twenty-four hours. Priests who are married cannot. This is particularly true if the married priests have working wives and children in school.

Pope Benedict can, of course, continue to reaffirm tradition and avoid experimentation. Until now, he has done exactly that. However, if he simply reaffirms the status quo, he faces a tough dilemma. He is convinced that the Catholic church can only be renewed by a fresh dedication to the Eucharist, the sacramental meal of bread and wine in which Catholics believe the risen Christ is present and accessible to them.

But the Eucharist can be offered to the laity only after it has been consecrated by priests. And the shortage of priests stands in the way of the fulfillment of Benedict's dream of renewal. The pope could, of course, authorize the ordination of celibate women, but that is the least traditional and, therefore, least likely solution to his problem. Or he could increase the rate at which priests are transferred from dioceses where there is a surplus of clergy to dioceses in which there is a shortage, a strategy that he has already adopted but that may prove inadequate to meet long-term needs.

He might also turn to married ex-priests for help, though that is unlikely. Former priests are allowed under canon law to function as priests in an emergency. An ex-priest who is a stockbroker or car mechanic can absolve a dying Catholic colleague if no other priest is present. To what extent does the current shortage of priests constitute, in itself, a continuing emergency?

Or the pope could authorize the ordination of the kind of mature married men who are now sometimes chosen as deacons. These seasoned men could be ordained as priests, but restricted in their functions to offering the Eucharist only when celibate priests are not available. After some discussion, this idea has been shelved—at least for now.

I

Perhaps the question of married priests needs to be put in a larger historical context, Marriage, after all, is not an institution invented by Christians. Long before the birth of Jesus, the ancient Romans had a clearly defined institution of marriage, with rights and privileges protected by law. Roman marriage was not primarily about sex. In the ancient world, where a large proportion of the population were slaves, sex was readily available outside marriage. Marriage was about children, property, politics, and the orderly succession of generations.

The ancient Romans did not much care with whom they mated—men, women, or children—though some disgruntled critics thought the pedophilia of the dour emperor Tiberius unworthy of his exalted office. Still, an elite Roman male who had sex with a slave girl in the morning, a young male in the afternoon, and his wife at night would not have been thought unusually per-verse—not even by his wife.

All of this changed when the Roman Empire was Christianized. Christians banned nonreproductive sex (whether with a same-sex partner or a child), limited sexual activity to a potentially reproductive relationship between hus-band and wife, severely restricted the possibility of divorce (usually limited to separation from bed and board), and extolled the virtues of sexual abstinence. The change would have startled Julius Caesar.

The new Christian ideal of marriage embraced at least three elements: (1) an openness in all sexual activity to the procreation, nurture, and education of children; (2) a covenant of mutual fidelity in which husband and wife, "for-saking all others," pledge to care for each other through thick and thin; and (3) a recognition that the bond between husband and wife is as indissoluble as the bond between Christ and the church.

This is heavy-duty stuff, and it would be disingenuous to assume that everyone lived up to such high ideals. Human beings are, after all, prone to fall short of their own lofty rhetoric. Nevertheless, even unattainable ideals have consequences that matter.

In time, the Christianized Roman Empire fell into political ruin, but its culture did not collapse. The ideals of Christian Rome became the ideals of the barbarian nations that succeeded it, and its culture laid the foundation of European civilization. In due course, this Christianized civilization was exported to the New World and so to us.

Christian civilization exalted the institution of marriage but also praised virginity as a higher moral state and required its clergy to be celibate. Though some late medieval figures, such as Nicholas de Blony, taught that marriage was as meritorious as celibacy, the majority of late medieval clergy agreed with the opinion of the famous Strasbourg preacher John Geiler of Kaysersberg, who observed that marriage is honorable but not preferable to the state of celibacy.

In the Bible there were, after all, plenty of sayings that lent support to the development of a celibate ethic. Paul had indicated that celibacy was preferable to marriage, not because of a general world-weariness, but because the celibate minister was delivered from family cares and responsibilities and was therefore free to devote himself completely to the work of the Gospel. Jesus had praised those disciples who became eunuchs for the Kingdom of Heaven, even though it is impossible to regard Jesus as an ascetic in the ordinary sense of the term. And after the triumph of Christianity in Europe, celibacy was one of the few forms of martyrdom still accessible to the grandchildren of Cyprian and Perpetua.

The celibate ethic was reinforced by a distinction between commands and counsels. Commands are ethical requirements binding on all Christians, such as the prohibition of murder or adultery. Counsels, on the other hand, are moral requirements binding on an elite within the church who have obligated themselves by a vow to a more rigorous standard of Christian discipleship. Among the counsels are the sayings of Jesus on nonretaliation, the renunciation of private property, and the desirability of a celibate life. Ever since canon 33 of the Council of Elvira (ca. 300) celibacy had been enjoined on all clergy in the West, though there were de facto exceptions, like the Anglo-Saxon church in Britain. The laity, however, were required only to keep the commandments, including the sexual prohibitions of adultery and fornication.

The celibate ethic received important encouragement from the writings and example of Augustine, who could find for himself no middle ground between asceticism and sexual license. Augustine taught that original sin was transmitted from generation to generation not by the sexual act itself (that would be Manichaean), but by the inordinate self-regard of the sexual partners, who think of themselves more highly than they ought to think and who seek their own good rather than the good of their spouses. Biology was not the culprit, though original sin was connected with human sexual activity in the broader sense. While the celibate Christian did not participate in the admitted goods of marriage, the celibate was also free of responsibility for its unfortunate side effects.

The emphasis on celibacy as the preferred state for the serious Christian and the obligation of the clergy to remain celibate created a permanent class of men not fully integrated into society. Because the clergy had no wives and family of their own, they were regarded by the suspicious laity (and not always unjustly) as a perpetual threat to the stability of the home. Instances of anticlerical sentiment relating to the alleged sexual offenses of some of the clergy are all too easy to find in the sources.

For example, in 1519 a group of canons in Strasbourg, returning from a drunken party, were attacked by a group of citizens who regarded them as a danger to the moral purity of their wives and daughters. John Murner, brother of the rabidly anti-feminist Franciscan friar Thomas Murner, accused the canons of Young St. Peter's Church in Strasbourg of seducing his sister. In January 1520 two women charged three members of the clergy, including the vicar of the Strasbourg cathedral, with breaking into their homes at midnight and making improper sexual advances. When the women resisted, they were beaten. Needless to say, the guilty clergy were fined and imprisoned by the Strasbourg city council.

Even the confessional was regarded with suspicion by some laity. The Eisenach preacher Jacob Strauss attacked the confessional practice of the late medieval clergy as profoundly unsettling to the peace and stability of Christian family life:

> In the confessional simple folk learn things about sin and evil which
> have never occurred to them before, and which need not ever have
> occurred to them! The confessional is a schooling in sin. It is known
> and many thousands can attest how often mischievous and perverse
> monks out of their shameless hearts have so thoroughly and
> persistently questioned young girls and boys, innocent children, and
> simple wives about the sins of the flesh in their cursed confessional
> corners that more harm was done there to Christian chasteness and
> purity than in any whorehouse in the world. He is considered a good
> father confessor who can probe into every secret recess of the heart
> and instill into the innocent penitent every sin his flesh has not yet
> experienced. They want to know from virtuous wives all the
> circumstances of the marital duty—how their husbands do it [certain
> "unnatural positions" were very serious sins], how often, how much
> pleasure it brings, when it is done, and the like. In this way new
> desires and lusts are simulated within the weak. They even teach
> poor wives not to submit to their husbands on certain holidays and
> during Lent.[1]

If clergy were regarded by the laity as a threat to the stability of the home, women were regarded by the clergy as a threat to their celibacy and moral purity. Sebastian Brant, himself a layman, gave expression to this sentiment when he wrote his masterpiece, *The Ship of Fools* (1494):

Who sees too much of women's charms
His morals and his conscience harms;
He cannot worship God aright
Who finds in women great delight.[2]

In a time of moral decline and disintegration (and Brant, like Geiler of Kaysersberg, was convinced that he lived in such a time of moral decay), the "frailty" of women constitutes a perpetual temptation for a celibate clergy, whose vows require them to abstain from sexual activity, but whose vocation brings them into constant contact with the wives and daughters of laymen. Not all clergy were able to resist the temptations strewn in their path. Friar Martin Luther, OESA, had no difficulty keeping his celibate vows; Father Huldrych Zwingli and Friar Martin Bucer, OP, were not so morally heroic.

Some clergy took concubines, a practice winked at by some ecclesiastical superiors and even taxed by a few bishops as a way of raising additional revenue for the diocese. The Protestant reformer Heinrich Bullinger was born into such a clerical "family." But clergy who took concubines rather than place themselves in the path of a temptation that they did not trust themselves to resist placed themselves in another kind of moral dilemma. The relationship between a priest and his housekeeper, however regularized and accepted, was still fornication in the eyes of the church. Men and women who lived in this relationship had to do so in the knowledge that they were committing mortal sin and in danger of punishment by God. Furthermore, when a priest died, his widow was left without inheritance and his children without a name. As far as civil and canon law were concerned, the pastor's wife—no matter how faithful she had been to him—was only the priest's whore. She had no claims against the estate that she could prosecute and no position in society that she could occupy. On the other hand, fornication, while a mortal sin, was according to late medieval sexual morality a lesser crime against God than adultery (which violated the sacrament of marriage) or masturbation (which, as a crime against nature, was more heinous than rape). And so the practice of concubinage, if not condoned, was at least tolerated.

II

The Protestant Reformation constituted a sustained attack on the celibate ethic and a reemphasis on the dignity of the institution of marriage. Protestants did not deny that some men and women are called to a celibate life, though they regarded all claims to a celibate vocation with considerable suspicion, but they rejected the contention that celibacy should be made a law binding on all clergy.

A vow in the very nature of the case destroys Christian freedom. While some Christians may be called to celibacy, all Christians are assuredly called to a life of freedom. Therefore celibacy that is received as a gift and exercised in freedom may be celebrated as an authentic form of Christian discipleship, but celibacy that is made a law and enforced by a binding vow destroys the freedom that belongs to the essence of the Christian life and must therefore be rejected. Celibacy may be a charism; it may never be a law.

The distinction between commands and counsels was also rejected by Protestants, though not by all Protestants in exactly the same way. The Anabaptists, for example, concluded that nonresistance and pacifism were binding on all Christians, who were excluded by the teachings of Jesus in the Sermon on the Mount from all participation in public and political life. Luther, on the other hand, distinguished between what Christians were permitted to do in all matters that touched their own case exclusively (here the rigorous precepts of Jesus apply directly) and what they were obliged to do for the sake of their neighbors, who would be left at the mercy of sinful and rapacious men if they refused in such cases to resist evil forcibly. Christian love and responsibility may even permit one to discharge the role of public executioner, though Christ forbids one to take revenge or to seek justice in a purely personal matter. But whether one followed Luther or the Anabaptists or any of the shades of Protestant opinion in between, all Protestants agreed that the distinction between commands and counsels was unacceptable in principle. They regarded the gifts and demands of the Gospel as equally relevant for all Christians, clerical and lay alike. For them there was no heroic elite in the church; or, perhaps one should say, they considered all Christians as called to join that heroic elite. There was one standard of sanctity, and one only, for all Christians.

The Protestants could find no reason for urging celibacy on their clergy. The pastor (only men were ordained in the sixteenth century) was not ontologically distinct from the laity. He received no indelible character that communicated to him a sacramental power denied to the laity. The ministry of Word and sacrament belonged inherently to the common priesthood conferred on all Christians, male and female, in their baptism. Lay Christians exercised that ministry in private as they carried God's Word of judgment and grace to their neighbor. The pastor was ordained to preach that Word in public and preside at the church's celebration of baptism and the Eucharist. The distinction between clergy and layperson was primarily functional within the Body of Christ, though no one might exercise the clerical function who had not been called to do so by God and acknowledged and confirmed in that office by some local congregation of believers. There was no reason, therefore, why the pastor, who differed from the laity only in function and vocation, should not marry and rear his own family. Indeed, the exercise of his vocation might be helped rather than hindered by his family life and participation in ordinary social responsibilities.

Together with the rejection of celibacy as a law, the dissolution of the distinction between commands and counsels, and the stress on the functional character of the pastor's office, Protestants emphasized the interdependence of men and women in a joint task of creating a Christian society. Marriage stood at the center of a God-given order. Matthew Zell, a Protestant preacher at the cathedral in Strasbourg, argued in a famous sermon that, since woman was made from man, her origin proved not that women are subordinate to men but that men can only attain their full perfection in marriage. As Christ loved the church, so men and women are to love one another and to seek their perfection in an interdependent relationship.

Just as marriage was the ordinary and proper state of life for the Protestant pastor, so, too, were laywomen called to a more active role in the life and public ministry of the church. Protestants did not advocate the ordination of women, though the stress on the common priesthood conferred in baptism and the redefinition of ordination in functional terms laid the foundation for the ordination of women in another place and time. Almost all of the arguments used today to defend the practice of the ordination of women were known in the sixteenth century, though none of the people who used them advocated such a radical break with the long-standing practice of the Christian churches. Nevertheless, the arguments were advanced, if only to support a more active role for women among the laity of the church. When Katherine Zell, for example, was told by a critic that Paul told women to be silent in the church, she responded that the same apostle had also taught that in Christ there is neither male nor female, bond nor free. Furthermore, the prophet Joel predicted that in the last days daughters as well as sons would prophesy. And no one who reads Luke's Gospel could fail to be impressed by the fact that Elizabeth was filled with the Holy Spirit while her husband, Zechariah, was struck dumb because of his unbelief. Women have a priesthood to discharge as well as men; like men, they are to be Christ to their neighbor.

This Protestant teaching led to the initiation of certain social changes and sanctioned others, though one should be careful never to confuse the intention to effect a change with the change itself. One can, however, safely observe that the celibate ethic was utterly abandoned by Protestants, who nevertheless preserved the notion of an occasional charism of celibacy (which was forced to prove its credentials before a largely skeptical audience). Protestants turned the full force of their attention to the institution of marriage and emphasized the interdependence of men and women within it. Women were no longer regarded as simply dependent on their husbands, but were expected to assume an active role in the relationship to them. Martin Bucer once observed that the only defect of his second wife was that she did not criticize him. Mutual criticism is an expression of mutual love. Christians are called to seek their perfection in society rather than in isolation.

Protestant clergy were thus expected to marry (save in very rare and exceptional cases), and were thought by their parishioners to be more fully integrated into their society by family lufe than their celibate predecessors had been. The home and not the cloister became the arena for the exercise of the gentler Christian virtues. Marriage was not a concession to human weakness, but the chosen institution for the expression of the interdependence of male and female described in chapters 1 and 2 of Genesis. Not only the sexual act but the mutual society of male and female antedated the Fall as the God-given purpose of marriage. "It is not good for man to be alone" was spoken not of human nature in a state of sin, but of man as male and female before the Fall. Thus procreation and mutual society take precedence over the "remedy for concupiscence" as the principal purpose of marriage.

The downside of all this was that the new emphasis on the home and family was not an unmixed blessing for women, who over the course of the sixteenth century lost many of the rights and privileges they had enjoyed in the fifteenth: the right to work outside the home, to buy and sell property, to own businesses in their own name, and so on. The dissolution of religious houses for women also reduced women's opportunities to exercise control over their own societies with minimal interference from men—though the lively debate between Marie Dentière and Jeanne de Jussy over the positive and negative effects of the cloistered life for women indicates that women were themselves deeply divided over this issue.

Protestants also backed the possibility of real divorce with the right of the "innocent party" to remarry, though divorce was not easy to obtain and very grudgingly granted. Furthermore, by rejecting the celibate ethic and emphasizing the institution of marriage as a means for the hallowing of human life, the Reformation re-created for the Western church the office of pastor's wife, a role never abandoned by the Eastern church. Women who had lived a shadowy existence as a priest's concubine were able to enter into a sexual relationship with their husbands within officially acknowledged bonds of matrimony. This was a gain not simply in the sense of delivering these women from an intolerable burden of guilt (which on Protestant grounds there was no conceivable reason for them to carry), but also in the sense of recognizing and honoring their inheritance rights as widows and the legitimacy of their children. It may be difficult for women who are currently seeking ordination to regard the creation of the pastor's wife as a step forward in the liberation of women from unjust restrictions, but for the women involved in unofficial clerical "families" the Reformation was a profoundly liberating event.

At the end of her life Katherine Zell described her role as a pastor's wife in Strasbourg. Katherine had no children and was able to assume far more duties in church and community than the average laywoman; nevertheless, she claimed only in practice a freedom accessible to other women in principle:

> That I learned to understand and helped to acknowledge the Gospel
> I shall let my God declare. That I married my pious husband and for
> this endured slander and lies, God knows. The work which I carried
> on both in the house and out is known both by those who already rest
> in God and those who are still living—how I helped to establish the
> Gospel, took in the exiled, comforted the homeless refugees,
> furthered the Church, preaching and the schools, God will remember
> even if the world may forget or did not notice.... I honored, cherished
> and sheltered many great, learned men, with care, work, and
> expense.... I listened to their conversation and their preaching, I read
> their books and their letters and they were glad to receive mine...and
> I must express how fond I was of all the old, great learned men and
> founders of the Church of Christ, how much I enjoyed listening to
> their talk of holy things and how my heart was joyful in these things.[3]

III

By this point it has become clear that the stories of marriage in Europe and America are intertwined. The Christian ideal of marriage is found in American culture (and not merely in American churches). It was not put there in recent years by an aggressive and humorless religious Right. It was there from the very beginning, a cultural heritage of Christian Rome.

That said, "traditional" American-style marriage is a good deal less traditional than one might suppose. Often couples marry later in life. Many of them are survivors of relationships that went sour and ended in separation. While no one thinks divorce is a good answer to a marital problem, fewer and fewer couples believe marriage is indissoluble, given the possibility of irreconcilable differences.

Furthermore, the Pill uncoupled sex from the unwanted procreation of children. To an extent never before possible, women could avoid the biological consequences of casual sex. These technological advances occurred in a society that prizes self-realization over fidelity to others. The results were not hard to predict.

In short, marriage as "the union of one man and one woman" is an American institution in trouble. Although no one has proposed that marriage vows be altered to say "I take thee, George, to be my first husband," the words "till death do us part" have an increasingly hollow ring.

None of which means that the old ideal has lost its persuasive force, even in a society uncertain of its cultural norms. Far from it. A woman comic recently joked that if women published an erotic magazine, it would be called *Commitment* and have a foldout picture of a man ironing a shirt. Which is only another way of saying that the ancient ideal of marriage as a stable and exclusive relationship in which mutual promises are freely made and faithfully kept is still enormously appealing.

In other words, some items in the bumpy history of Christian marriage may still be worth contemplating, even in our changed circumstances.

1. It is at least arguable that the Protestant churches were not entirely wrongheaded to accept celibacy as a gift and resist it as a law. Celibacy is an authentic form of Christian discipleship, and the freedom of the Gospel means at the very least that some Christians, for whatever reasons, will be led to adopt this style of life. The Protestant churches are in error, therefore, when they reject celibacy and make marriage a law for all clergy.

2. The Protestant emphasis on the interdependence of men and women in marriage and the common calling of men and women to seek the will of God in mutual relationship is an important corrective to theologies that subordinate women to men, on the one hand,[4] or that dispense with the relationship between male and female as trivial, on the other. Men and women are created for each other; they are bound to each other by ties of mutual dependence within the institution of marriage and outside it. The *imago dei* is an *imago trinitatis* in the sense that the society of Father, Son, and Holy Spirit is reflected in the society of man, who is created male and female. Mutual dependence involves, for most Christians, the task of living a faithful covenant in sexual partnership. For Christians who choose celibacy, it involves caring and sacrificial relationships with men and women in the full range of our common life together. There is no room in the church for misanthropy or misogyny. God who created human beings male and female calls Christians to perfection in mutual society.

3. The Reformation did not sanction the ordination of women to the public ministry of Word and sacrament. Nevertheless, the fundamental arguments that sanction that act are already articulated in the Reformation era. Women share in the common priesthood committed to all the faithful by baptism.

When women are ordained, they are only authorized to exercise in public a charism granted to them for private exercise by virtue of their incorporation into Christ. Katherine Zell had a point when she argued that women may be forbidden to preach and celebrate the Eucharist only if it may be demonstrated that in Christ there is indeed male and female (contra Paul) and that in the last days sons shall prophesy while daughters shall demurely keep silent (contra Peter). Women already belong to a royal priesthood; otherwise they are not even members of the church.

4. That a Christian is a female is no bar to valid ordination in the church. But neither is it the basis on which ordination may be granted. Only those persons—whether male or female—may be ordained for the public ministry of Word and sacrament who have been called to the ministry of God and who have demonstrated to the church that they have, in the happy Wesleyan phrase, "gifts, grace and the promise of usefulness." The office may be discharged by any baptized Christian, male or female; its discharge should be restricted, however, to those Christians who have been called to that ministry and whose vacation has been acknowledged by the church. When all is said and done, calling—not gender—is the only indispensable precondition for authentic ministry.

12

Christ and the Eucharist

There was no quest for the historical Jesus in the sixteenth century, because the necessary precondition for such a quest was lacking. For Luther and Calvin, to say nothing of their Catholic and Protestant contemporaries, the historical Jesus was precisely the Jesus who was portrayed in the Gospels. They saw no slippage between the biblical portrait of Jesus and the historical reality that lay behind it, even though they were well aware of some difficulties in the biblical text. In the end, they regarded such difficulties as theologically trivial and capable of satisfactory resolution through renewed study.

Debates over the identity of Jesus in the early Reformation were therefore not prompted by the kind of historical-critical questions that interest biblical scholars in the present. The issue for sixteenth-century theologians was the import of Jesus' teaching in the Gospels and not its historical reliability. Debates over the identity of Jesus in the Reformation occurred primarily in the context of debates over the nature of the Eucharist. Critics of Catholic sacramental theology found they could not talk about the presence of Jesus Christ in the Eucharist without clarifying what they believed about his identity. Who was Jesus, after all, and what could he have meant to imply about himself when, as the Gospel of Matthew reports, he broke bread and told his disciples, "Take, eat, this is my body"?

Early Protestants were fairly certain they knew what Jesus did not mean. In their view he did not mean to suggest that bread and wine had been miraculously transformed or "transubstantiated" into his body and blood. The word "transubstantiation" describes the medieval Catholic theory of Christ's real presence. It rests on a distinction between the substance of a thing (what it really is) and its accidents (how it appears to observers). Ever since the Fourth Lateran Council in 1215 the Catholic Church had insisted that consecrated bread and wine were transformed by the power of God into the substance of Christ's body and blood without any alteration of their accidental qualities. Observers could detect no change in the consecrated elements or distinguish consecrated from unconsecrated by taste, appearance, weight, or smell.

Jesus Christ and the Eucharist in Zwingli's Theology

For Huldrych Zwingli, the principal reformer of Zurich, the theory of transubstantiation seemed fatally flawed.[1] While he conceded that Christ was in some way present when the Eucharist was celebrated, he denied that Christ was present in the bread and wine. Zwingli's eucharistic theology was heavily influenced by his reading of four biblical texts: one from Paul (Rom. 1:25), two from John (4:24, 6:63), and a final one from Matthew (26:26). Romans 1:25, which complains that the Gentiles "served and worshipped creatures rather than the Creator," was a warning to Zwingli that reverence for consecrated elements might prove to be an ascription to creatures (namely, bread and wine) of an honor that belongs only to the invisible and transcendent God. In his view the common practice of honoring the Eucharist by reserving consecrated elements for adoration was an inexcusable lapse into the primal sin of idolatry.[2]

Zwingli's distrust of the material culture of late medieval religion was reinforced in his mind by John 4:24, a text which affirmed that "God is a Spirit" and should therefore be worshipped "in spirit and in truth." Incense, images, candles, holy water, stained glass windows—even music—represented for Zwingli an externalization of worship that obscured the immaterial character of God and the internal nature of Christian worship. God transcends material objectification, and spiritual worship requires a radical simplification of its external forms.

Zwingli's principal objection to material things as means of grace was encapsulated in his reading of John 6:63: "The flesh" (or, as Zwingli understood it, "the material world of which flesh is a useful symbol") "counts for nothing," since it is "the Spirit" who "gives life." The soul or inner person can only be touched and moved by the direct action of the Holy Spirit. External rites, including baptism and Eucharist, are incapable of conveying grace. They belong to the world of "flesh" and are therefore spiritually incompetent.

Whatever grace is given when the Eucharist is celebrated must be directly given by the Holy Spirit to the souls of the faithful rather than channeled through bread and wine. Why this distrust of sacraments as means of grace was not extended to preaching—which is, after all, itself a material act—remains an unresolved question in Zwingli's theology. Perhaps, for Zwingli, the invisibility of speech separated it from the world of "flesh" to which the more obviously material sacraments belonged.

The problematic text for Zwingli was the so-called words of institution in Matthew 26:26: "Take, eat, this is my body." If the consecrated elements were creatures rather than the Creator, if God was to be worshipped without material objectification, and if bread and wine belonged to the spiritually impotent world of "flesh," then what could Jesus have possibly meant by calling the bread his body? Zwingli was not impressed by the argument of Andreas Bodenstein von Carlstadt that Jesus was simply pointing to his body when he uttered these words to his disciples.[3]

Zwingli found help in a letter from a Dutch jurist, Cornelius Hoen, who claimed to have been inspired by the fifteenth-century Dutch theologian Wessel Gansfort. Hoen suggested that the verb "is" in the phrase "this is my body" should be read as "signifies." There is certainly precedent in the "I am" sayings from the Gospel of John for reading the verb "to be" in a metaphorical sense. When Jesus called himself the Good Shepherd, the Gate of the sheepfold, or the True Vine, he was not speaking literally. The verb "to be" in these cases indicates not identity but a very important similarity. So, too, argued Hoen, when Jesus said, "This is my body," the statement should not be taken literally. Jesus meant only that the bread and wine signified his body, not that they were identical with it. Zwingli was persuaded by Hoen's reasoning and embraced his interpretation as his own.

With these four texts in mind Zwingli constructed a complex doctrine of the Eucharist that had past, present, and future dimensions.[4] The past dimension of Zwingli's eucharistic theology is the aspect most frequently cited, though, unfortunately, not always correctly. Zwingli understood the celebration of the Lord's Supper as a "remembrance" of the life, death, and resurrection of Jesus Christ, though Zwingli's eucharistic liturgy was not a wistful recollection of things past and gone. Memory for Zwingli was a faculty that took a datum from the past and made it a living part of the present. It did so in order to enable a person or a group to function properly in the here and now.

Children provide a good example of what Zwingli had in mind. In Zwingli's world children learned at an early age to manage a variety of common tasks: ride a horse, lace a shoe, even fix a broken shelf. When they were middle-aged, they used such lessons from their youthful past to ride their own horses, lace their own shoes, and fix their own broken shelves. Memory brings past lessons into the present to enable human beings to function. Otherwise—to quote a German proverb—Johann may never do as an adult what little Hans failed to learn as a child.

What is true of individuals is also true of groups. Groups need to remember why they were constituted in order to achieve their goals in the present. Nothing is more pathetic than a once vigorous political party that has forgotten its first principles. Loss of memory is the first stage in the dissolution of a human personality or the decline of a particular social group.

The church that celebrates the Eucharist is not engaging in a nostalgic escape from the present to another place or time, where the problems of the present do not matter. The primary movement of memory for Zwingli is not from present to past but from past to present. The Holy Spirit takes a crucial datum from the church's past (in this case, the death and resurrection of Jesus Christ) and makes it as real to believers in the present as the bread and wine they share. It does so in order to prevent the dissolution of the church's identity and so enable it to achieve in the space and time in which it lives the purposes for which it was established. The Eucharist is about memory because memory is essential to proper human functioning.

But the Eucharist is also about hope. It is a simple meal eaten in anticipation of the lavish banquet to be shared in heaven at the end of time. Participation in the Eucharist is a public confession that God's Kingdom will come and God's commandments will be done, all evidence to the contrary notwithstanding. For Zwingli the Eucharist underscored the church's conviction that history is never out of control but always subject to God's providence. The future, like the past, belongs to a God whose purposes are benign and whose promises are reliable.

Zwingli reserved his most complicated argument for his discussion of the relation of the Eucharist to the present. That Christ is remembered and the Kingdom of God is anticipated are certainly important themes in any eucharistic theology. But the faithful gathered around the host—especially the newly hatched Protestant faithful, who a few short months before had attended Catholic Mass—expected Christ the Lord to appear at his own eucharistic celebration. Was that a hope Zwingli shared, or was the price of reform in Zurich the loss of Christ from the Eucharist? Was the Eucharist for Zwingli nothing more than an inner psychological event, a mnemonic device established to remind a church, always tempted to amnesia, of the central tenets of the Gospel, lest it forget who and what it is? Was Zwingli nothing more than the prophet of an absent Christ? Zwingli certainly didn't think so.

However, in order to explain how Christ was and was not present, it was essential for Zwingli to insist on a sharp distinction of the two natures of Christ.

His starting point was the orthodox Christology of the ancient creeds. With the early fathers he confessed that in the incarnation the divine Word, the Second Person of the Trinity, assumed human nature. The human nature of Christ was "anhypostatic" in the sense that it did not exist prior to, or apart from, its assumption by the divine Word, and "enhypostatic" in the sense that its continued existence depended on its continued union. Moreover, it was finite. Finitude marked Christ's humanity at every stage of his life: his incarnation, death, resurrection, and ascension. At no time, in Zwingli's view, was Christ's human nature divinized, except, of course, in the limited sense that the humanity of the risen Christ was no longer subject to death.

Confessing the finitude of Christ's human nature made what Zwingli regarded as an essential soteriological point. Christ assumed human nature, not angelic, and human nature is indisputably finite. Only if Christ bore the finite nature common to all men and women (sin alone excepted) could he stand in the presence of God as their high priest and intercessor. He could not be the perpetual representative of a group of which he was not a member or to which he no longer belonged. When the creed proclaimed that the risen Christ is "seated at the right hand of God, the Father Almighty," Zwingli understood this affirmation quite literally. In his view Christ's risen humanity could be in one place at a time, and one place only. X marked the spot. Any blurring of the line between the divine and human natures would threaten the integrity of the saving work of Christ.

Not that Zwingli knew exactly where "the right hand of God the Father" was. What was clear was that it was remote, transcendent, inaccessible—a distant place that could not be reached by human initiative. If Christ were to be present in the eucharistic service (leaving to one side the question of the locus of his presence), he could be present only in a way that did not threaten the claim that his humanity remained "seated at the right hand of God."

Zwingli made three suggestions to address the problem this affirmation created. The first suggestion focused on the Eucharist as a sign of a present reality. The Eucharist is not merely a remembrance of Christ's past death and resurrection or a foretaste of his future coming in glory—though it is both of those things. It is also a sign that the redeeming work of Christ as mediator and intercessor continues unabated in the present. The risen Christ is never idle, and the "right hand of God" is a place of endless activity on behalf of the redeemed. The confession that Christ's finite humanity is "seated at the right hand of God" is therefore very good news for the church and ought to be celebrated.

The second suggestion rested on the doctrine of the Trinity. Zwingli thought the role of the Holy Spirit was crucial in any sound eucharistic theology.

He believed the Spirit could make Christ so present to his followers that the seemingly unbridgeable gap between the finite human being "seated at the right hand of God the Father" and the congregation gathered around the eucharistic elements could in fact be bridged. Where the Spirit of the Lord was present in the church, there, too, Christ was present.

Zwingli turned to the doctrine of the two natures of Christ for his third suggestion. While the human nature of Jesus Christ remained finite even after the resurrection, his divine nature continued to be infinite. That meant that Christ could be present to the church not only by the action of the Holy Spirit, but also by the immediate presence of his divine nature itself. Of course, Christ's divine nature never appears in disembodied form. Because it is hypostatically united to Christ's human nature, the bond uniting them can never be severed. Wherever Christ is present, he is always present in both natures.

Zwingli centered the locus of Christ's presence in the worshipping community. Worshippers were the many grains formed by the action of God into one loaf. Zwingli scholars even suggest that what took place in the Eucharist was for Zwingli a kind of "transubstantiation" of the worshipping community into the body of Christ. This action took place prior to (or, at the very least, apart from) eating and drinking the consecrated bread and wine—which, as Zwingli made painfully clear on more than one occasion, could never be for him a means of grace.

Zwingli saw the Eucharist as a "visible sign of an invisible grace." In his view the "invisible grace" normally antedated the "visible sign." Worshippers ate the bread and drank the wine not in order to receive grace, but because they already had. At its core the Eucharist was an act of "thanksgiving." Believers shared the elements to express gratitude for what they had received and to confess their faith publicly. The material objects used in Zwingli's Eucharist belonged, in other words, to the visible response of the church to the invisible action of God. At no time were they regarded by Zwingli as channels of the grace they celebrated.

Jesus Christ and the Eucharist in Luther's Theology

Luther did not reject out of hand all of the propositions about the Eucharist Zwingli defended.[5] He agreed with Zwingli that transubstantiation was an unsatisfactory explanation of the mystery of Christ's real presence, though like his Catholic opponents he located Christ's presence in the elements of bread and wine. The problem with transubstantiation from Luther's point of view was that it required the faithful to believe two miracles: (1) that Christ was really present and (2) that his presence required the reduction of bread and wine to their accidents. For Luther one miracle sufficed. Christ was substantially present in the Eucharist, but so, too, were the bread and wine.[6]

Luther also agreed with Zwingli that the Eucharist was not a sacrifice. It was not something the priest offered to God for the sins of his congregation, not even when understood as a re-presentation of the unique sacrifice of Christ in unbloody form. The Eucharist was a gift God gave to the church. That is why both Luther and Zwingli preferred to regard it as a "benefit" or "testament" rather than a sacrifice.

"Testament" was a particularly important word for early Protestants. A testament is a one-sided contract that offers bequests to a beneficiary on the death of the testator. The contract is made not with a beneficiary but on his or her behalf. When Christ the testator died, he fulfilled the condition of his one-sided contract and offered to the church the benefits of his death and resurrection. The church did not in any sense merit such gifts, but received them as the undeserved bequest of the testator. The Eucharist is therefore, for Luther and Zwingli, not a place where sacrifices are offered, but where benefits are received.

Rejection of the doctrine of transubstantiation and the notion that the Eucharist was a sacrifice marked negative points of agreement between the two reformers. Positively, they agreed to regard the Eucharist as a visible Word of God: that is, as a proclamation in visible rather than audible form of Christ's death and resurrection. The Eucharist therefore offers Christ, not to God the Father, but to the worshipping congregation. The Word of God—that is, the lively and life-giving voice of the living God—is the instrument by which God created the world and through which he will renew it. It is the fundamental sacrament of which baptism and Eucharist are visible forms.

But there the agreements end and the disagreements begin to multiply. Luther dismissed Zwingli's reading of John 6:63: "The Spirit gives life," but "the flesh counts for nothing." The "flesh" which God condemned was not the material world, but the self-centered self that stands in opposition to God. Flesh in this text has to do with alienation, not materiality, and idolatry is a sin that can be committed in the complete absence of material objects. Whenever fallen human beings—whom Luther characterized as hearts turned in on themselves—trust what is not God as God (even if it is something as good as human love or as enduring as human friendship), they commit the primal sin of idolatry. No one commits idolatry by trusting the material channels for grace God has established in baptism and the Eucharist. They are trustworthy because they rest on God's promise. Not to trust the promise is not to trust God.

Luther was also not impressed by Zwingli's understanding of the phrase "seated at the right hand of God the Father" in the creed. The "right hand of

God" is obviously metaphorical language. In biblical language the "right hand" is the place of honor from which a ruler reigns. Since God reigns everywhere, "the right hand of God" is not so much a place as an assertion of God's universal sovereignty. Whereas Zwingli thought of the "right hand of God" as remote, transcendent, incredibly distant, Luther thought of it as immanent. That the risen Christ is at God's right hand is another way of asserting that Christ is everywhere present in his risen humanity.

Luther's view of the risen Christ rests on a Christology markedly different from Zwingli's. While Zwingli insisted on the finitude of Christ's risen humanity, Luther was willing to concede that something unprecedented had happened in the resurrection. Although Christ continued to bear a human body, it was a body no longer subject to limitations of space and time. Indeed, the body of the risen Christ could even walk through the door of a locked room to appear suddenly in the midst of his disciples. Luther thought what had occurred in the resurrection was a transfer of attributes (*communicatio idiomatum*) in which Christ's human nature took on some of the characteristics of his divine nature—including the trait of ubiquity.[7]

The chasm Zwingli posited between the congregation of believers on earth and the finite humanity of Christ in heaven dissolved for Luther. Luther saw no need to bring Christ down from heaven. Christ was already present on earth. He was present in the bread and wine, even before they were consecrated. Luther taunted Zwingli with the claim that the ubiquity of Christ's body meant it could be found everywhere, even in a peasant's bowl of pea soup (though—as Luther warned wryly—no one could locate Christ by stirring vigorously). If the risen Christ is where the Father reigns, he is never distant from the worshipping congregation. The ascension did not mean for Luther, as it did for Zwingli, that Christ had left the world's space and time, only that the mode of his continuing presence in the world had changed. The central problem for Luther's eucharistic theology was therefore not distance from the world, but inaccessible immanence within it.

Luther drew a simple distinction in German between a thing being present (*da*) and being accessible (*dir da*). The risen Christ is present (*da*) in ordinary bread and wine. But he is accessible to the church (*dir da*) only in the Eucharist. God has attached his promise to the Eucharist. It is there and not in ordinary bread and wine that Christ is savingly present in the full reality of both natures, truly human and truly divine. Luther affirmed the physical real presence of Christ and therefore insisted on a literal reading of the verb "is" in the words of institution. The Eucharist is not a mere sign pointing to a distant reality or even an icon through which the power of a distant divine reality is present. It is the thing itself. When Jesus said "this is my body," he meant what he said.

The question of whether unbelievers receive the body and blood of Christ when they participate in the Eucharist was largely moot for Luther's opponent, Zwingli. After all, in his view Christ was not present in the bread and wine at all. Believers received grace directly from God and participated in the Eucharist as an expression of their gratitude for grace already received. Believers and unbelievers alike, when taking the elements, received only bread and wine.

But Luther answered the question of whether unbelievers receive the body and blood of Christ with a resounding yes. The presence of Christ depended not on the faith of the communicant or the piety of the celebrant but on the reliability of God's promise. Even if an irrational creature—say, a mouse—were to eat the consecrated host, it would eat the body and blood of Christ. Nevertheless, faith was essential in order to receive the saving benefits of Christ's presence. Unbelievers received the body and blood of Christ, but they ate and drank to their own damnation. Benefits, Luther warned, were restricted to believers.

Jesus Christ and the Eucharist in Calvin's Theology

Calvin was appalled by Luther's doctrine of the ubiquity of the body of Christ.[8] A ubiquitous body was, in Calvin's view, no human body at all, only a "monstrous body" that had lost its proper form. While Calvin was critical of Zwingli on many points, he agreed with him that either Christ's humanity was finite or it was no longer human. Christ was, as Zwingli had correctly argued, "seated" in his finite humanity "at the right hand of God," a remote and distant place. The problem for Calvin, as for Zwingli, was how to bridge this chasm.[9]

Nevertheless, Calvin agreed with Luther that the material elements of bread and wine were in fact means of grace, a point Zwingli energetically denied. When the consecrated elements were offered to a worshipping congregation, Christ was offered. Christ was offered even if the congregation lacked faith. Indeed, Calvin wanted to argue for a real presence of Christ in the Eucharist, though his Christology forced him to argue for what he called a "spiritual real presence," an apparent oxymoron that bemused and annoyed Calvin's Lutheran critics.

Calvin offered four explanations to support his view that Christ was substantially present in the Eucharist. His first explanation rested on a redefinition of the word "substance." What, asked Calvin, was the substance of Christ's body? It was certainly not its bones, sinews, and tissue. The substance of Christ's body was its power and effect for human salvation. Wherever the power and effect of Christ's body was present, the substance of Christ's body was truly present.

Calvin's second explanation depended on a characterization of faith as an ecstatic act. When believers received the Eucharist, they were in Calvin's view elevated by faith to the "right hand of God," where they gazed on the risen Christ. In this account the chasm between heaven and earth was bridged not by the descent of Christ, but by the ascent of the church. Calvin obviously did not have in mind a literal ascent. However, to what extent this "ascent" was an inner psychological act of the human imagination and to what extent a gift of fresh insight by the Spirit was left unclear.

Calvin adopted his third and fourth explanations from Zwingli—though he revised them sharply on one crucial point. For Zwingli the locus of Christ's presence was the church; for Calvin it was the Eucharist itself. Nevertheless, both argued that Christ's presence depended on the action of the Holy Spirit (Calvin's third explanation) and the hypostatic union of Christ's divine and human natures (Calvin's fourth). Indeed, the whole Christ was present in the Eucharist, even if the finite human body remained at the right hand of God.

The Lutherans christened Calvin's fourth explanation as the *extracalvinisticum* because of a passage in the *Institutes* which suggested that Christ's divine nature continued to perform after the incarnation all the functions the Second Person of the Trinity had performed prior to it. So even while Jesus was asleep in a boat on the Sea of Galilee, his divine nature continued to function as the ordering principle of the universe, regulating wind and wave and tide. The Latin phrase Calvin used to describe the undiminished divine activity of the God-man, Jesus of Nazareth, was *etiam extra carnem*, "also outside the flesh." *Extra carnem* was another way of saying the God-man never ceased to do what God the Son had always done.

For Calvin the humiliation of the kenosis was that Christ hid his divine power, not that he surrendered it. Indeed, Calvin found it impossible to see how Christ's death could have been a totally free act of submission if he had relinquished his boundless power. Because he retained throughout his suffering and death the power to terminate it, his passion was an absolutely free choice. In this respect the divine nature guaranteed the undiminished integrity of the human. Christ chose to be victim; he was not victimized.

This state of affairs did not change with the ascension. Christ's divine nature continued to operate "outside the flesh," even in the Eucharist. And if Christ was present in the Eucharist, he was present in both natures. How could he not be, given the hypostatic union? Calvin asked only that theologians grant that (1) Christ's human nature was finite and (2) his infinite divine nature was hypostatically united to it, and they had conceded the possibility of a "spiritual real presence." In short, for Calvin the "whole Christ" was present in both natures, "but not wholly," so long as the finite humanity remained seated at the right hand of God. *Totus Christus sed non totum.*

Calvin's argument seemed like nonsense to Lutherans like Joachim Westphal and Tilemann Hesshusen, who suspected that Calvin was a "crafty sacramentarian," whose "spiritual real presence" was another form of "substantial real absence." At the very least Calvin seemed to them to have taken away with one hand what he conceded with the other. Lutheran theologians insisted on a glorification of Christ's risen humanity that overcame the finite limitations so crucial to the arguments of Zwingli and Calvin. Calvin did not accommodate them.

Calvin did agree with Luther that Christ was truly offered to the worshipping congregation in the Eucharist, even if the members of the congregation lacked faith. What he did not accept was the notion that unbelievers could receive Christ's body and blood. To explain what he had in mind, he posited the doctrine of a "double mouth." In order to receive bread and wine, one only needed a physical mouth. In order to receive Christ's body and blood, one needed the additional mouth of faith.

Faith did not make Christ present. Calvin was adamant on that point. Christ was offered to the congregation, whether it received him or not. But there was an important difference for Calvin between offering and receiving. Unbelievers were offered Christ, but received only bread and wine. Believers were offered Christ and received both Christ and the consecrated elements. In his rejection of the notion that unbelievers do in fact receive Christ, Calvin broke decisively with Luther.

Conclusion

If Zwingli, Luther, and Calvin were asked to identify Jesus, they would undoubtedly have pointed to what they regarded as the historically reliable narrative of his life, death, and resurrection in the four Gospels, a narrative anticipated in the Old Testament and further explicated in the New. As they saw it, Christians were called to obey this Jesus and no other.

At the same time, explaining Jesus as he was offered to them by the Gospels was no simple task. It compelled them to use the complex language of the ancient creeds. In their view, the Bible taught—in substance if not in words—that the Second Person of the Trinity assumed humanity, though not a human being, in Jesus of Nazareth. This incarnate Lord bore two natures, fully human and fully divine, hypostatically united in one person. When Luther indicated at the beginning of the Smalcald Articles that he had no quarrel with the Catholic church over the doctrine of the Trinity or the two natures of Christ, he could have been speaking for Zwingli and Calvin as well.

Their differences emerged in the context of their discussions of the Eucharist. Zwingli and Calvin argued that it was essential for Christ's humanity to remain finite, even after the resurrection and ascension. Christ could not be our high priest, if he no longer bore our humanity. However, they rejected as faulty reasoning the claim that the presence of Christ's finite humanity in heaven precluded its presence on earth. In the end both defended a kind of "spiritual real presence," though Zwingli located it in the church and Calvin in the bread and wine.

Luther thought there was ample evidence in the New Testament that the risen Christ had undergone a transformation. His body was no longer subject to temporal and spatial limitations. Therefore it could be physically present whenever the Eucharist was celebrated. The good news for Luther was that Christ was not only present but also accessible. As Luther saw matters, the problem for eucharistic theology had never been a chasm between heaven and earth, but the existence on earth of a presence that eluded human grasp.

The disagreements among the Protestant reformers richly illustrate the point that debates about the nature of the Eucharist are so intertwined with debates about the identity of Jesus that it is impossible to separate them for very long. This line from a hymn, "O young and fearless prophet of ancient Galilee, thy life is still a summons to serve humanity," evokes one kind of eucharistic theology. This line from a Christmas carol, "Veiled in flesh the Godhead see, hail the incarnate deity," evokes quite another. While it is not clear that the eucharistic encounter with Jesus depends on having the theory exactly right, it is clear that ideas do matter. Martin Kähler may have been right when, faced with the limitations of human reasoning about God, he suggested that the intellectual as well as the moral life of Christians needs to be justified by faith. But his suggestion does not change the fact that eucharistic theologies have no obvious way to transcend the theories about Jesus on which they rest. Theories about Jesus inspire exactly the eucharistic theologies they deserve. It could hardly be otherwise.

13

World Christianity under New Management?

It's no secret, of course, that Christianity is an international movement. But it is an international movement that has been dominated by Christians in the developed West. Christians from Asia, Africa, and Latin America (the region known as the Global South) have taken their cues from the settled churches of Europe and North America.

There are signs, however, that this relationship is changing. Take, for example, the recent debate in the United States and Canada over gay ordination and same-sex marriage. While mainline churches in the West have taken an increasingly liberal stance on gay and lesbian issues, churches in the Global South have not. With very few exceptions the South opposes the ordination of gay clergy and the blessing of same-sex unions.

The English newspaper the *Guardian* urged Anglicans in the developed West to "ignore the bigots" in the Global South and to continue to support gay and lesbian issues. But ignoring the Global South is increasingly hard to do.

At its triennial convention in 2004, the Anglican Church of Canada decided to postpone its debate on the approval of same-sex unions until 2007, even though the liberal provinces of Quebec, Ontario, and British Columbia had by then already approved same-sex marriage. The reason was the opposition of the Global South.

The case for postponement was argued by the Rev. Canon Gregory Cameron, speaking on behalf of the Archbishop of Canterbury. Such a postponement could buy time for the beleaguered Anglican Communion and reduce the strains brought on by the unilateral decision of the Episcopal Church (the American branch of the Anglican Communion) to consecrate an openly gay man, the Rt. Rev. V. Gene Robinson, as the bishop of New Hampshire. The Canadians grudgingly agreed to wait.

In 2007 the Canadians took the matter up again and this time narrowly defeated a proposal to bless same-sex unions, even though such unions are legal throughout Canada. In the end, it was the opposition of the Canadian bishops, who were unwilling to become the cause of a permanent division in the Anglican Communion, that did the proposal in.

The Canadian bishops found the Global South hard to ignore, not least because it is the fastest-growing area in Christendom. In 1900 there were only 10 million Christians in Africa. Africa now has 360 million, Latin America 560 million, and Asia 313 million. There are at least 30 million Christians in China, perhaps as many as 50 million. Korea has a large Christian minority, and Korean missionaries can be found throughout Asia.

The figures for attendance at Sunday worship are even more striking. Archbishop Peter Akinola presides over an Anglican church in Nigeria with more than 17 million members. But Anglican services in Nigeria can be attended on any Sunday by twice that number of worshippers. By contrast, the Church of England and the American Episcopal Church each have an average Sunday attendance of roughly 800,000 to 1 million.

The African churches in particular are now working on American soil. On May 5, 2007, Martyn Minns, a former rector of an Episcopal parish in Truro, Virginia, was installed as an Anglican bishop at a ceremony held in the suburbs of Washington, DC. His installation came just two days before the four hundredth anniversary of the arrival of the first Anglicans in Virginia.

But the installation of Bishop Minns was not so much a celebration of Anglicanism's past as an attempt to redefine its future. Minns was installed not as the successor of Peter Lee, then bishop of the Episcopal diocese of Virginia, but as the first missionary bishop of the Anglican Church of Nigeria. The service was led not by Katherine Jefferts Schori, the presiding bishop of the Episcopal Church, but by Archbishop Peter Akinola, the primate of Nigeria.

The consecration was another step in a conservative response to the decision of the Episcopal Church in 2003 to consecrate a divorced gay man as a bishop and to permit, as a local option, the blessing of same-sex unions. Of course, bitter controversy is nothing new to the churches of the Anglican Communion, which have managed to hold together through thick and thin despite long-standing theological differences between liberals, evangelicals, and Anglo-Catholics. But the consecration of Robinson as bishop was a turning point for conservatives. It reminded them how deep those differences in the Episcopal Church had become, how unlikely the church was to change, and how remote, therefore, was the possibility of ultimate reconciliation.

The churches in Africa were particularly sensitive to what they understood as the plight of a conservative minority in liberal American churches. They were also sensitive to the general Anglican concern with pedigree. After all, it is never enough for Anglicans to have bishops. They must have bishops in apostolic succession.

Apostolic succession means that proper bishops are consecrated by bishops who were consecrated by bishops who were consecrated by bishops who were consecrated by apostles. Anglicans—even evangelical Anglicans who sing praise songs, speak in tongues, and listen to Christian rock bands—want bishops in an unbroken succession to the first century. It is a non-negotiable point.

Which is exactly what the Africans could provide for American conservatives. Bishop Henry Orombi of Uganda took under his wing disaffected Episcopalians who wanted the spiritual direction of a conservative archbishop who clearly stood in apostolic succession. Archbishop Emmanuel Kolini of Rwanda even started the Anglican Mission to America, an alternative evangelical church for Anglicans, complete with its own missionary hierarchy and evangelistic zeal.

But in all these developments, Archbishop Akinola held back. To be sure, he became the principal defender of American conservatives and their most outspoken champion. Still, he waited to make his most important move. The reason for Akinola's delay seems to have been that he wanted there to be no doubt that the leadership of the Episcopal Church would refuse to comply with the demands of the worldwide Anglican Communion before he acted—especially the demand that it accept a "primatial vicar," or alternative chief presiding officer, for conservatives. Once the door to a primatial vicar was closed, Akinola offered a Nigerian alternative.

Liberal Episcopalians were not amused. They pointed to the fact that very few congregations had at the time actually withdrawn from the Episcopal Church and that Akinola's initiative outside his own diocese violated ancient Christian tradition. But the protest seemed to miss the real significance of the African initiative—namely, its aim to revitalize Anglicanism in America on the model of Anglicanism in Africa. Neither Akinola nor Kolini intends to limit the growth of their churches to already disaffected members of the Episcopal Church, competing for ever smaller slices of a shrinking pie. Both know how to grow new churches in unlikely places with new converts. Each assumes that the beautiful liturgy, evangelical theology, and contagious faith that drew new converts to African-style Anglicanism will draw Americans as well.

There is also an anticolonial edge to the new African initiatives. Christians in the West are well aware of the reaction against Western values by Islamic militants but seem far less sensitive to the anticolonial thinking of Christians in the Global South. Africans in particular regard the imposition of the sexual morality of the West on their traditional societies as a new and insidious form of intellectual colonialism that must be resisted.

As painful as the cross-cultural argument between Christians in the West and Global South may be, it is unavoidable. One of the oldest tests for authentic Christian teaching is to ask whether it is universally accepted. The old rule was that it should have been taught "everywhere, always, and by all."

According to that rule a theological opinion was thought to fail the test of universality if it could be embraced in Canada but not in Kenya, or in England but not in Hong Kong. On the other hand, it passed a crucial test if it showed staying power over time. Even then, it could not be accepted as correct if promoted by only one sociological group—by men but not by women, by whites but not by blacks, or by rich but not by poor. Christians thought that truth is by definition boundary-transcending: either a teaching transcends boundaries, or it is an error. "Local option" is another name for heresy.

Judged by the ancient standard of "everywhere, always, and by all," the international debate in mainline Christian churches over human sexuality is a long way away from achieving a consensus. The temptation of the liberal West will be to give up on dialogue with the more conservative Global South, surrender any hope of consensus, and fall back into the comfortable old ways of colonial thinking. We teach; they listen.

But falling into the bad old ways is a formula for disaster. Unless the emerging consensus of the churches over human sexuality is international, it will not last. You can count on it.

14

Religion in the Public Square

The 5,300-pound stone monument of the Ten Commandments was removed in 2003 from its place in the Alabama Judicial Building, to the consternation of the demonstrators who had camped for more than a week on the courthouse steps to protest its removal. State Supreme Court Chief Justice Roy Moore, who defied a court order to remove the monument, was suspended from office and eventually relieved of his post.

The whole episode clearly made a statement in the long-standing debate in America about the role of religion in public life. But what kind of a statement it made is anything but clear. If the Alabama monument had been installed in 1828, one could reasonably argue that the federal government ought to leave it alone as part of the cultural heritage of Alabama, even though the granite monument is, to say the least, not museum-quality art. But "Roy's Rock" was not a cultural heirloom. It was installed in the Judicial Building two years before it was removed as an aggressive challenge to prevailing cultural trends of which the chief justice disapproved.

Moore claimed that he had installed the monument, and subsequently opposed its removal, because it was a public symbol of his conviction that the Ten Commandments are the moral foundation of American law. But as Christians and Jews already know, American law and Mosaic law diverge on many issues. Take the commandments concerning adultery and Sabbath-keeping as prime examples. Marital infidelity is not punishable in America with the death penalty (even though some offended spouses may wish it were). And the Mosaic rules concerning Sabbath-keeping, once codified in America in the so-called blue laws, would be immensely unpopular among Sunday shoppers if reintroduced by state legislatures.

Even the claims for the Christian roots of the American form of government can be vastly overstated by the zealous. It is true that the principle of separation of powers is partly derived from a Calvinist reading of the Christian doctrine of original sin (the natural tendency of human beings to think more highly of themselves than they ought to think, and to act accordingly). But it is also true that it derives partly from English constitutional history, especially from the bitter clashes between Crown and parliament, and partly from some ancient theories about government advanced two millennia ago by the Roman statesman Marcus Tullius Cicero.

Even so, one might inquire whether the installation of a large and ugly monument to the Ten Commandments, absent the religious intent of Chief Justice Moore, constitutes by itself an establishment of religion. Or it is merely a violation of the norms of good taste? Would the monument be acceptable to its critics if the Alabama Supreme Court had installed additional monuments to other great moments in the history of law, from Solon to the Code Napoleon? What if the offending monument were a magnificent work of art by Michelangelo? Did removing the Ten Commandments represent, as Justice Douglas Johnstone suggested, a necessary stand against the danger that America will become a theocracy (an event in my view as improbable as the loss of New York City to a rogue glacier)? Justice Johnstone needs to watch the *Jerry Springer Show.*

Americans on both sides of the cultural divide appear more confident about where to draw the line between religion and the state than anyone really can be at this stage of our political discourse. We are still trying as a society to figure out the best course of action and to trample on as few consciences as possible in the process. The consensus we seek (but has thus far eluded us) lies somewhere between the religious extremists, who want to impose Christian values, mainly Protestant, on everyone else, and their secular counterparts, who want to ban religion completely from public life and make it a purely private matter, like a passion for scuba diving or a taste for boiled okra. This society is both too religious and too tolerant to accept either extreme.

What we need to do is exactly what we are doing; we need to argue it out. The good news is that we still live in a robust democracy, however flawed. It will survive the disagreement. Down the road we may arrive at a new social contract with each other that will define a reading of the nonestablishment clause of the Constitution we can all live with. If not, we can survive that, too.

Part of the argument revolves around the question of the original intention of the Constitution. Some senators always want to quiz Supreme Court nominees about their views on the "original intention" of the framers of the Constitution. They particularly want to know what role nominees assign to such an "original intention" in determining the outcome of cases brought before the court.

No one expects the candidates to say (even in the unlikely case they thought it) that the original intention of the framers is of no relevance whatever in deciding cases before the Supreme Court or that the Constitution is a blank whose entire meaning is filled in by the current Justices.

On the other hand, discerning the original intention of historical documents, especially one agreed to by a large body of politicians long dead, is not as simple as it might first seem. After all, not everyone who first read the Constitution or had a hand in its writing had exactly the same thing in mind. Diversity of opinion is not a twenty-first-century invention. Disagreement and compromise were alive and well in the eighteenth century.

Take, for example, the Constitution's First Amendment, which forbids Congress (though not the states) to pass any laws that establish religion or hinder its free exercise. The first problem is terminological. The word "religion" was often used in the early republic as a synonym for Christianity, especially in its Protestant forms. "Getting religion" was another way of talking about converting to Christianity. Although the framers were aware of non-Christian religions, they were not the primary focus of the First Amendment.

What worried Thomas Jefferson and James Madison were the various Christian establishments that had once existed in colonies like Virginia and continued to exist in Europe. In the sixteenth century, Christian Europe had picked specific churches to back, usually with tax money gathered from the purses of the willing and unwilling alike. England was Anglican, Sweden Lutheran, France Roman Catholic, Holland Reformed, and Russia Eastern Orthodox.

Where one form of Christianity was supported by the state, very little breathing room was left for all the others. John Bunyan wrote his classic, *Pilgrim's Progress*, while imprisoned in Bedford jail for his activities as a Baptist minister in Anglican England. Establishment of religion and the prohibition of free exercise were two sides of the same coin.

Even among people who opposed the establishment of religion, there was a diversity of opinion. Some supporters, like Patrick Henry in Virginia, thought that the Anglican Church should be disestablished but that church taxes should continue to be collected. Henry wanted to share the tax revenues with all the churches, not just the once-established Anglicans.

American refugees from state churches (like the Mennonites of Pennsylvania) thought that any government support was bad for churches, which should remain completely independent from all government support and entanglement.

Other Americans, like Thomas Jefferson, thought entanglement with churches was bad for the state. He even opposed the right of clergy to run for political office, a position successfully defeated by James Madison. In Madison's view such a position would deprive a group of citizens—namely, clergy—of a natural right conferred on them by God, or, at the very least, not conferred by the state.

Madison thought that establishment was bad for both state and church. In his view (which proved to be correct) religion would thrive if the smothering hand of the state were withdrawn. The state, after all, is almost comically incompetent in theological matters and should stick to the more mundane business it understands.

What Madison promoted was neutrality, an American state that neither embraced one religious group at the expense of all others nor restricted the free religious practice of its citizens. As Madison saw it, establishment was bad because it was contrary to natural rights and inevitably drove some forms of religious belief and practice from the public square.

In other words, the eighteenth century saw not one, but several "original intentions," from Henry, who wanted to support all religious groups, to Jefferson, who thought it better to support none. Madison took the middle road by envisioning a state that is religiously neutral rather than religiously unfriendly.

So perhaps the question the senators should ask nominees for the Supreme Court is this: "Of all the framers of the Constitution, whose understanding of its original intention do you find most persuasive?"

Which bring us back to religious monuments. The monument in Alabama had hardly been removed before Florida decided to join Alabama in testing the boundaries between religion and the state.

A group of private citizens in Polk County, Florida, installed a 6,000-pound granite monument to the Ten Commandments in the rotunda of their administration building to rival the 5,300-pount granite monument to the Ten Commandments removed from display in the Alabama Judicial Building. Unlike the Alabama monument, however, the so-called Foundation Rock in Polk Country has inscriptions from the Magna Carta, the Bill of Rights, and Hammurabi's Code, as well as from the Bible, thus making its constitutionality difficult to challenge.

The controversies in Florida and Alabama over religious symbols in public places serve as a pointed reminder that America, when judged by European standards, is still a very religious country. The sociologist Peter Berger once quipped that America is the India of the West (with, he added, an intellectual class imported from Sweden). While talk-show pundits immediately agreed that the monuments should be removed, most Americans were apparently not convinced that a replica of the Ten Commandments constitutes a clear and present danger to the well-being of the Republic. According to a USA Today–CNN poll, 77 percent of the 1,009 Americans interviewed disapproved of the order by a federal judge to remove the offending monument from the Alabama courthouse.

The debate about unwarranted intrusion is usually framed by stressing the doctrine of the separation of church and state. Public policy, it is argued, should be determined in a religion-free zone by reasonable people, who examine the options available to them and make rational choices on the basis of convincing evidence. Religion as a system of beliefs and values has no place in the corridors of power.

The late Paul Tillich took a different line. He wanted to discuss religion under the heading of "ultimate concern." In his view, all human beings are religious in the sense that they cherish deeply held convictions about the nature of the universe and the moral standards appropriate for human behavior. Religious institutions address such questions directly, but they are not questions human beings can successfully escape by avoiding organized religion.

From this perspective, political debates in America are not between people who hold religious views and people who do not, but between people who hold different and sometimes sharply conflicting religious views. Since everyone is committed to such core beliefs, however loosely formulated, the notion of a value-neutral, religion-free zone in which public discourse can take place is a myth.

One does not have to accept Tillich's generous definition of religion to admit that public-policy debates are arguments between people who are already deeply committed. Some things are not up for a vote. Political discourse in a democracy is passionate precisely because it is not neutral. It is about things that really matter—about beliefs and values and visions of the good society.

Which means, of course, that religion in both the broad and narrower sense never intrudes into public life, because it is already there. Democracy moves forward not by excluding religious values or suppressing fundamental beliefs, but by risking the outcome of unrestricted debate. It is a risk free people should be willing to take.

15

The Necessity of the Past

Americans are not as a matter of course oriented toward the past. There are any number of historical reasons why they are not. America represented for the immigrant populations of Europe an attempt to break with the Old World and to make a fresh start, untrammeled by the past. Most of the immigrants to the New World had good reasons for trying to begin again, for wanting to forget the past. Some had been persecuted for their faith, some for their politics. And those who had not been persecuted left because they faced a bleak economic future and believed they could improve their situation in a land hospitable to new beginnings and careless of the past.

After all, why would potential immigrants want to leave Europe and face the dangers and uncertainties of the American frontier if life in their native land was comfortable and secure? There were, of course, adventurers who found excitement in the harsh American frontier lands, and indentured servants, especially African slaves, who were compelled to come. But more frequently, the immigrant was a person who wanted to begin again and who had good reason to forget the past.

I

Nation-building consumed energies and talents in America that in Europe could be devoted to culture and the arts. Art requires leisure, and there was little of that on the frontier. The frontier was radically egalitarian. It judged people by what they could do and not by what they had been. If men and women could bear their share of the work and were honest in their dealings with their neighbors, no one was inclined to be inquisitive about their past. The talents valued on the frontier were talents that were immediately useful for survival in a harsh and primitive situation. If thoughtful people wanted to write novels or read ancient history, that was their business— provided they knew how to make an immediate contribution to frontier society and did not expect others to do their work while they read and thought. Folk could live on the frontier without knowing how to read; they could not live without knowing how to hunt, fish, spin, weave, trap, farm, clear land, carpenter, shoe a horse, and defend themselves.

Preoccupation with practical tasks did not mean that Americans lived altogether without a sense of history. They commemorated their national heroes and events. But the past played a lesser role for them than the future. There were no Roman ruins in Kentucky, no castles of robber barons along the Missouri River. Americans were not surrounded by memorials of the past. The great fact for American life was the frontier. Or perhaps I should put that differently: the great fact that confronted Americans on every hand was seemingly limitless space. There were new lands to be opened up, new resources to be exploited, and new possibilities for movement and migration. The future offered rugged individuals who were willing to take risks the chance to make their fortunes in a land their ancestors had never seen.

In Europe, the land had been divided centuries before; movement and migration were restricted; national boundaries were clearly known, as were social and economic boundaries. Children born in Europe knew what the future held; largely, it held what the past had held for the generations of men and women born before them. The possibilities were clearly marked out, and they were limited. Not so the American frontier. The future on the American frontier was a time of limitless possibilities, or so at least it seemed. And not only so, but the possibilities that confronted children were always believed to be better than the possibilities that confronted their parents and grandparents.

Americans were future-oriented. The future was hopeful, fraught with new and unknown possibilities. And there was in the indeterminate and hopeful future a solution for every problem. Europeans might feel in advance that a problem was insoluble, if for no other reason than their forebears thought it was insoluble. But Americans were not burdened with such respect for the opinions of the past. They did not know that a problem was insoluble until they themselves tried to solve it and failed. Even then they were convinced that their own failure did not rule out the possibility of the later success of someone else. The future was hopeful; no one knew in advance the limits of its possibilities, and for every problem—no matter how complex—there was a practical solution.

The American attitude toward Europe and toward the European past was complicated by still another fact: the belief in American innocence and boundless goodwill. Puritans came to America to found a Holy Commonwealth, a city that should be set on a hill as an example to the nations. Americans in every generation since have been seeking to build the Kingdom of God in America. Europe represented for America not only the past, which they were eager to forget, but what they regarded as a corrupt past, from whose contamination they wished to escape. The ocean served as insulation against the influences of a decadent Old World. Here in America they could build the Holy Commonwealth or the Great Society (a secular version of the same thing), unhindered by the baleful influences of the past. Americans believed that God was making in their country a new beginning. Therefore Americans regarded the past not so much something to be studied as something to be overcome.

These attitudes toward the past place the American church in an awkward position. The plain fact is that the church cannot escape the past, however much it may wish to. It cannot escape the past because of the nature of the Christian faith, which rests on an appeal to certain past events. Those events have been claimed by the church to be not only decisive for its own faith, but absolutely crucial for the history of the world—for the history and destiny even of people who have no interest at all in these events or who have never heard about them. The Apostles' Creed, recited in Christian churches, is itself evidence of this appeal to history. Consider the verbs that are used: "conceived…born… suffered…crucified…buried…descended…rose again." When Christians recite the creed, they point to this history, to this story of Jesus of Nazareth, whom the church claims to be the Word and Deed of God in history. The church confesses that the salvation of the world was effected in the life, death, and resurrection of this man. Not all Christians understand these events in the same way. But regardless of how they explain them, they all appeal to them.

Of course, there are some people who are radically skeptical about knowledge of the past, especially the past that the church confesses to be important, but also, when pressed, about the past in general. In the nineteenth century, radical historical skepticism was in great vogue. The critical intelligence of historians, for a brief period at least, ran amok. Radical skepticism eventually died a natural death. No one refuted it; indeed, no convincing arguments could be adduced to refute it. As a philosophical position it was airtight. What finally did it in was common sense. Historians found that people who began by doubting whether Caesar crossed the Rubicon ended by doubting whether their latchkeys would fit their front doors. If radical skepticism concerning the first problem did not lead them in time to radical skepticism concerning the second, it was either because they were not logically consistent or because they were cursed with a lamentably pragmatic disposition, unswayed by philosophic reasoning and probably unswayable. In short, the arguments of the radical historians proved to be very much like the arguments of a madman. They were logical, flawless in their rational consistency, but much too small to fit reality. Human life is not possible without memory, neither in the short run nor in the long.

Memory is not, however, a faculty that enables us to escape from a present that we find distressing or boring into a past no longer strange and therefore manageable. Even Zwingli, who liked to stress the memorial aspect of the Lord's Supper, its intractably past dimension, did so not because he thought memory was a faculty for taking us out of the present. Zwingli was too much of an Augustinian for that. Memory is a faculty that takes some aspect of the past and makes it a datum of my present, as real and tangible as the pew on which I am sitting or the neighbor who is seated beside me. Memory grasps the past and makes it a part of my present. It does so because I need that past in order to function in the present. It is for the sake of the present that memory lays hold of the events of the past.

II

Christian faith is based on certain remembered events in history—above all, on the resurrection of Jesus Christ from the dead. The resurrection is the key event on which all else depends. First Corinthians 15:14 is a text the church cannot circumvent: "If Christ has not been raised, then our preaching is in vain and your faith is in vain." No resurrection, no Christianity.

This means that Christianity is not, first of all, an appeal to philosophy. Early Gentile Christians were not terribly interested in history. They were frequently under the influence of an outlook that tended to depreciate what happened in history. It stressed instead the importance of eternal and unchanging truth, a realm of ideas above history that could be penetrated by a philosopher's disciplined reason. In explaining the Christian faith and in recommending it to their contemporaries, Gentile Christians made use of philosophical ideas and categories so deeply ingrained in them that they could not imagine a way of looking at the world that dispensed with them entirely. But however useful Gentile Christians imagined philosophy to be, they did not lose, except perhaps momentarily, their hold on history. Greek philosophy was used by Christians to explain to themselves and to the pagan world how God had entered history in Jesus of Nazareth. There were, then as now, philosophical ideas on which Christians and non-Christians could agree; and Christians used philosophy with varying degrees of adequacy as a means of interpreting the Christian faith. But Christian faith does not rest on any single philosophy—not on Platonism, Aristotelianism, Kantianism, Hegelianism, existentialism, process thought, or language analysis. The Christian faith rests on past events, which it believes to be crucial.

This also means that Christianity is not an appeal to ethics divorced from history. There have been attempts to locate the significance of Christianity in the ethical precepts of the teaching of Jesus, precepts that existed before he enunciated them and that are valid apart from all consideration of the events of his life. History is denigrated in favor not of metaphysics (with its abstract arguments) but of morality (with its well-scrubbed and respectable face). But to praise the moral teaching and dispense with the figure of Jesus is to turn the New Testament on its head. From the standpoint of the Christian faith, the importance of Jesus of Nazareth is not that he uttered the Golden Rule, but that he was conceived, born, suffered, crucified, died, buried, and rose. This means that my faith as a Christian is inextricably bound up with those events of the past. To be a Christian is by definition to be involved in the past, if only for the sake of the present and future.

III

There is, of course, a catch. Whether we know it or not and whether we think it is a good idea or not, our understanding of the Christian faith is influenced by the Christian tradition in which we stand. We inherit more than a New Testament account of the life, death, and resurrection of Jesus Christ; we inherit a traditional understanding of it. What we sometimes naively assume to be a biblical idea may not be directly stated in the Bible at all (at least not in the meaning we attach to it), but is either a deduction from selected data or a probable explanation of certain muddy and ambiguous passages. Our understanding of the Christian faith, quite apart from the question of whether we find this desirable or not, has been influenced by postbiblical developments in the Christian church.

The doctrine of the Trinity provides a good example of the way in which the early church reflected on the Bible and shaped our understanding of it. We are all acquainted, more or less, with the outcome of the Trinitarian controversies. It is reflected in the concluding line of a familiar hymn: "God in three persons, blessed Trinity." Is the word "Trinity" a biblical term? Do we find it anywhere in the Old or New Testaments? The answer, of course, is no. What do we find in the Bible? The Greek fathers would have said that in the Old Testament we find the confession that God is one, and in the New Testament we find the three names Father, Son, and Holy Spirit. How are these three names related to the confession that God is one? The Bible does not answer that question. The doctrine of the Trinity is the answer that the early church hammered out as it tried to reconcile its belief in the oneness of God with its conviction that God was revealed as Father, Son, and Holy Spirit. Anyone who has studied theology knows how difficult this question was to answer and how reluctantly the church came up with its solution.

The doctrine of the Trinity is not directly found in the Bible, but it represents the attempt of the church to make sense out of what it did find there. In arriving at its position the church weighed and rejected dynamic and modalistic Monarachianism, Tritheism, and Arianism, all of which offered alternative explanations of the biblical evidence. When I read the baptismal formula in the Gospel of Matthew ("Make disciples of all nations, baptizing them in the name of the Father and of the Son and of the Holy Spirit," Matt. 28:19) and think to myself, "Aha, the doctrine of the Trinity!" I do so because my understanding of the primitive faith of the church has been influenced and shaped by all the generations of Christian interpreters who stand between me and the apostolic age.

Church history helps us become self-conscious concerning our dependence on the traditions of the past. It thereby gives us the freedom, when necessary, to become critical of those traditions. People who believe that they have no creed except the Bible will, I am sorry to say, be victimized by the past. So, too, will those innocent souls who believe that the history of the world begins with the birth of their own consciousness.

Let me quickly add that I do not think that it is a bad thing for the Christian church in the present to be influenced by the church of the past in its understanding of the Christian faith. Quite the contrary: it is not only inevitable that the church in the present will be influenced by the past, it is even desirable. What is intolerable in a Christian theologian or pastor is a lack of awareness of that influence. As long as Christians do not understand the role of tradition in shaping their faith and influencing their actions, they will allow it to control them unconsciously. That is not to say that this is always reprehensible and may not be turned to good use by a wise providence. Christians may be under the influence of traditions that lead them into a faithful apprehension of the Gospel and that provide reliable guidelines for responsible action in the present. But they may also be misled and misguided by tradition. As long as they accept uncritically what they have received from the past, they put ourselves unreservedly in its power. Tradition can obscure as well as clarify the Gospel. The study of history gives the church freedom vis-à-vis its past: freedom to appropriate its past wisdom, when it can, and overcome its faithlessness and sin, when it must. The aim of church history as a theological discipline is to provide the church with a more universal and self-critical perspective within which to make responsible theological and pastoral decisions in the present. The study of the church's past ought to be a liberating experience as Christians learn, in the phrase of Adolf von Harnack, "to overcome history with history," always bearing in mind that unexamined history operates as fate.

IV

Church history has an indispensable role to play as a theological stimulus and corrective. In freeing Christians from theological parochialism, it also results in a loss of innocence. Students see how the traditions they learned in a parish or parachurch group evolved over the course of the centuries and discover, sometimes to their chagrin, that their tradition, whatever else it may be, is not simply a repristination in the twenty-first century of the primitive apostolic faith. As they become acquainted with traditions other than their own, they are painfully disabused of the idea that tradition A (their own) is the only possible option that the church has followed or, indeed, can follow. When they place tradition A alongside traditions B, C, and D, they realize for the first time what tradition A really is. Through the study of history they become aware of the diversity of traditions in the Christian church and self-critical of their own tradition. The very existence of other traditions, all claiming to be faithful to the Gospel (and each with some undeniable right to do so), puts their own tradition in question. If at the end of this self-criticism they once again affirm, albeit in a modified form, tradition A, they do so because they have tested it in the light of divergent and often conflicting interpretations that challenge their own point of view. This loss of innocence is absolutely essential to responsible theological work.

It is not the task of historians to reformulate the Christian faith anew for this generation or to prescribe policies for the church's action in the present. But by interpreting what the church did in the past, by clarifying what it believed, they provide Christians with a more universal perspective within which to clarify their own faith and to formulate our own actions in the present. The first task of church history as a theological discipline is to free Christians from their own parochialism and make them truly catholic.

The study of church history also teaches Christians to make modest claims for their theology. There is a sense in which theology is a humble science. It is human reflection about divine revelation. No one can, by taking thought, initiate divine revelation, nor is there any way to bypass it. Even theologians who are keen on constructing a natural theology only do so because they believe that God has previously been revealed in nature and is therefore prehensible to human reason and imagination. The Christian church has claimed from the beginning that there is no knowledge of God apart from revelation. Theology waits humbly, hat in hand, for that revelation.

Perhaps that is not the best image. Christian theologians are not waiting for divine self-revelation, because they believe it has occurred already. Revelation is the presupposition and precondition of theology. Theology begins with a given: unless there is revelation, no authentically Christian theology is possible. Theology is a human enterprise. God is revealed in nature and history, and theology is reflection in time about that revelation. All theological decisions are historically conditioned: that is to say, they are the decisions of people who live and think in the categories of their own time. Christians do not simply borrow their philosophical categories from non-Christians in order to make their faith intelligible. They are converted along with their intellectual categories, which are embedded in their own existence. These categories partly obscure and partly clarify the revelation of God with which they deal.

Church history reminds us that all Christian doctrine, including the theologies of hope, revolution, the future, play, virtue, and the city, is historical. The norm for Christian theology is not logical consistency but faithfulness to its origin: God's revelation occurs in time and under the conditions of finitude. Church history forces us to admit that reflection about that revelation is inevitably a human enterprise and therefore only partly true. It is not simply the weight of the past from which the study of church history frees Christians, but also the weight of an undue and inauthentic attachment to the present.

In part Christians study the history of the church in order to find answers to the questions that perplex them. But in the process of finding answers to their questions, they are opened up to new problems and learn questions that had never occurred to them before. That means that though they study the past for the sake of the present, they proceed methodologically as though they were studying the past for the sake of the past alone. Their questions drive them to the sources in the first place. But if they hope to learn from those sources, they must discover the questions they were originally written to answer. Only arduous labor, an active application of the historical imagination to the writings of the past, will teach them what they hope to learn. It is not true that the documents of the past speak to readers without any involvement on their part. The past is mute until it is cross-examined. A merely passive reading of an old theological text will teach readers very little. They must learn to ask it the kind of questions that will spark it into life. If they ask it wrong or foolish questions, they will be given misleading or foolish answers.

It is both necessary and dangerous for readers to ask their questions of the past. Unfortunately, if they search the past with their questions uppermost in their minds, but do not trouble to learn the context in which those questions were first raised, they will, to be sure, find some light on their questions. But they will misunderstand much of what they read, and unnecessarily and prematurely limit what they can learn from the wisdom of the past. If, however, they learn to come to the past on its terms and not on theirs, and if they learn to ask the questions the documents were written to answer, they will find more than answers to their questions. They will find themselves in turn questioned by their sources. Through strange and unfamiliar debates of the past, on the pages of ancient commentaries, in dusty and unread books, they will suddenly find themselves engaged by the insights of men and women long forgotten or at best dimly remembered. In a flash, their questions will be transformed by the older questions of others. Over the bridge of the past they will enter a newer and richer world.

Historians, unlike systematic theologians, are left with historical materials that will not conform to their finer theological instincts and with results that force them to conclusions that they find personally disagreeable. There is one commandment and one only that church historians must scrupulously observe: namely, honor thy father and thy mother. Historians must accept the past as it offers itself to them. They have no godlike prerogative to bowdlerize and "improve" history. It may be true that we understand the arguments between disputants in the past better than they themselves did, but we also labor under handicaps that they did not have. Luther and Eck may have lacked sympathy with each other, but they shared the same language, the same undivided church, and similar educational and cultural opportunities, were acquainted personally, and must assuredly have had friends in common. With all that in their favor, they still disagreed, not once but repeatedly. I may applaud that disagreement or bemoan it; I may understand it or explain it away; but one thing I cannot do: I cannot alter it. The historical event is beyond the reach of the historian at the level of its sheer givenness.

We study the past for the sake of the present and the future, though we proceed methodologically as if the present were not our real concern. We study the past because it is able to instruct us, if we learn to ask it the right questions and discover how to engage it on its own terms. It opens us to insights, ideas, and questions we would have encountered in no other way.

V

I once attended a party where I was called on to introduce all the guests. I knew everyone there, so that was not an unreasonable request. I went around the circle of guests easily calling off the names. Then I noticed from the corner of my eye a young woman sitting on a window ledge. Suddenly I panicked. I could not remember her name. There were five guests to go, then four, three, two, and at last, in shame and confusion, I had to ask her to introduce herself. My lapse of memory meant that I could no longer function effectively in the present.

I thought at the time what an awful thing it must be to lose one's memory completely. People who have lost their memories can no longer remember who they are. That means that they can no longer function effectively in the present and have no secure plans for the future. They have lost their past, and that has emptied their present of meaning and clouded their future. We must have contact with the past, if only for the sake of the present and the future.

The church could, I suppose, lose its memory as well. It is certainly tempted to do that often enough. But a church that has lost its memory of the past can only wander about aimlessly in the present and despair of its future. The church needs the past, if only for the sake of the present and the future.

The invitation to study the history of the church is not an irrelevant call to forsake the mission of the church and to lose oneself in a past no longer recoverable. It is, rather, a call to abandon peripheral matters, to put an end to aimless meanderings and nervous activism, to learn once again who we are and to whom we belong. Only when we have regained our identity from the past can we undertake our mission in the present.

16

Taking the Long View

Taking the long view was a way of life for two of the twentieth century's finest historians of Christianity: Jaroslav Jan Pelikan (1923–2006) and Heiko Augustinus Oberman (1930–2001). Pelikan was always more difficult than Oberman to characterize. Most historians of Christianity pick some limited subfield from the past, which becomes the focus of their research and writing. The really good historians among them will push back the boundaries of what is known in their subfield or find new and imaginative ways to read old evidence from it. That was the path Oberman chose.

Pelikan chose a different path. Although he was associated in his early life with Reformation studies—especially with Luther studies— and in his later life with the study of early Christianity, he is unlikely to be remembered primarily as a Reformation scholar or as a historian of the early church.

Pelikan had a larger ambition. He aspired to be an interpreter of the entire Christian past and to explain its development from its earliest beginnings to the present. He seemed determined to understand it all, every twist and turn, and to explain what he understood as clearly as he could to the cultured elites, inside and outside the church, who were ignorant of it.

In that sense Pelikan was not a historian's historian. He did not write primarily for other members of the historical guild (though, undoubtedly, professional historians were among his readers). As a historian Pelikan was very much an inner-directed man. Only an inner-directed historian would have decided to write a new history of doctrine to correct the classic history of dogma written in the late nineteenth century by the great Protestant church historian Adolf von Harnack. It was a project from an earlier age, the kind of massive multivolume study that even Germans, who love massive multivolume works, were no longer attempting.

Pelikan intended to challenge Harnack's interpretation on several fronts. Whereas Harnack did not discuss Byzantine Christianity and stopped his history at the Reformation—as though the development of doctrine after Augustine was primarily a Western phenomenon that ended in the sixteenth century—Pelikan included both Byzantine and post-Reformation Christianity.

Furthermore, Pelikan regarded Harnack as a "reductionist liberal" who studied the past not to cherish it, but to liberate himself from its power. Chief among the past errors Harnack deplored and wished to overcome through historical study was the use of Greek metaphysics by the early church.

Metaphysics obscured rather than clarified the heart of the Christian Gospel as Harnack understood it. For him the center of the Christian faith was a set of moral values embodied in the preaching of Jesus. Jesus came preaching the "Fatherhood of God" and the "brotherhood of man." It was a simple message, easy for the German middle class to understand, and light years away from the metaphysical speculations of Nicaea and Chalcedon about "substance" and "person," speculations that lost the historical Jesus and substituted an "imagined" Christ.

Not so, argued Pelikan. Harnack's misguided correction to the Christian past needed itself to be corrected. While theology involves ethics, it can never be reduced to a moral code, however radical or grounded in the preaching of Jesus. Harnack's attempt to do so rendered him tone-deaf to the rich theological melody of the Christian past. It was a mistake that Pelikan (who was always comfortable within the boundaries of classical Christian orthodoxy) did not intend to repeat.

Writing a comprehensive work brings with it enormous difficulties for historians intent on mastering details and avoiding a superficial treatment of their complex subject. All historical writing requires historians to "go native." They must learn the languages, the customs, the intellectual assumptions, and even the humor of the people they are studying. This is particularly true for historians of Christianity, who attempt to interpret a movement that adapts well to new cultures and has been adapting over and over again for two millennia.

Most historians shy away from projects that place too heavy a linguistic burden on their research. But Pelikan did not only know the classical theological languages of Greek, Hebrew, and Latin; he was also a master of Slavic languages, from Slovakian to Russian. He was therefore uniquely equipped to interpret the Orthodox East as well as the Catholic and Protestant West.

Anyone who has read Pelikan on the Czech reformer Jan Hus knows how important his mastery of Slavic languages was for the success of his project. Suddenly, it was no longer sufficient to talk about the history of doctrine and omit all reference to eastern Christianity after Chalcedon. Thanks to Pelikan, any new history of Christian thought that omits the Slavs and the Greeks would be regarded by the scholarly community as a truncated and therefore fundamentally misleading history.

"Going native," however, is only part of the historian's task. Interpreters must interpret. They must explain to their readers in language and categories their readers can understand what they have learned from studying the writings and artifacts of an alien place and time.

What they are not allowed to do is correct the opinions of the past or reclothe long-dead figures in the fashions of the present. Calvin was not a feminist or a Barthian, however much some modern historians might want him to be. The past is always unalterable. Historians may misinterpret what happened, but they cannot change it. Furthermore, "going native" never means that historians should serve as cheerleaders for past figures of whom they particularly approve or misrepresent other figures of whom they disapprove. Their task as historians is to enable the voices of Christians from distant ages to be heard again by a church that may have forgotten them and desperately needs to hear them again.

This does not mean that historians of Christianity have been deprived of the right to make normative judgments about the past—only that they must make those judgments as theologians, speaking constructively to the church, rather than as historians, clarifying what was once believed and taught. Pelikan knew that he was not doing his job properly if he did not explain Arius and Athanasius with equal enthusiasm and clarity. Being an orthodox Christian was no excuse for writing bad history.

In short, historians must be methodologically humble, even if they are not humble in any other way. They must accept the past on its terms rather than on their own. If they do so, they will find that the past can prove enormously instructive, often in unexpected and boundary-breaking ways. But if they do not, they will hear in their interpretation of the past only the echo of their own voice.

In all these respects Pelikan was a master of his craft. He met the past on its own terms, learning the languages, customs, and intellectual assumptions of Christians who inhabited a world very different from his own. He wrote what he learned in a lucid and elegant prose easily accessible to general readers, whatever their worldview. Pelikan's long career demonstrated that it is possible to combine a broad vision of the Christian past with an astonishing mastery of historical detail. As a result, his work has instructed readers inside and outside the church in ways that often sundered old intellectual boundaries, especially the boundaries between East and West.

Heiko Oberman followed the more conventional route of finding a period in the history of the church that fascinated him and sticking with it through thick and thin. In Oberman's case the period was late medieval and early modern Europe. It was the period of Thomas Bradwardine and Gabriel Biel, of Martin Luther and John Calvin.

In the years that I was at Harvard (1961–66), Oberman never offered a seminar on John Calvin. The seminars he did offer—at least the three seminars I took—were devoted to the theology of Gabriel Biel, Jan Hus, and the Council of Trent. But the fact that Heiko's research was centered elsewhere did not mean that he neglected Calvin entirely. He twice offered a lecture course on Calvin: once in the fall semester of 1961 and again in the spring semester of 1966. I know because I was a student in the first class and his teaching fellow for the second. Heiko also supervised two Harvard dissertations on John Calvin: the first on the *extracalvinisticum* written by David Willis, now retired from Princeton, and a second on Calvin's relationship to scholastic theology by Armand LaVallee, then an Episcopal priest in Rhode Island.

If Oberman was planning at the time to write a book on Calvin, he never mentioned it to me. In 1966 he seemed fully absorbed with questions of Luther's beginnings, especially Luther's relationship to the theological traditions stemming from Gregory of Rimini in the Augustinian order. It was not even clear that Heiko would eventually write a biography of Luther rather than a monograph on Luther's thought. There were no real grounds to believe that he would develop at Tübingen a concern for what he later called "the social history of ideas." Oberman described himself at Harvard on more than one occasion as a historian of Christian thought from the school of Reinhold Seeberg.

The Calvin I met in Oberman's class was not the Calvin with whom I had become familiar in a seminar on Calvin's theology taken the semester before I moved to Harvard. The Calvin to whom I had been introduced was primarily a dialogue partner for neo-Reformation theology. The context for understanding this neo-Reformation Calvin featured the issues prominent in mainstream Protestant theology in the mid-twentieth century: the possibility or impossibility of natural theology, the relation of reason and revelation, the inspiration of scripture, the critique of theological liberalism, and the recovery of Christology. The authors who mattered most were theologians like Karl Barth,

Emil Brunner, T. H. L. Parker, and Edward Dowey who were deeply concerned with the impact of Calvin's thought on the doctrinal debates then raging. They were joined by a large company of Barthian and erstwhile Barthian interpreters of Calvin, from Thomas Torrance and Wilhelm Niesel to Ronald Wallace and Paul Van Buren, theologians who often found it difficult to draw sharp lines of demarcation between Calvin's theology and the theology of Karl Barth.

It would be too much to say that Oberman had no interest in these theological debates. He was, after all, a minister of the Nederlands Hervormde Kerk, a doctor of theology from the University of Utrecht, and a representative of what the Dutch then called the Middle Orthodox party. I remember how years later in Tübingen he remarked with considerable amusement that "some Germans" (whether faculty or students he did not say) had decided to label him a "crypto-Calvinist." "This is, of course, nonsense!" he added as though dismissing an entirely preposterous suggestion. "I am quite openly a Calvinist!"

What was different about the Calvin Oberman presented in his lectures was the historical context in which he placed him. Gone were the dominating concerns of neo-orthodox theology! Whatever relevance Oberman's Calvin might have had for theology in the early 1960s could only have been as a by-product of his careful historical work. For Oberman, Calvin must first be located in his own time and space. Students therefore found themselves listening to lectures on Calvin's education at the Collège de la Marche and the Collège de Montaigu, his subsequent legal education at Orléans and Bourges, the teachers with whom he did or did not study—Cordier, Wolmar, Alciati, Coronel, Major—his brush with the law and his flight to Basel, his relationship to Bucer and Farel, his marriage in Strasbourg to Idelette de Bure, the multiple editions and publishing dates of his *Institutes of the Christian Religion*—in short, all the details of Calvin's life and setting that the present-minded and impatient students of the 1960s preferred to sidestep in their rush to get as quickly as possible to the central issues of Calvin's mature theology. While it would be an exaggeration to claim that Oberman was already launched on his own quest for the historical Calvin, it would not be an error to see some of his later historical interests already reflected in his passion for proper historical context.

Oberman's early methodology required historians to understand as far as possible the documents of the past on their own terms and within their own intellectual universe. It was, of course, not easy to develop such a historical empathy, and impossible to achieve it perfectly; but empathy could not be achieved at all without an immersion in primary sources. I can still remember my astonishment when I was told that I ought to spend my first summer in graduate school reading through the *opera omnia* of Augustine in Latin, starting with *De doctrina christiana* and proceeding on through the anti-Pelagian writings. Needless to say, I did not make it through the whole body of Augustine's Latin writings in one summer, but I made it through enough volumes to enrich my understanding of Augustine forever.

Oberman was particularly keen that students develop a sensitivity to the details of the language used by an author, what he called the shape and smell and feel of words. Is there a difference between the words *mereri* and *promereri* in the decrees of the Council of Trent, and, if so, what is it? Do these words provide another way of distinguishing between *meritum de congruo* and *meritum de condigno*? If not, what is their purpose? And when Calvin spoke of his *conversio subita*, his sudden conversion to evangelical Christianity, did he mean "sudden" in the sense of "within a very brief period of time" or "sudden" in the sense of "wholly unexpected" or both? Words matter, and the historian who does not weigh them carefully will write bad history.

The historical enterprise Oberman envisioned required a rethinking of historical periodization. The Reformation did not begin in 1517 but was part of a long story that began much earlier. For Oberman all Reformation thinkers, Luther and Calvin chief among them, needed to be put in their late medieval context in order to make their thought intelligible. I can remember very little on Oberman's part during the Harvard years that might have passed for a fascination with *das Moderne*. Nor can I remember anyone suggesting that Professor Oberman was an early modernist. It would have seemed odd at the time, since his overwhelming emphasis was on the Reformation as a medieval event. The most commonly used words during those years to describe the Oberman research agenda were the "history of Christian thought in the late Middle Ages and Reformation."

There were several themes in Oberman's early approach to Calvin, many of which were repeated in his later essays. For example, in his early lectures Oberman was interested in promoting a late date for Calvin's conversion. He did not argue the case for 1533 over 1529 but simply accepted as more persuasive the arguments of historians who supported the earlier date. He regarded as the two most important texts for gaining insight into the nature of Calvin's conversion Calvin's *Reply to Sadoleto* (1539) and the preface to his *Commentary on the Psalms* (1552), and he spent considerable time in class interpreting them at length. One can catch a glimpse of his early thinking in his later essay "*Subita Conversio*: The Conversion of John Calvin."

There is, however, a textual problem with the *Reply to Sadoleto*. Can one be certain that the purportedly autobiographical section of Calvin's reply was in fact autobiographical? After all, Cardinal Sadoleto's original letter to the Genevans contained what appeared to be an autobiographical section as well. In Sadoleto's case it is clear that he was using a rhetorical device, speaking less in his own person than in the person of a representative but fictitious Catholic believer, one bemused by the hostility and ambition of the new heretical teachers. Why should historians assume that Calvin was not doing the same thing, using a rhetorical device to give voice to a generation that had converted from Catholicism to the new evangelical movements? While the matter can never be settled definitively, there are important parallels between the *Reply to Sadoleto* and the preface to the Psalms commentary that are mutually reinforcing. On the whole I am inclined to believe that Oberman's intuitions were right and that the *Reply to Sadoleto* does in fact contain genuine autobiographical passages, whatever role it might have played as a sounding board for a broader generation of disaffected Catholics.

But the importance of the *Reply to Sadoleto* for Oberman extended far beyond its importance as a source for Calvin's life. Oberman believed that the best way to understand the *Institutes* was to read it through the lens of book IV, the section of the *Institutes* dealing with the church and its sacraments. And the best introduction to book IV and its doctrine of the church was the *Reply to Sadoleto*, in which Calvin articulated his vision of the church and its history in opposition to the rival Catholic view of Cardinal Sadoleto. I can still remember Oberman writing on the board for the largely Latinless students in his class Calvin's Latin definition of the church from the *Reply* and demonstrating that it was point for point an institutionalization of the Vincentian canon: *quod semper ubique ab omnibus creditum est.* Sadoleto had already made this shift from the Vincentian canon to a definition of the church in his letter to the Genevans, and Calvin adopted and revised it.

Although Oberman referred to some treatises, letters, and commentaries by Calvin, his lectures focused on the 1559 Latin *Institutes*, an edition Calvin regarded as definitive. Heiko relished Calvin's metaphors in the *Institutes*. I still cannot think of Calvin's doctrine of providence without immediately thinking of Oberman's pleasure in Calvin's derisive caricature of the position of the Epicureans as belief in a God in a watchtower. Calvin wanted to assert that providence pertains to God's hands and not merely to his eyes and to affirm that God was the steersman who directed history through stormy seas to its ultimate destination. Calvin could have expressed these ideas more abstractly, but did not, and Oberman did not suppress the literary rather than philosophical character of his thought. Calvin was not Thomas Aquinas, though he made many of the same points in his doctrine of providence, and Oberman cherished both the similarities and the differences.

Although Oberman later became suspicious of what he dismissed as the search for pedigree, he did nevertheless spend some time identifying sources of Calvin's thought. He was particularly impressed by the recurrence of themes from John Duns Scotus in Calvin's thought, among them his doctrine of double acceptation, his affirmation that whatever is good is good because God wills it (and not the reverse), and his construction of a doctrine of election that gave priority to predestination to glory over predestination to grace. At the time Oberman seems to have thought that Calvin might have been influenced in his theology by the lectures of John Major, a Scot by nationality and a Scotist by conviction, who lectured at Paris during the years Calvin was in residence. Oberman later abandoned this notion, largely as a result of reading Alexandre Ganoczy's careful study of the young Calvin.

In view of the many Scotistic themes in Calvin's theology it was all the more mystifying to Oberman that Calvin almost willfully misunderstood the important distinction between the *potentia dei ordinata* and *potentia dei absoluta*, a misunderstanding traced by Oberman's student Armand LaVallee. Calvin dismissed the scholastic distinction between the two powers of God as a distinction between what he called the *potentia dei ordinata* and the *potentia dei inordinata* (the "ordered" and "disordered power" of God). It seemed to Calvin that the distinction between absolute and ordained power separated God's will from his justice. Of course, no such separation was ever intended by Scotus (as Oberman has amply proven in the case of Gabriel Biel), and Calvin's reading still seems tendentious.

During the years at Tübingen Oberman's interests shifted from intellectual history in isolation from other forms of history to what he called "the social history of ideas." One ought not to be misled by this language. Oberman did not suddenly become a social historian, nor did he ever lose his interest in theology. What he did attempt to do was to broaden the context of intellectual history to include the whole human reality in which ideas were embedded: social, political, psychological, economic, and cultural. When Oberman left Harvard for Tübingen, one might very well have expected him to have written a traditional theological monograph titled, say, *Luthers Theologie als Ausdruck und Kritik der theologischen Traditionen des Augustinerordens*. That is what a historian of Christian thought from the school of Reinhold Seeberg might have been expected to do. What he wrote instead was a lively biography of Luther that attempted to capture the full human reality of his subject and to put Luther's fascinating ideas in their larger and compelling historical context.

In the 1980s and 1990s Oberman composed a series of essays on Calvin that Jane Dempsey Douglass has carefully summarized in her essay "Pastor and Teacher of the Refugees: Calvin in the Work of Heiko A. Oberman." I do not want to duplicate her work here, only to call brief attention to two themes in Oberman's later research. In general one could say that Oberman's essays on Calvin have been marked by his quest for the historical Calvin and by his fascination with what he labeled "the Reformation of the refugees."

Oberman remarked in my presence more than once that the trouble with Calvin research was that Calvin had fallen into the hands of his friends. Luther research had not been left to Lutherans, and Catholic scholars had periodically cast a cold eye on some doubtful tendencies in traditional Luther research. But Calvin research had all too often been left to Calvinists, who sometimes lacked the critical distance to ask uncomfortable questions about Calvin. Too much Calvin research was intellectual history divorced from the larger historical reality in which Calvin participated. Not to pay attention to that larger historical context was in the end to be unfair to Calvin and to reduce his rich historical reality to a dogmatic locus. That was why Oberman greeted William Bouwsma's study of Calvin with considerable enthusiasm. Whatever Bouwsma's limitations (and Oberman differed with him on several matters) he was making in Oberman's view a serious and imaginative attempt to recover the historical Calvin.

Oberman saw the historical Calvin not as a leader of a city Reformation, but as a spokesman for the emerging Reformation of the refugees. For Oberman Calvin was not so much a reformer of Geneva as a reformer out of Geneva whose real object of reform was France and, beyond France, the whole of Europe in distress (*Europa afflicta*). He was not a city reformer like Zwingli or Bucer. What Calvin was interested in developing were self-governing reformed communities within the larger civil communities that could dominate the civil community when they were in the majority and survive under persecution when they were not.

Oberman had intended to develop these ideas in a full-length study of Calvin. In the end he was unable to write the book he planned before he died. We shall therefore have to be satisfied with his essays, which have been edited by Peter Dykema in a single volume for Librairie Droz in Geneva. Oberman's contribution to Calvin studies, though substantial, remains incomplete. In death as in life Oberman continues to be a seminal thinker who sets other historians in motion. He has left the next generation of Calvin scholars a rich collection of stimulating ideas and suggestions and defined for them unfinished tasks to do.

The differences that divided Pelikan from Oberman were, in the end, far less important than the convictions that united them. Although Pelikan chose to be a historian who ranged widely over several historical periods, while Oberman elected to remain more sharply focused on one, both men attempted to understand the past on its terms and not on their own. They agreed that the first duty of a historian is to go native, and they refused to interpret the past to their contemporaries until they understand its culture, its forms of discourse, its languages, and even its sometimes odd sense of humor.

They were, in other words, living refutations of the proposition that only distance from a subject gives reliable insight into it. Affection can distort a subject, but so can too much distance. After all, who sees my faults better than someone who loves me? G. K. Chesterton argued a century ago that love is not blind, it is merely bound. And that binding is the source of insight available in no other way.

Make no mistake about it: Pelikan and Oberman had a grand time studying the Christian past. By the end of their lives, it was hard to imagine them doing anything else that could have given them such seemingly endless pleasure. But they were never uncritical. And their critical reading of the Christian past, born of genuine affection for it, still challenges the church to remember its past and, by doing so, take the long view on its present.

17

Concluding Notes for a Pilgrim People

The recent revelation that Mother Teresa of Calcutta suffered from long periods of spiritual desolation in which she felt utterly abandoned by God has—to say the least—met with a mixed response from the media. Skeptics like Christopher Hitchens took the revelations as further proof that Mother Teresa was an incorrigible fraud, a crypto-atheist who knew there was no God but who lacked the common decency to admit it. Other critics, more favorably disposed to Mother Teresa, reacted with shocked disbelief at the news of her spiritual struggles, as though saints were never allowed a bad day and the life of faith, properly handled, was a life of unending bliss.

Not that bliss is entirely lacking from the quest for sanctity. Christian mystics over the centuries have reported ecstatic experiences marked by incredible joy, experiences that seem to have eluded Mother Teresa. Her period of spiritual desolation (what St. John of the Cross would have termed her "dark night of the soul") seems by any measure unusually long and therefore atypical, but not every quest for sanctity is the same. Still, what struck me most forcefully about Mother Teresa's spiritual struggles was the extent to which her experiences resembled similar struggles by Martin Luther with his *Anfechtungen* or "spiritual trials."

Take, for example, Mother Teresa's sense of having made no progress whatever in the life of holiness. Luther thought it was a fundamental principle of the spiritual life that saints and not sinners were the real authorities on sin. If any inquiring mind wants to know what makes sin sinful, it should ask St. Francis or St. Clare and not a roomful of hormonally charged late adolescents at a college frat party.

The reason for this is very simple. To understand what sin is, one has to oppose it. The more strenuously one opposes it, the more powerful and pervasive it seems. One barely notices a current with which one is swimming. But one cannot fail to notice what is happening when one struggles to swim against an opposing tide.

Which means that the more one progresses in the spiritual life, the more one may develop a sense of making no progress at all. In point of fact the would-be saint is often making considerable progress. But "making progress" and "feeling one is making progress" are two quite separate things.

In some ways the struggle for sanctity resembles the old fairy tale about the princess and the pea. The storyteller assumes that royalty would be particularly sensitive to any foreign object left where it should not be, especially in one's bed. A genuine princess would therefore notice a tiny object (like one very small pea), even if it were placed under her mattress. The princess in the fairy tale proves her royal lineage to skeptics by noticing an offending pea lodged not only under one mattress, but under a pile of mattresses heaped up to the ceiling.

The genuine saint displays the same sensitivity in the presence of the tiniest sin. The more saintly the saint, the more sensitive he or she is to the least infraction of God's will. Saints see their own imperfections with a dazzling clarity. The unfortunate effect of this sensitivity is that real progress in the spiritual life may strike the saint as no progress at all, and a robust faith may feel like hypocrisy or unbelief. Each step forward may feel like a step back. But the motion of saints is in fact forward, however retrograde they may feel.

Luther borrowed from St. Bernard of Clairvaux the dictum that a Christian is always a beginner. Christians are always beginners because they have to stick to what they learned first. And the most elementary and basic of first lessons is that there is no way to grow in grace by trying to grow out of it. In other words, Christians are always beginners because there is no way to grow beyond Christ. In the end, sanctity is God's gift to Christians and not any Christian's gift to God.

Medieval spiritual advisers often summed up their advice to Christians experiencing the unsettling feeling of an inexplicable and almost unbearable absence of God with the words "God does not deny his grace to those who do what is in them." The saying could, of course, mean several different things (some of which Luther regarded as positively toxic). But such advice in this pastoral context was meant to be a form of gentle encouragement. From time to time everyone endures a barren period in the life of faith. Prayers bounce off the ceiling unanswered. Hymns stick in one's throat, and whatever delight one once felt in the contemplation or worship of God withers away.

In such circumstances Christians should "do what is in them." That is, they should keep on keeping on. They should keep on with their prayers, their hymns of praise, and their daily round of duties. Even though it seems like they are walking through an immense and limitless desert, with oases few and far between, they should plod on, knowing that obedience is more important than emotional satisfaction and a right spirit than a merry heart.

To such people, "God does not deny grace." They live in hope, however, that sooner or later the band will strike up a polka and the laughter and the dancing will start all over again. But if it does not—and it did not in Mother Teresa's case—the grace that was in the beginning will be at the end as well. Of that, one can be sure.

Undoubtedly, Mother Teresa would have preferred to walk a less desolate path through life, one marked by inner joy and not just by outer virtue. But as Luther confessed many times, he found more help in the contemplation of the imperfections and limitations of the saints than in a recitation of their heroic achievements. An all-too-human Mother Teresa was an impressive witness to a grace that brought her through spiritual trials that she had not anticipated and might have failed. She did not abandon the God who seemed to have abandoned her, as she very well might have done. By doubting vigorously but not surrendering to her doubts, she became a witness to a faith that did not fail and a hidden God who did not let her go. That is what sanctity is all about.

Appendix

Footnotes to an Old Complaint

In 1979 I gave a public lecture to the Kearns Seminar at Duke University on the theme "The Superiority of Pre-critical Exegesis." The lecture was published in *Theology Today* in 1980, probably to the dismay of some biblical scholars and theologians, who feared I had lost my way and rejected historical criticism in principle (which, of course, I had not done). Other readers were not so sure I was wrong. They, too, were unhappy with some aspects of historical criticism as then practiced, understood the specific nature of my complaint, and used the opportunity to voice their own criticisms of assumptions and practices of biblical study that seemed to them to need rethinking. The essay was anthologized a number of times, less, I suspect, as an invitation to agree with my specific point of view than as an invitation to join the discussion.

When the program committee of the Society of Biblical Literature (SBL) asked me to comment nearly thirty years later on my old essay, I suspect they were offering me an opportunity to correct, amplify, or renounce positions I advanced in 1979. While I would certainly be happy to be corrected where I was in error and amplify arguments when asked, I am still in fundamental agreement with the positions I took then.

What the essay argued was not that the so-called pre-critical exegesis was superior to historical-critical exegesis in every way but that it was clearly superior to it in some respects. I took as my starting point a famous essay by Benjamin Jowett published in 1859 which suggested that "Scripture has one meaning—the meaning which it had in the mind of the Prophet or Evangelist who first uttered or wrote, to the hearers or readers who first received it."[1] Scripture should be interpreted like any other book (by which Jowett meant books like the ancient classics), and the later accretions and venerated traditions surrounding its interpretation should, for the most part, be either brushed aside or severely discounted: "The true use of interpretation is to get rid of interpretation, and leave us alone in company with the author." Jowett regarded Jesus in particular as a "teacher...speaking to a group of serious, but not highly educated, working men, attempting to inculcate in them a loftier and sweeter morality."

For me Jowett's words created as many problems as they purported to solve. While he was not speaking for contemporary biblical scholars when he appealed to the nonapocalyptic and rather tamely bourgeois Jesus so effectively debunked by Albert Schweitzer in *The Quest of the Historical Jesus*, he did represent an enduring consensus of a different kind. Like Jowett, biblical scholarship in the late twentieth century still hoped to recover the original intention of the author of a biblical text and still regarded the pre-critical exegetical tradition as an obstacle to the proper understanding of the true meaning of that text. For them the most primitive meaning of the text was its only valid meaning, and the historical-critical method was the only key that could unlock it. I devoted the bulk of my essay to exploring the problems with an exegesis that rested on what I had come to regard as questionable assumptions: namely, that all biblical texts have a single meaning, that this meaning is defined solely by the intention of the author, that there are no serious barriers between an author's intentions and proper reception by the original audience, that audiences are passive and contribute nothing to the act of understanding, that ecclesiastical and rabbinic traditions as a general rule misunderstand biblical texts and should be ignored, that the most primitive meaning of a text is its only valid meaning, and that this meaning can be recovered by the historical-critical method alone.

I did allude briefly, if vaguely, to literary theory. Perhaps I should have said more. What I had in mind were New Criticism, with its debunking of the "intentional fallacy"; reader-response criticism, with its focus on the agency of audiences; and deconstructionist criticism, with its attempt to subvert a straightforward theory of intention. But I passed over literary studies quickly in favor of concrete historical examples drawn from the church's exegetical past. My thesis was that literary texts, including biblical texts, may create a field of legitimate meanings, none of which in principle excludes the rest, even if some proposed interpretations of a text may prove for various reasons better than the alternatives. To the extent that medieval exegesis recognized the multiple possible meanings of some texts, to that extent it seemed to me superior to any exegesis that in principle denies such a possibility.

I am aware that hermeneutical discussions among biblical scholars and theologians have moved in new directions since 1979 and do not presume to suggest that I have followed them all. At the very least one needs to take into account a new and widespread appreciation of what was once summarily dismissed as useless (or, at best, misleading) traditional exegesis. As a sign of the times, Intervarsity Press has sold over 450,000 sets of its Ancient Christian Commentary Series and is following up this astonishing success with a new Reformation Commentary Series. Eerdmans has its own series of ancient commentaries called The Church's Bible, which uses a different scholarly paradigm. Ambrosiaster (or Origen) on Romans and Chrysostom (or Augustine) on John have begun to create the kind of buzz among younger theological students once restricted to Karl Barth on Romans and Rudolf Bultmann on John. Still, there is no consensus how best to use the new insights from the past, and there is a seductive Whig temptation (always to be resisted) to hail in the past precisely those insights that most agree with ours.

I have often reflected on the way in which the sixteenth-century slogan *ad fontes* morphed from a philological principle (one should prefer the original writing to any translation, however well done) to a theological axiom (one should prefer scripture to later tradition or even the most primitive layer of the Bible to all subsequent layers). What if, instead of the image of a stream that is purer near its source, European imaginations had been dominated by an organic image of an acorn, sapling, and tree? Which then is the true oak? Should the later stage of growth be preferred to the earlier, and, if so, on what grounds?

The defenders of the Latin Vulgate, who eventually won at the Council of Trent, used a different image. They argued that the Latin text of the Vulgate should be preferred to the original Greek and Hebrew texts as a finished cabinet should be preferred to the raw materials from which it was constructed. Ironically, the Protestants, who had put more of their eggs in the Bible basket than their Catholic opponents had, broke with a millennium of Western church practice and opted for the original Hebrew and Greek texts, thus destabilizing the text to which they appealed at a time when stability was particularly crucial.

The European elites in the sixteenth century were as matter of course trained to read, write, and speak Latin. Henry VIII could woo a new wife (or girlfriend) as easily in Latin as in French or English. Martin Luther reported that any boy in his Latin school who was heard to speak German instead of Latin on the school grounds was summarily whipped. The Latin Bible was as such no problem for the educated classes of Europe. Even some educated women learned to read and speak Latin through private lessons. Latin made it possible for a German student to study in Paris and a French student to study in Heidelberg, as well as to ease communication between Bavarian and Saxon students (representatives of two peoples divided by a common tongue).

In part, Protestants met the challenge of the displacement of a Latin Bible by offering, as Theodore Beza did, new and (hopefully) improved Latin translations for the Hebrewless and Greekless Latin-speaking elite. Or they broadened the curriculum. Early on, in Zurich under Zwingli, the boys in the Latin school were taught Greek and Hebrew as well as Latin. But for the vast majority of the European laity in Protestant territories the de facto source and norm for Christian teaching was not the Greek and Hebrew originals, but the authorized vernacular translations in common use.

At the same time early Protestants coined a phrase, "the plain sense of scripture," which, amazingly, they did not regard as ironic. What they seemed to suggest was that the "plain sense" was what older theologians had called the literal sense of scripture, the storybook or narrative line believed to lie very close to the surface. What they really meant was something more. They collapsed what earlier theologians had called the allegorical, tropological, and anagogical senses into a greatly expanded literal sense. The so-called plain sense became anything but simple, a big-bellied literal sense, eight months pregnant with hidden meanings. Why? Did the advocates of the "plain sense" fear the loss of some theological gains that had been achieved in the older hermeneutic, whatever its faults? They certainly worried that theologians might in the end lose the link between the testaments and transform an Old Testament that was Christian scripture into a Hebrew Bible that was not. Would a focus on the literal sense in a very narrow perspective open the way for a Jewish rather than Christian reading of the whole Bible? What is clear in the sixteenth century is that even the very cautious John Calvin, who was repeatedly accused of judaizing by his Lutheran critics, spent some time spinning out an account of the Hebrew Bible as Christian scripture. In the end, the so-called spiritual senses were transformed by early Protestants rather than abandoned. The plain sense of the Bible could never be allowed to become too plain.

One colleague, puzzled by my seeming fondness for Origen and Nicholas of Lyra, wondered whether it would not be more accurate to say that scripture has one meaning and many applications. Unfortunately, that suggestion will not work. I remember listening to Barbra Streisand singing "Happy Days Are Here Again" very slowly—andante, maybe even adagio. The original song had once served as the campaign theme for FDR in the 1930s and was never sung more slowly then than a fast march. Its normal tempo was allegro vivace.

Whatever its original setting, the New Deal version was a celebration of a nation recovering from the Great Depression. But Streisand did not sing FDR's song; she sang a different song. The words were the same, but the meaning of the words had shifted. After all, the words "Happy days are here again" (like the words "Yes we can") can be spoken or sung enthusiastically, dismissively, ironically, angrily, derisively, nostalgically, or sadly. What took place when she sang is simply not covered by the term "application." What she offered was a new meaning, a new song with old familiar words, all the more complex because of the obvious abandonment of its old meaning. Her song left me asking, Why should scripture be exempted from the multivalence that belongs to language as such?

It has also become increasingly unclear to me what biblical scholars mean by the words "historical reconstruction." If one were to write a historical reconstruction of the Regensburg Colloquy between Catholics and Protestants in 1541, one would have an enormous amount of evidence to sift through and evaluate: official dispatches, personal letters, diaries, acta and memoirs, chronicles, histories, partisan propaganda, cartoons, posters, pamphlets, and marginal annotations, to say nothing of the relevant writings of such figures as Gasparo Cardinal Contarini, John Eck, John Gropper, Philip Melanchthon, John Calvin, Martin Bucer, and the Imperial Chancellor Nicholas Granvella. People wrote about the colloquy who were there at the time and who were elsewhere, who favored the colloquy in principle and who bitterly opposed it, who welcomed the compromise formula for double justification and who scorned it as a theological dead end. Historians are accustomed as a general rule to large amounts of often contradictory material which they are expected to reduce to some kind of intelligibility. They have to deal with truthful people and habitual liars, wise counselors and complete fools, people devoted to the public good and to their own self-advancement. Even intellectual historians cannot do their work without understanding the social, political, and intellectual environment of an alien place and time.

Some of this is surely involved in biblical studies as well. On the other hand, biblical scholars often find themselves dealing with texts for which any kind of external evidence is skimpy or nonexistent. When Hermann Gunkel attempted to define the social and liturgical setting of the Psalms, he was thrown largely on internal literary evidence. He used source criticism to reconstruct the hidden literary history of the Psalms and to re-create their *Sitz im Leben*. It was brilliant and imaginative work, though as Rolf Rentdorf of Heidelberg observed at a meeting of the SBL some years ago: "You know, we *know* none of this!" By which, of course, he meant that Gunkel lacked the kind of external evidence for the setting of the Psalms that Hubert Jedin had in abundance for his "historical reconstruction" of the Regensburg Colloquy. In other words, Gunkel's achievement was literary in fact, though historical in aspiration. By "literary," I do not mean simply written evidence, but written evidence for which there is little or no corroborating evidence, whether written or unwritten, outside the source text itself.

The reason this is worrying to historians outside the biblical guild is that they regard it as a very dangerous practice to rely too heavily on internal literary evidence for the reconstruction of random external events. It may be unavoidable in certain cases, but always needs to be accompanied by the cautions and caveats that accompany any inference for which the historical evidence is thin. One need not go as far as my college friend who suggested that the universal answer to all philosophical questions was "Yes, yes, indeed, unless, of course, the contrary be true!" But some moderate disclaimer is clearly needed.

Take, for example, the career of one of the chief participants in the Regensburg Colloquy, the Catholic theologian John Eck from the University of Ingolstadt. In 1525 Eck wrote a polemical treatise entitled *Enchiridion of Commonplaces against Luther and Other Enemies of the Church*. The book was a bestseller among parish priests, who found themselves attacked by laity drawn to the teaching of Luther and the views of other early Protestants like Martin Bucer and Huldrych Zwingli. The book tried as much as possible to argue against the Protestants on their own scriptural grounds, offering Catholic interpretations of the biblical texts cited frequently by advocates of the new theology and quoting other texts against Protestants that were more problematic for them.

In 1542 Eck delivered his last lectures on book I of the *Sentences* of Peter Lombard. The lectures were models of late medieval theology, tranquilly discussing problems in the doctrine of God with nary a mention of "Luther and other enemies of the church." One could never guess from any internal evidence in the lectures that Eck had just returned from Regensburg and his disappointing encounter with such Protestant heavyweights as Melanchthon and Bucer. The lectures could have been delivered as easily in 1442 as 1542. Indeed, one would be justified to conclude on the basis of internal literary evidence that the lectures on the *Sentences* were an early work of Eck and the polemical *Enchiridion* a later one. That would be a reasonable inference. But, of course, it would have been dead wrong.

Even obvious literary clues can be misleading. Historians are right to be suspicious of too many coincidences in a text. An overabundance of coincidences suggests that the editor or author may have shaped a text in illegitimate ways, perhaps to make a text more edifying than it would have been if left unedited. But even here one has to exercise caution, for the simple reason that coincidences *do* happen in the real world outside of texts, sometimes with surprising frequency.

So, as you can see, I am still unrepentant, still muttering under my breath *non revoco*. In 1979 I found a long list of hermeneutical assumptions problematic: namely, that all biblical texts have a single meaning, that this meaning is defined solely by the intention of the author, that there are no serious barriers between an author's intentions and proper reception by the original audience, that audiences are passive and contribute nothing to the act of understanding, that ecclesiastical and rabbinic traditions as a general rule misunderstand biblical texts and should be ignored, that the most primitive meaning of a text is its only valid meaning, and that this meaning can be recovered by the historical-critical method alone. To which I have added a new worry: that it seems to me extremely difficult to do a successful historical reconstruction of any text on the basis of internal literary evidence alone, save for the occasional and often unreliable intervention of sheer good fortune.

Notes

CHAPTER 1

1. Benjamin Jowett, "On the Interpretation of Scripture," *Essays and Reviews*, 7th ed. (London: Longman, Green, Longman, & Roberts, 1861), 330–433.

2. Ibid., 378.

3. Ibid., 384.

4. Ibid., 412.

5. Helen Gardner, *The Business of Criticism* (London: Oxford University Press, 1959), 83.

6. Origen, *On First Principles*, ed. G. W. Butterworth (New York: Harper & Row, 1966), 288.

7. For a brief survey of medieval hermeneutical theory that takes into account recent historical research see James S. Preus, *From Shadow to Promise* (Cambridge, MA: Harvard University Press, 1969), 9–149; see also the useful bibliography, 287–93.

8. W. H. Lewis, ed., *Letters of C. S. Lewis* (New York: Harcourt, Brace & World, 1966), 273.

9. Jowett, "Interpretation," 337.

10. This quotation is cited by E. D. Hirsch, Jr., *Validity in Interpretation* (New Haven, CT: Yale University Press, 1967), 1, at the beginning of a chapter that sets out to elaborate an alternative theory.

CHAPTER 2

1. Some very obvious instances of such second narratives can be found in Acts 2:14–36, Acts 7:2–53, and Hebrews 11.

2. *De praescriptione hereticorum* 19.

3. *De praescriptione hereticorum* 16.

4. *De praescriptione hereticorum* 15–19.

5. On this subject see particularly the third book of *Adversus haereses* by Irenaeus.

6. For the English translation see Athanasius, "On the Incarnation of the Word," in *Christology of the Later Fathers*, ed. Edward R. Hardy (Philadelphia: Westminster Press, 1954), 55–110, esp. 110.

7. Josephine Tey, *The Daughter of Time* (New York: Macmillan, 1951).

8. Marc Bloch, *The Historian's Craft* (New York: Vintage, 1953), 123.

9. Johannes Eck, *Enchiridion locorum communium adversus Lutherum et alios hostes ecclesiae (1525–1543)*, ed. Pierre Fraenkel, Corpus Catholicorum 34 (Münster: Aschendorffsche Verlagsbuch handlung, 1979), 97–98.

10. Walter L. Moore, ed., *In primum librum sententiarum annotatiunculae D. Iohannes Eckio praelectore*, Studies in Medieval and Reformation Thought 13 (Leiden: E. J. Brill, 1976.

11. Benjamin Jowett, "On the Interpretation of Scripture," in *Essays and Reviews*, 7th ed. (London: Longman, Green, Longman & Roberts, 1861), 378.

CHAPTER 3

1. In this connection, see the illuminating discussion by Georges Florovsky, "The Function of Tradition in the Ancient Church" and "The Authority of the Ancient Councils and the Tradition of the Fathers," both in *Bible, Church, Tradition: An Eastern Orthodox View* (Belmont, MA: Nordland, 1972), 73–103.

2. On the doctrine of creation, see Georges Florovsky, "St. Athanasius' Concept of Creation," in *Aspects of Church History* (Belmont, MA: Nordland, 1975), 39–62.

CHAPTER 5

1. The addition of the phrase "Mother of God" to the *Ave Maria* grows out of the Nestorian controversy of the fifth century. The Orthodox fathers ascribed to Mary, the mother of Jesus, the title of *Theotokos* or God-bearer, which better preserved the Word-flesh Christology of Alexandria against the Word-man Christology of Antioch. Curiously, the West did not use the exact Latin equivalent, *Deipara*, but rather the phrase *Dei Genetrix* or Mother of God. The intention, however, was the same: to preserve the high Christology of Chalcedon rather than to ascribe special honor to Mary herself. The later medieval theologians saw in Mary's role as *Theotokos* the basis of her work as intercessor.

2. The suggestion that John 1:13 is an indirect allusion to the Virgin Birth was first made by Hans von Campenhausen in his book *Die Jungfrauengeburt in der Theologie der alten Kirche*, Sitzungsberichte der Heidelberger Akademie der Wissenschaften, Phil. Hist. Klasse, Abh. 3 (1962), 12.

3. Because of the opposition of Thomas Aquinas and the Dominicans to the doctrine of the immaculate conception, it was not promulgated as a dogma until the Council of Basel (1439). Since it was proffered in a session that was not confirmed, the teaching did not become official dogma of the Roman Catholic Church until restated by Pius IX in 1854 in the papal bull *Ineffabilis Deus*. Martin Luther and Huldrych Zwingli were raised in a late medieval tradition that supported the doctrine of the immaculate conception.

4. The doctrine of the bodily assumption of Mary into heaven did not gain official status as a dogma until 1950, when it was promulgated by Pius XII in the bull *Munificentissimus Deus*. The bodily assumption did have vigorous support among certain

theologians in the late Middle Ages; Gabriel Biel (d. 1495), for example, tied the doctrine of the bodily assumption to the role of Mary as intercessor. He did not, however, believe that faith in the bodily assumption of Mary was necessary to salvation. The contention that belief in the assumption is necessary to salvation is a modern problem.

CHAPTER 6

1. For an excellent analysis of early Catholic criticism of Luther see David Bagchi, *Luther's Earliest Opponents: Catholic Controversialists, 1518–1525* (Minneapolis: Fortress Press, 1991).

2. Older but still important is Adolf Herte, *Die Lutherkommentare des Johannes Cochläus* (Münster, 1935).

3. Heinrich Denifle, *Luther und Luthertum in der ersten Entwicklung* (Mainz, 1904).

4. Hartmann Grisar, *Luther*, 3 vols. (Freiburg, 1911–12).

5. Joseph Lortz, *Die Reformation in Deutschland*, 2 vols. (Freiburg, 1939–40).

6. Otto Hermann Pesch, *Theologie der Rechtfertigung bei Martin Luther und Thomas von Aquin.: Versuch eines systematisch-theologischen Dialogs* (Mainz, 1967).

7. Reinoud Weijenborg, "Miraculum a Martino Luthero confictum explicatne eius reformationem?" *Antonianum* 31 (1956): 247–300.

8. For a brief introduction to some of the controversies concerning Luther see E. Gordon Rupp, *The Righteousness of God: Luther Studies* (London: Hodder and Stoughton, 1953); David C. Steinmetz, *Luther and Staupitz: An Essay in the Intellectual Origins of the Protestant Reformation* (Durham, NC: Duke University Press, 1980); Kenneth G. Hagen, "Changes in the Understanding of Luther: The Development of the Young Luther," *Theological Studies* (1968): 472–96.

9. Erich Vogelsang, *Die Anfänge von Luthers Christologie nach der ersten Psalmenvorlesung*, AKG 15 (Berlin and Leipzig, 1929); Emanuel Hirsch, "Initium Theologiae Lutheri," in *Lutherstudien II* (Gütersloh, 1954), 9–35.

10. Ernst Bizer, *Fides ex Auditu*, 2nd rev. ed. (Neukirchen Kreis Moers, 1961); Uuras Saarnivaara, *Luther Discovers the Gospel* (St. Louis: Concordia, 1951).

11. On this and related topics see my *Calvin in Context*, 2nd ed. (New York: Oxford University Press, 1995, 2010).

12. Irena Backus, "The Bible and the Fathers according to Abraham Scultetus (1566–1624) and André Rivet: The Case of Basil of Caesarea," in *Die Patristik in der Bibelexegese des 16. Jahrhunderts*, ed. David C. Steinmetz (Wiesbaden, 1999), 231–58.

13. Instructive in this respect is Calvin's heavy citation of the fathers in his "Prefatory Address to King Francis I of France" at the beginning of the *Institutes*.

14. David Yeago, "The Catholic Luther," in *The Catholicity of the Reformation*, ed. Carl E. Braaten and Robert W. Jenson (Grand Rapids, MI: William B. Eerdmans, 1996).

CHAPTER 7

1. *D. Martin Luthers Werke: Kritische Gesamtausgabe* (Weimar, 1993), 56,449.1–6.

2. John C. Olin, ed., *John Calvin and Jacopo Sadoleto: A Reformation Debate* (New York: Harper & Row, 1966), 82.

3. *Institutes* III.iii.1.

CHAPTER 9

1. This essay under a different title was given as the 2006 Roland Bainton Lecture at Yale Divinity School. I am grateful to Dean Harold Attridge and the members of the Yale community for their warm reception and generous hospitality.

2. Which is not to deny that a Reformation of some kind might have occurred without Luther or to reduce the Reformation to a footnote in his life. It is only to affirm with Luther's contemporaries that the Reformation that did occur bore, for better and for worse, the marks of his active agency.

3. Older but still useful is E. Gordon Rupp, "Word and Spirit in the First Years of the Reformation," *Archive for Reformation History* 49 (1958): 3–26.

4. It is sometimes easy to overlook how much Luther had to say about the Holy Spirit. See especially the classic study by Regin Prenter, *Spiritus Creator* (Philadelphia: Muhlenberg Press, 1953).

5. WA 18.83.

6. For introductions to Muentzer's life and thought see E. Gordon Rupp, *Patterns of Reformation* (Philadelphia: Fortress Press, 1969), and Eric W. Gritsch, *Reformer without a Church: The Life and Work of Thomas Muentzer, 1488?–1525* (Philadelphia: Fortress Press, 1967).

7. WATR 6.16.

8. Franz Hildebrandt discussed this distinction in *Est: Das lutherische Prinzip* (Göttingen: Vandenhoeck & Ruprecht, 1931).

9. Still important for understanding Geiler is E. Jane Dempsey Douglass's study *Justification in Late Medieval Preaching: A Study of John Geiler of Keisersberg* (Leiden: E. J. Brill, 1966).

10. Hedio provides one of the important accounts of the debate between Luther and Zwingli over Christ and the Eucharist at the Marburg Colloquy in 1529.

11. On Christ as prophet see John Calvin, *Institutes of the Christian Religion* (Latin edition of 1559), II.xv.1–2.

CHAPTER 11

1. Jacob Strauss, *Ein neuw wunderbarlich Beychtbeuchlin* (Augsburg, 1523), as quoted by Steven E. Ozment, *The Reformation in the Cities* (New Haven, CT: Yale University Press, 1975), 52–53.

2. Sebastian Brant, *The Ship of Fools*, trans. E. H. Zeydel (New York: Columbia University Press, 1941), 91.

3. Katherine Zell, *Ein Brief an die gentz Burgerschaft der Stadt Strassburg betreffend Hern Ludwig Rabus* (1557), as quoted by Miriam U. Chrisman, "Women and the Reformation in Strassburg 1490–1530," *Archive for Reformation History* 63 (1972): 157.

4. I do not mean to imply that traditional Protestant theology did not teach the subordination of women to men within the context of family and the home; it certainly did. But it was combined with an emphasis on spiritual equality in Christ, a common priesthood, companionship as a fundamental purpose of marriage, and the rejection of celibacy. These motifs also had historical consequences even within the sixteenth century itself. In his commentary on Genesis, Calvin observed that the male was only half a man and that Adam saw himself completed in his wife. That is frequently overlooked in the rush to condemn Protestant teaching on the obedience of women to men. I cannot agree with the judgment of George Tavard that Protestantism has contributed little original insight to a theology of womanhood (cf. *Woman in Christian Tradition* [Notre Dame, IN: University of Notre Dame Press, 1973], 171). It is Protestantism and not Eastern Orthodoxy or the Roman Catholic Church that has found a rationale for the ordination of women, not by rejecting its tradition, but by taking the implications of its tradition seriously.

CHAPTER 12

1. For an introduction to Zwingli's eucharistic views see Jaques Courvoisier, *Zwingli: A Reformed Theologian* (Richmond: John Knox Press, 1963), 67–78; Gottfried W. Locher, *Zwingli's Thought: New Perspectives* (Leiden: E. J. Brill, 1981), 20–23, 220–28.

2. For important texts from Zwingli in English translation see "On the Lord's Supper," in *Zwingli and Bullinger*, ed. G. W. Bromiley (Philadelphia: Westminster Press, 1963), and *Commentary on True and False Religion*, ed. S. M. Jackson and C. N. Heller (Durham, NC: Labyrinth Press, 1981).

3. For a brief introduction to Carlstadt see my *Reformers in the Wings*, 2nd ed. (New York: Oxford University Press, 2001), 123–30, or E. Gordon Rupp, *Patterns of Reformation* (Philadelphia: Fortress Press, 1969). Ronald J. Sider offers a sympathetic interpretation in *Andreas Bodenstein von Karlstadt: The Development of His Thought, 1517–1525*, Studies in Medieval and Reformation Thought 11 (Leiden: E. J. Brill, 1974).

4. The Anabaptists were clearly indebted to Zwingli, rejecting with him a bodily presence of Christ in the Eucharist and stressing the presence of his glorified body at the right hand of the Father. Some Anabaptists allowed for a spiritual presence of Christ and emphasized solidarity with him in his suffering. Faith, memory, gratitude, and suffering were the words underlined by Anabaptists. See John D. Rempel, *The Lord's Supper in Anabaptism: A Study in the Christology of Balthasar Hubmaier, Pilgram Marpeck, and Dirk Philips* (Scottsdale, PA: Herald Press, 1993).

5. For a brief treatment of Luther's eucharistic theology see Paul Althaus, *The Theology of Martin Luther* (Minneapolis: Fortress Press, 1966), 375–403. See also chapter 7, "Scripture and the Lord's Supper in Luther's Theology," in my *Luther in Context*, 2nd ed. (Grand Rapids, MI: Baker Books, 2002), 72–84.

6. The most important English translations of Luther's polemical works against Zwingli are found in *Luther's Works* 37 (Minneapolis: Fortress Press, 1962).

7. The radical Reformer Caspar Schwenckfeld argued against Luther that Christ brought his own heavenly or "uncreaturely" body with him in the incarnation and that it was possible to engage in an internal eating of Christ's body and blood that could precede, accompany, or follow any external eating. For a brief introduction and bibliography see my *Reformers in the Wings*, 131–37.

8. The best general introduction to Calvin is still François Wendel, *Calvin: Origins and Development of His Religious Thought* (Grand Rapids, MI: Baker Books, 1950; 3rd ed., 1997). Especially important on his eucharistic thought is Killian McDonnell, *John Calvin, the Church and the Eucharist* (Princeton, NJ: Princeton University Press, 1967). See also Brian Gerrish, *Grace and Gratitude: The Eucharistic Theology of John Calvin* (Minneapolis: Fortress Press, 1993), and my *Calvin in Context* (New York: Oxford University Press, 1995).

9. In addition to Calvin's *Institutes of the Christian Religion*, ed. John T. McNeill, Library of Christian Classics 20–21 (Philadelphia: Westminster Press, 1960), one should consult Calvin's treatises against Lutheran theologians Joachim Westphal and Tilemann Hesshusen in *Selected Works of John Calvin: Tracts and Letters 3*, ed. J. Bonnet and H. Beveridge, reprint ed. (Grand Rapids, MI: Baker Books, 1983).

APPENDIX

1. See chap. 1 above for the text, footnotes, and quotations from Jowett.

Scripture Index

Genesis
1–2, 37, 42, 111
1:3, 83–84
2:18, 111
3:15, 48
17:15–16, 46

Deuteronomy
32:11, 35

I Samuel
2:4–7, 46

I Chronicles
17:13, 7

Psalms, 165
19:1, 40
30, 61
31:2, 61
33:9, 84
70:2, 61
117, 7
131:2, 35
137, 5, 6–7

Job
38:29, 35

Isaiah
7:14, 47
42:14, 35

43:19, 64
49:14–15, 35
61, 88
66:13, 35

Jeremiah
29:13, 71

Joel
2:28, 110, 114

Zechariah
1:3, 71

Gospels, 73, 115, 125

Matthew, 46, 47
3:16–17, 31, 88
4:17, 76
9:12, 106
20:1–6, 9–12
23:37, 35
26:26, 115,116, 117
28:19, 31, 142

Mark
1:9–11, 31
3:32, 45

Luke, 46, 47, 49, 110
1:28, 46, 51
1:37, 47

1:42, 46, 51
3:21–22, 31
4:16–19, 88
11:9, 71
11:27, 45
15:8–10, 35

John, 46, 117, 163
1:3, 28
1:13, 35, 47
3:5–8, 35
4:24, 116
4:29, 73, 99
6:63, 116, 121
15:1–27, 31
16:1–15, 31

Acts
1:7–8, 31
2:14–36, 88, 169n1
2:17, 114
7:2–53, 169n1

Romans, 163
1:16–17, 56, 61
1:25, 116
8:9–11, 31

I Corinthians
7:32–34, 106
12:4–6, 31
15:14, 140

II Corinthians
  3:6, 4
  13:14, 31

Galatians
  3:28, 110, 114
  4:4–7, 31

Ephesians
  4:4–6, 31

II Thessalonians
  2:13–14, 31

I Timothy
  2:12, 110

Hebrews, 88
  11, 169n1

James
  4:8, 71

General Index

Abortion, 76
Abraham (patriarch), 10, 17, 46, 48
Absolution, 66, 104. *See also* "Keys."
Abstinence, sexual, 105
Ad fontes (principle), 163
Adam, 5, 10, 32, 38, 48, 49, 83,
    173n4
Adoptionism, 32
Adultery, 106, 108, 131
Africa, 127, 128, 129–130
Akinolo, Peter Jaspar, 128, 129
Alabama Judicial Building, 131,
    134–135
Alciati, Andrea, 151
Alexandria (Egypt), 170n1
Allegory, vii, 6, 164
Ambrosiaster, 163
American culture, 70, 112–113, 132,
    135, 137–139
Amish, 79–80
Anabaptists, 76, 80, 109, 173n4
Anagogy, 6, 164
Analogy, 6, 24–25, 35
Anglican Church of Canada,
    127–128
Anglican churches/communion,
    103, 127, 128, 129, 133
Anglican Mission to America, 129

Anna (*Luke* 2), 51
Anne, Saint (mother of Virgin
    Mary), 59
Antioch, 170n1
Apophatic theology, 35
Apostles, 7, 18–19, 22, 23, 24, 25, 30,
    62, 83, 84, 129
Apostolic succession, 18–19, 30, 129
Aquinas, Thomas. *See* Thomas
    Aquinas.
Arianism, 30, 31, 33, 142
Aristotelianism, 7, 141
Aristotle, 38, 69
Arius, 149
Arminius, James, 100
Art, 137
Asbury, Francis, 70
Asceticism, 106
Asia, 127, 128
Assumption. *See under* Mary.
Athanasius, Saint, Patriarch of
    Alexandria, 19, 34, 149
Atheism, 38, 40, 157
Augustine, Saint, Bishop of Hippo,
    4, 5, 6, 33, 34, 40, 73, 88, 106,
    148, 151–152, 163
    De doctrina Christiana, 7, 151
    Milleloquium veritatis, 73

Augustinian Hermits, 54, 55, 59, 150
Augustinianism, 61, 70, 71, 140
Auschwitz (Poland), 79
Authority, 73, 94
Ave Maria (prayer), 170n1

Babylon, 5, 7, 83
Bangkok Assembly (1973), 70
Baptism, 31, 32, 35, 64, 65, 66, 75, 84, 92,
    94, 95, 101, 109, 110, 113, 116, 121
    infant, 54, 88
Baptists, 133
Barnes, Robert, 63, 76
Barth, Karl, 150, 163
Barthianism, 149, 151
Basel (Switzerland), 151
Basel, Council of (1439), 170n3
Benedict XVI, Pope, 104
Berger, Peter Ludwig, 135
Berlin (Germany), 22
Bernard of Clairvaux, Saint, 158
Beza, Theodore, 164
Bible, 18, 23, 24, 29–30, 31, 41, 42, 65, 77,
    83–84, 85, 89, 100, 134, 141–142,
    150, 163
    New Testament, 17, 18, 23, 29, 31,
        45–46, 62, 92, 100, 141
    Old Testament, 5, 8, 17, 26, 51, 125, 164
    Septuagint, 19, 87
    translation, 83, 164
    Vulgate, 163–164
Biel, Gabriel, 58, 70–72, 150, 154, 171n4
    Collectorium, 70
Bill of Rights (U.S.), 134
Birth control, 112–113
Bishops. *See* Apostolic succession;
    Episcopacy
Bizer, Ernst, 61
Bloch, Marc Léopold Benjamin, 20
Blony, Nicholas de, 105
Blücher, Gebhard Leberecht
    von, 22
Bodenstein, Andreas. *See* Carlstadt,
    Andreas Bodenstein von.
Boehme, Jakob, 13
Boehmer, Heinrich, 61

Böhner, Theophilus, 59
"Born-again" Christians, 35
Bourges (France), 151
Bouwsma, William James, 155
Bradwardine, Thomas, 150
Braght, Thieleman Janszoon van.
    Martyrs' Mirror, 76
Brant, Sebastian. *Ship of Fools*, 86,
    107–108
Brès, Guy de, 63
Brunner, Emil, 151
Bucer, Martin, 21, 108, 111, 151, 155,
    165, 166
Buchenwald (Germany), 79
Bullinger, Heinrich, 85, 108
Bultmann, Rudolf Karl, 61, 163
Bunyan, John. *Pilgrim's Progress*,
    74, 133
Bure, Idelette de, 151

Calvin, John, 39–43, 60, 62, 63, 64–65,
    70, 73, 76, 77, 87, 89, 91, 115,
    123–126, 149–155, 164, 165
    Commentary on Genesis, 173n4
    Commentary on the Psalms, 76, 152, 153
    Institutes, 63, 124, 151, 153, 171n13
    Reply to Sadoleto, 62, 72–73, 152–153
Calvinism, 70, 98, 132, 151, 155
Cameron, Gregory, 127–128
Campion, Edmund, Saint, 76
Canada, 127, 128, 130
Canterbury (English archbishopric), viii
Capreolus, John, 58
Carlstadt, Andreas Bodenstein von, 20,
    117
Cassian, John, Saint, 6
Catholicity, 64, 65–66, 92–93, 143
Celibacy, 103–106, 108–109, 110,
    111, 113
Chalcedon, Council of (451), 148, 149,
    170n1
Charity, viii, 53, 96
Charles V, Emperor, 53
Chesterton, Gilbert Keith, 91, 156
Chiles, Robert Eugene, 98
China, 128

Christianity, 23, 127, 130, 132, 139, 140–141, 148, 158, 159

Christie, Agatha Mary Clarissa Miller, 18, 25

Christology, 51, 61, 66, 88, 118–119, 120, 122, 124, 125–126, 150, 170n1

Church, the, viii–ix, 6, 31, 47, 49, 50, 51, 61, 64–65, 71–74, 77, 84, 89, 91–94, 97–98, 99, 101, 102, 105, 110, 118, 121, 124, 126, 139, 142, 144, 146, 149, 153, 156

Church history, 62, 142–146, 147–150, 152, 153, 154, 156

Church of England, 128

Church of Nigeria (Anglican), 128

Cicero, Marcus Tullius, 132
De natura deorum, 40

Clare of Assisi, Saint, 158

Clement IX, Pope, 20

Clement XIV, Pope, 20

Clergy. See Ministry; Priesthood.

Cochlaeus, Johannes, 55, 57, 60
Commentary on . . . Luther, 55

Code Napoleon, 132

Coincidences, 20, 166–167

Cologne (Germany), 54, 58

Colombini, John, Blessed, 20

Colonialism, 130

Commands, 106, 109, 110

Communicatio idiomatum, 122

Compassion, 50, 51, 96

Concubinage, 108, 111

Concupiscence, 111

Confession of sin, 88, 95. See also Penance.

Confessional, 107

Congregationalists, 93–94

Conscience, 56, 60, 93

Constitution (U.S.), 22–23, 42, 133, 134
First Amendment, 132, 133, 135

Contarini, Gasparo Cardinal, 165

Context, historical, 13, 145, 148, 151, 152, 154, 155–156, 165

Contraception, 112–113

Conversion, 9–10, 12, 35, 70, 72, 74–76, 77, 152

Cordier, Mathurin, 151

Coronel, Antonio, 151

Corvinus, Anton, 63

Cotton, John, 70

Councils, 100

Counsels, 106, 109, 110

Covenant, 49, 50, 71, 93, 105

Creation, 12, 28, 33–34, 35, 38–39, 43, 83

Creation story, 8, 37, 38, 39, 42, 48

Creeds, 18, 30, 46, 65, 66, 101, 119, 121, 125, 139

Cross, 46, 49, 50
theology of, 58

Cyprian, Saint, Bishop of Carthage, 106

da / dir da, 122

D'Ailly, Pierre, 58

Dalgliesh, Adam (character), 16

Daniel (prophet), 83

Darwin, Charles Robert, 42

David, King of Israel, 7, 10

Deacon (office), 96, 104

Death, 10, 12, 32, 119

Deconstructionism, 162

Delahaye, Albert, 20

Denifle, Heinrich, 55–57, 58, 61, 67

Dentière, Marie, 111

Detective stories. See Mystery stories.

Dilthey, Wilhelm, 61

Discernment, 19

Discipline, 95, 96, 102

Divorce, 105, 111, 112

Doctor (theological teacher), 93

Dominicans, 56, 58, 69, 75, 170n3

Donatists, 99

Dordrecht, Synod of (1618/19), 100

Double acceptation, 154

Double justification, 165

"Double mouth" (doctrine), 125

Douglass, E. Jane Dempsey, 154

Dover (Pennsylvania), 37

Dowey, Edward A., Jr., 151

Drechsel, Thomas, 82

Drew University, 99

Düsseldorf (Germany), 22

Duffy, Eamon, 24
Duke University, vii, 161
Duns Scotus, John, 21, 48, 54, 154
Dykema, Peter Alan, 155

Eastern Orthodoxy. *See* Orthodox
    Churches.
Eastern Rite Catholic churches, 103
Eck, John, 20–21, 145, 165, 166
    Enchiridion, 20–21, 166
    Lectures on the *Sentences* (1542), 21,
        166
Eden, Garden of, 38, 83
Education, 87–88, 100–101, 112
Edwards, Jonathan 70
Eerdmans (publisher), 163
Einsiedeln (Switzerland), 86, 87
Eisegesis, 8
Eisenach (Germany), 107
Eisleben (Germany), 81
Elba (island), 21
Elder (office), 96, 100
Election, 71, 154
Elizabeth, Saint (mother of John the
        Baptist), 47, 51, 110
Elton, Sir Geoffrey Rudolph, 67
Elvira, Council of (ca. 300), 106
Engels, Friedrich, 12
England, 23, 87, 103, 106, 130, 132, 133
Epicureans, 42, 153
Episcopacy, 18–19, 66, 92–93, 100, 103,
        129
Episcopal Church (U.S.A.), 128–129
Epistemology, 41
Erfurt (Germany), 55, 56, 58
Erikson, Erik Homburger, 12, 55
Eschatology, 118
Established churches, 133–134
Ethics, 106, 141. *See also* Morality.
Eucharist, 31, 32, 49, 50, 53, 54, 60, 61,
        63, 64, 66, 72, 84–85, 86, 88, 95,
        104, 109, 114, 115–126, 140, 172n10
    unbelievers, 123, 125
Europe, 127, 133, 137, 138–139, 155
Evangelical awakening (U.S.), 70
Eve, 38, 48, 173n4

Evolution, 37, 38, 39, 43
Exegesis, vii, 3–4, 8, 13, 20, 36, 83,
        162, 164, 165, 167. *See also*
        Historical-critical method.
    traditional, vii–viii, 4, 6, 7–9, 12, 13–14,
        15, 17, 19, 25–26, 161–163
Existentialism, 61, 141
Extracalvinisticum, 124, 150

Faith, 6, 32, 39, 42, 45, 51, 53, 60, 74, 123,
        124, 125, 129, 159, 173n4. *See also*
        under Justification.
    implicit, 101
Family life, 107
Farel, Guillaume, 62, 151
Fathers (church), 18, 19, 22, 23, 62–64,
        65, 87, 98, 101, 142
Feminism, 51, 149
Finitude, 97, 119, 122, 124, 126, 144
Finney, Charles Grandison, 70
Fisher, John, Saint, 76
Flesh, 76, 116, 121
Florida, 134–135
Florovsky, Georges, 23
Forgiveness, 72, 80
Forgiveness of sin, 32, 77
Fornication, 106, 108
France, 5, 21, 133, 155
Francis of Assisi, Saint, 158
Francis I, King of France, 57
Franciscans, 7, 58, 59, 75, 107
Freedom, human, 60, 109, 113
French language, 70, 87, 163
Frontier, 137–138
Frye, Northrop, 13

Ganoczy, Alexandre, 154
Gansfort, Wessel, 117
Geiler of Kaysersberg, John, 86, 87, 106,
        108
Geneva (Switzerland), 152, 153, 155
Gentiles, 10, 23
George III, King of England, 23
George, Duke of Saxony, 55, 69
German language, 60, 83, 163
Germany, 12, 61

Global South, 127–128, 130
Gloria Patri (doxology), 27–28
Glory, 40, 43, 154
Gnosticism, 18, 38
Goch. See Pupper of Goch.
God, 5, 7, 11, 29, 32, 33–34, 35, 37–39, 40,
    41, 42, 46, 48–49, 56, 71, 76, 83–84,
    85, 90, 97, 98, 100, 116, 118, 121,
    142, 153, 154, 158. See also Trinity.
  aseity, 29, 33, 34
  aseity, 33, 34
  goodness of, 11, 12, 34
  judgment of, 74, 76, 86, 89, 95,
    96, 109
  righteousness of, 56, 61, 154
God the Father, 18, 28, 30, 31, 33, 34, 35,
    119, 121–122
Goodness of creation, 34, 35
Gospel, the, viii, 56, 60, 62, 70, 71, 72,
    73, 74, 75, 77, 89, 91, 93, 99, 100,
    101, 106, 112, 142–143
Government, 132, 134
Grace, 4, 7, 10, 12, 33, 42, 50, 58, 59, 62,
    69, 71, 74, 75, 84, 89, 95, 96, 98,
    109, 116–117, 120, 121, 123, 154,
    158, 159
  preparation for, 70, 71, 72, 77
  prevenient, 98
Graham, William Franklin (Billy), 70
Grant, Alan (character), 19
Granvella, Nicholas, 165
Greek language, 70, 83, 87, 88, 148,
    163, 164
Gregorios III Laham, Patriarch, 104
Gregory of Rimini, 150
Grisar, Hartmann, 12, 57, 59
Gropper, John Cardinal, 165
Guardian (newspaper), 127
Guinness, Sir Alec, 30
Gunkel, Hermann, 165–166

Hallard, Marta (character), 19
Hammurabi's Code, 134
Hannah (mother of Samuel), 47, 51
"Happy days are here again" (song),
    164–165

"Hark! the herald angels" (hymn), 126
Harnack, Karl Gustav Adolf von,
    143, 148
Harrisburg (Pennsylvania), 37
Harvard University, 150, 152, 154
Hebrew language, 70, 83, 87, 148,
    163, 164
Hedio, Caspar, 86
Hegelianism, 141
Heidelberg (Germany), 164, 165
Heisselwörter, 83, 84
Helvetic Confession, Second, 85
Henry VIII, King of England, 57, 163
Henry, Patrick, 133, 134
Heresy & heresies, 18, 29, 54, 58, 59, 62,
    63, 99, 130
  virtual, 35
Heretics, 54
  use of the Bible, 17–18, 29
Hermeneutics, 4, 5, 6, 7–8, 14, 30, 164,
    163, 167, 169n7
Hermogenes, 28
Herte, Adolf, 55
Hesshusen, Tilemann, 125, 174n9
Hirsch, Emanuel, 61
Historical-critical method, vii, viii, 4, 14,
    15, 115, 161, 162, 167
Historical reconstruction, 20, 165–166,
    167
History & historians, 5, 12, 19–20, 21–23,
    24, 25, 137–146, 147–149, 151–152,
    154, 165–167
Hitchens, Christopher, 157
Hoen, Cornelius Henrici, 117
Holland, 100, 133
Holmes, Sherlock (character), 16, 21
"Holy, Holy, Holy" (hymn), 141
Holy Spirit, 28, 31, 33, 35, 42, 82, 88, 89,
    92, 94, 97, 100, 101, 110, 116–117,
    118, 119–120, 124
Homer. Odyssey, 74
Homosexuality, 105, 127
Hong Kong, 130
Hope, 6, 118, 144
Horace (Quintus Horatius Flaccus), 18
Human nature, 33, 71, 105

Humanity, 33, 40–41, 50. *See also under* Jesus Christ.
Humility, 11, 51, 61, 86, 91
Humor, 148, 156
Hus, Jan, 149, 150

Ideas, divine, 21
Idolatry, 41, 116, 121
Ignatius Loyola, Saint, 20, 58
Images, 82, 116
Immaculate conception. *See under* Mary.
Imperial free cities, 12, 85–86
Incarnation. *See under* Jesus Christ.
Inclusive language. *See under* Language.
India, 135
Individualism, 72
Indulgences, 55, 63, 69
Ineffabilis Deus (1854), 170n3
Ingolstadt (Germany), 20, 21, 166
Inspiration, 82, 89
Intelligent design, 37–38, 39, 40, 42–43
Intention, authorial, vii, 3, 4, 7, 8, 12, 13, 14, 22, 26, 133, 134, 162, 167
Intervarsity Press, 163
Irenaeus, Saint, Bishop of Lyon, 9, 17, 18, 29, 30
Isaiah (prophet), 28, 64
    second, 26
Iserloh, Erwin, 59
Islam, 130
Israel (people), 17, 23, 24, 46, 48
Israel / Church, 5, 6, 46
Iustitia, 56

James, Phyllis Dorothy, 25
Jedin, Hubert, 165
Jefferson, Thomas, 60, 133, 134
Jefferts Schori, Katherine, 128
Jerusalem, 5, 6
Jesuates (Apostolic Clerics of St. Jerome), 20
Jesuits (Society of Jesus), 19, 20, 57
Jesus Christ, 3–4, 5, 7, 9, 10, 12, 17, 24, 25, 28, 30, 31, 32–33, 34, 39, 45–51, 69, 73, 80, 98, 105, 106, 109, 110, 115–126, 139, 141, 148, 162. *See also* Christology.
    ascension, 119, 122, 124, 126
    baptism, 31, 88
    birth, 46, 47, 48
    crucifixion, 26, 31, 38, 49
    humanity, 32, 119, 122, 123, 124, 125, 126
    incarnation, 32, 33, 46–47, 49, 119, 124, 125
    as priest & prophet, 88, 89, 90
    resurrection, 119, 122, 126, 140
    ubiquity, 122, 123
Jews, 10, 79, 131, 164
Jews / Gentiles, 9, 10, 12
Joel (prophet), 110
John the Apostle, Saint, 28, 45–46
John the Baptist, Saint, 47, 51
John, King of England, 23
John Chrysostom, Saint, Abp of Constantinople, 163
John of the Cross, Saint, 157
Johnson, Samuel, 12
Johnstone, Douglas Inge, 132
Jowett, Benjamin, 3–4, 7, 8, 12, 13, 22, 161–162
Judgment. *See under* God.
Judgment, private, 100, 101
Julius Caesar, 105, 139
Jussy, Jean de, 111
Justice. *See* God, righteousness of.
Justification, 56, 58–59, 60, 71, 165
    by faith, 53, 57, 59, 62, 63, 126

Kähler, Martin, 126
Kant, Immanuel, 71
Kantianism, 141
Kataphatic theology, 35
Kenya, 130
"Keys" (sacrament), 64, 66, 73
Kind Hearts and Coronets (1949 motion picture), 30
Kingdom of God, 7, 9, 118, 139
Knowledge of God, 39, 40, 41, 42, 54, 144
Kolini, Emmanuel M., 129
Korea, 128
Krauthammer, Charles, 43

Laity, 94–95, 101, 106–107, 109
Language(s), 3, 54, 85, 90, 95, 141,
    148–149, 152, 156, 165. *See also*
    Words.
  inclusive, 27–28, 34–35
Lateran Council II (1139), 103
Lateran Council IV (1215), 116
Latimer, Hugh, 76
Latin America, 127, 128
Latin language, 70, 83, 87, 148, 163–164
Lausanne Covenant (1974), 70
LaVallee, Armand Aime, 150, 154
Law, 11
  and gospel, 4
Lebanon, 103
Lee, Peter James, 128
Lefèvre d'Étaples, Jacques, 8
Leipzig (Germany), 20
Leo X, Pope, 53
Letter / spirit, 4, 5–6, 8, 13
Leutpriester, 86–87
Lewis, Clive Staples, 24
  Till We Have Faces, 12
Lewis, Robert (Robbie) (character), 17
Liberalism, 61, 150
Literal meaning of Bible, 6, 7, 8, 38,
    39, 164
Literary criticism, 13, 162, 166
London (England), 22
Lord's Prayer, 80
Lortz, Joseph Adam, 57–58, 59
Louvain (Belgium), 54
Love, 6, 9, 33, 49, 50, 51, 53, 71, 75, 76,
    110, 111, 121, 156
Luccock, Halford Edward, 92
Lucretius Carus, Titus, 42
Luke the Evangelist, Saint, 47
Lust, 47, 48
Luther, Hans, 55, 59
Luther, Martin, 11, 12–13, 20, 21, 50, 51,
    53–67, 69–72, 76, 81–85, 89, 90, 93,
    95, 108, 109, 115, 120–123, 125, 126,
    145, 147, 150, 152, 154, 155, 158, 159,
    163, 166, 170n3, 172n10
  Anfechtungen, 60, 157
  as prophet, 60, 81, 85, 90

  tower experience, 61
  Lectures on Psalms, 61
  Lectures on Romans (1515/16), 56
  Ninety-five Theses, 55, 69
  Small Catechism, 84
  Wider die himmlischen Propheten, 82
Lutherans & Lutheranism, 60, 61, 64,
    100, 123, 124, 125, 133, 155, 164

McSorley, Harry J., 59
Madison, James, 133, 134
Magna Carta, 134
Major, John, 154
Manichaeanism, 106
Manns, Peter, 59
Mansfeld (Germany), 59
Marburg Colloquy (1529), 172n10
Marcionites, 18
Maronite Church, 103
Marpeck, Pilgram, 100
Marple, Jane (character), 16, 25
Marriage, 47, 76, 105–106, 108, 110–113
  clerical, 103–104, 108, 109–110, 111, 113
  same-sex, 127–128
Martyrdom, 65, 106
Marxism, 12
Mary, Blessed Virgin, 32, 45–51
  assumption, 48, 170–171n4
  immaculate conception, 47–48
Masturbation, 108
Melanchthon, Philip, 63, 86,
    165, 166
Melchizedek, King of Salem, 88, 90
Melkite Church, 103, 104
Memory, viii–ix, 117–118, 140, 146,
    173n4
Mennonites, 79, 134
Mercy, 12, 74, 75, 76
Merit, 11, 33, 48–49, 50, 53, 121, 152
Messiah, 51
Metaphor, 5, 6, 117, 122, 153
Metaphysics, 98, 141, 148
Methodism, 98, 100
Michalson, Carl Donald, Jr., 99
Michelangelo Buonarotti, 132
Milton, John, 13

Ministry, ordained, 66, 87, 88, 89, 91–102, 106–107, 108, 109, 111, 134. *See also* Deacon; Priesthood.
Minns, Martyn, 128
Modalism, 142
Monarchianism, 142
Monasticism, 53, 61, 111
Moody, Dwight Lyman, 70
Moore, Roy Stewart, 131, 132
Morality, 6, 32, 33, 54, 71–72, 76, 95, 98, 100, 106, 108, 126, 130, 131, 135, 141, 148, 162
More, Sir Thomas, Saint, 76
Morse, Endeavour (character), 17, 24, 25
Moses, 17, 88, 131
"Mother of God" (Marian ascription), 170n1
Moynihan, Daniel Patrick, 22
Muentzer, Thomas, 82–83, 85, 89, 90
Munificentissimus Deus (1950), 170n4
Murner, John, 107
Murner, Thomas, 107
Musculus, Andreas, 63
Music, 116
Mystery stories, 15–17, 21, 23, 24, 25

Napoleon I, Emperor of the French, 21–22
Natural theology, 39–40, 41, 42–43, 144, 150
Nature, 39, 41–42, 43, 144
  theology of, 40
Nazareth (Israel), 88
Nederlands Hervormde Kerk, 151
Nestorianism, 170n1
New criticism, 162
New York City, 132
Nicaea, Council of (325), 148
Nicholas of Lyra, 6, 7–8, 13, 164
Nickel Mines (Pennsylvania), 79
Niesel, Wilhelm, 151
Nigeria, 128
Noah (patriarch), 6, 10
Nominalism, 58
Nonviolence, 79–80, 106
North America, 127, 129

"O young and fearless prophet" (hymn), 88, 126
Oberman, Heiko Augustinus, 147, 150–156
Ockham, William, 21, 58
Ontology, 31, 35
Ordination, 35, 72, 91, 94, 95, 100, 101, 104, 110, 114
  gay, 127
  women, 104, 110, 113–114, 173n4
Origen, 4–5, 9, 33–34, 38–39, 42, 163, 164
Orléans (France), 151
Orombi, Henry Luke, 129
Orthodox Churches, 59, 103, 111, 133, 148, 149, 173n4
Oxford University, 3, 54

Pacifism, 109
Pantheism, 40
Papacy, 53, 94
Parables, 38, 42
Paris (France), 5, 21, 22, 54, 151, 154, 164
Parker, Thomas Henry Louis, 151
Pastor (office), 66, 89, 93, 94, 96, 101, 109–110
Paul the Apostle, Saint, 4, 31, 46, 56, 92, 106, 110, 114
Peace, 86
Pearl, The (Middle English poem), 10, 11
Pedophilia, 105
Pelagianism, 33, 58, 70
Pelikan, Jaroslav Jan, 147–150, 155–156
Penance, 62, 64, 66, 70, 71, 84, 86. *See also* Confession of sin.
Penitence, 69, 71, 74. *See also* Repentance.
Pennsylvania, 134
Perpetua, Saint, 106
Pesch, Otto Hermann, 58, 59
Peter the Apostle, Saint, 46, 88, 114
Peter Lombard, Bishop of Paris. *Sentences*, 21, 70, 166
Pfürtner, Stephan Hubert, 59
Philology, 87, 163
Philosophy, 39, 98, 139–141, 144

Pietism, 60
Pius IX, Pope, 170n3
Pius XII, Pope, 170n4
"Plain sense," 164
Platonism, 141
Poetry, 18, 29
Poirot, Hercule (character), 18, 21
Polk County (Florida), 134
Polytheism, 29
Positivism, 14
Potentia dei, 154
Prayer, 19, 31, 50, 96, 158–159
Preaching, vii, viii, 64, 65, 66, 84–87,
    89, 90, 91–96, 99–100, 101–102,
    109, 112, 114, 117
Predestination, 21, 28, 98, 154
Presbyterians, 93
Priesthood, 64, 66, 84, 85, 86, 88, 90,
    103–104
Priesthood of all believers, 64, 94–95,
    109, 110, 113–114, 173n4
Princeton University, 150
Process thought, 141
Procreation, 47–48, 105, 111, 112
Prophecy, 81–82, 85, 87, 88, 89–90
Prophets, 7, 10, 22, 24, 81, 83, 84, 85
Prophezei (Zurich seminar), 87
Proportionality (doctrine), 10–11, 12
Protestantism, 20, 45, 46, 47, 50, 59,
    60–67, 70, 72, 74–75, 77, 85,
    87–90, 91–93, 95–97, 100–101,
    108–111, 113, 121, 132, 150–151, 163,
    164, 166
Providence, 118, 153
Prussia, 22
Psychology, 12, 57, 59
Pupper of Goch, John, 10, 11
Puritans, 87, 139

Race, 76
Rahner, Karl, 35
Rape, 108
Reader-response criticism, 162
Reason, 39, 42, 144, 150
Redemption, 8, 32, 33, 36, 39, 48,
    49, 50

Reformation, the, 58, 63, 70, 81–82, 90,
    93, 108, 112, 113, 152, 155, 172n2
    origins, 55, 57, 59, 69
Reformed tradition, 95–96, 100, 133
Regeneration, 8, 47
Regensburg Colloquy (1541), 165, 166
Religion, 40, 135
    and the state, 131, 132, 133–135
Rentdorf, Rolf, 165
Repentance, 69–72, 73,–74, 75, 76, 77
Revelation, 3, 39, 41, 82, 89, 90, 144, 150
Rhetoric, 87, 96
Richard III, King of England, 19
Ritschl, Albrecht Benjamin, 61
Roberts, Charles Carl, 79, 80
Robinson, Vicky Gene, 128–129
Roman Catholicism, 12, 20, 38, 53–67,
    88, 90, 93, 95, 100, 103–104,
    115–116, 125–126, 133, 153, 155, 166,
    170n3, 173n4
Rome, 20, 54, 103, 105, 112
Roosevelt, Franklin Delano, 164–165
Rule of faith, 25, 89
Russia, 133
Rwanda, 129

Saarnivaara, Uuras, 61
Sabbath, 131–132
Sabellianism, 28, 30–31
Sabellius, 30
Sacraments, viii, 31–32, 49, 50, 64, 66,
    82, 84, 85, 87, 89, 90, 93, 94, 95,
    99, 100, 109, 114, 115, 117, 153
Sadoleto, Jacopo Cardinal, 62, 152–153
Saints, 65, 75, 157, 158, 159
Salvation, 9, 10, 11, 29, 32, 33, 35, 45, 51,
    123, 171n4. *See also* Soteriology.
Same-sex marriage, 127–128
Sanctification, 74
Sanctity, 157–158, 159
Sarah (matriarch), 46, 47, 51
Sarcerius, Erasmus, 63
Schönborn, Cristoph Cardinal, 38
Scholasticism, 21, 69, 150, 154
Schweitzer, Albert. *The Quest of the
    Historical Jesus*, 162

Schwenckfeld, Caspar, 174n7

Science, 38, 43

Scotism, 154

Scotland, 154

Scotus. *See* Duns Scotus.

Scripture. *See* Bible.

Second narrative, 16–17, 18, 19, 21, 22, 23–24, 25

Seeberg, Reinhold, 150, 154

Sermon on the Mount, 109

Servus servorum dei (papal title), 94

Sex, 48, 105, 106, 111, 112–113

Sexuality, 35, 111, 113, 114, 130

Shakespeare, William, 13

Shamgar (son of Anath), 6

Siena (Italy), 20

Signs, 7, 84, 85

Simeon (*Luke 2*), 51

Sin, 32, 47, 71, 72, 75, 84, 86, 97, 107, 108, 111, 119, 157–158
    original, 39, 40–41, 48, 84, 106, 132

Sinners, 71, 72, 75, 132

Sisera (Canaanite leader), 6

Skepticism, 139–140

Slavery, 105, 137

Slavic languages, 148

Smalcald Articles, 66, 125

Society of Biblical Literature, 161, 165

Soldier Field (Chicago, Ill.), 65

Solomon, King of Israel, 7

Solon (Athenian statesman), 132

Soteriology, 31–32, 119. *See also* Salvation.

Source criticism, 165

Springer, Gerald (Jerry), 132

Steinmetz, Max, 12

Storch, Nicholas, 82, 85, 87, 89

Stotternheim (Germany), 59

Strasbourg (France), 86, 106, 107, 110, 112, 151

Strauss, Jacob, 107

Streisand, Babara Joan (Barbra), 164, 165

Stuebner, Markus Thomae, 82

Subjectivism, 14

Substance, 116, 123, 148

Suffering, 49, 50, 60, 76, 173n4

Sunday, William Ashley (Billy), 70

Supreme Court (U.S.), 133, 134

Sweden, 133, 135

Synods, 100

Syphilis, 57

Tavard, George Henry, 173n4

Taxation, 108, 133

Teaching office, viii, 89, 90, 92, 93, 95, 96, 101, 102

Ten Commandments, 131–132, 134, 135

Teresa of Calcutta, Mother, 157, 159

Tertullian, Quintus Septimus Florens, 17, 18, 28, 29
    De praescriptione hereticorum, 18

Testament, 121

Tetzel, John, 69

Tey, Josephine. *The Daughter of Time*, 19, 21

Theology, 21, 26, 35, 54, 143, 144, 145, 149, 166. *See also* Natural theology.

Theotokos (Marian title), 170n1

Thettelwörter, 83–84, 90

Thomae, Markus (Stuebner), 82

Thomas à Kempis, 97

Thomas Aquinas, Saint, 7, 10, 11, 13, 21, 39, 42–43, 48, 50, 58, 153, 170n3
    Lectura super evangelium Sancti Matthaei, 9–10

Thomas, Dylan Marlais, 32, 80

Thomism, 58

Tiberius, Emperor of Rome, 105

Tillich, Paul Johannes, 135

Tin Men (1987 motion picture), 34

Tolkien, Johan Ronald Reuel. *The Lord of the Rings*, 24

Torrance, Thomas Forsyth, 151

Tradition(s), 30, 62, 63, 65, 141, 142–143, 162, 163, 167

Translation, 98, 163. *See also under* Bible.

Transubstantiation, 53, 63, 64, 66, 115–116, 120–121

Trent, Council of (1545–1563), 64, 150, 152, 163

Trinity, 10, 21, 27–36, 61, 66, 113, 119, 126, 141–142

Tritheism, 142
Troeltsch, Ernst, 61
Tropology, 6, 164
Truro (Virginia), 128
Truth, 14, 38, 130
Tübingen (Germany), 70, 150, 151, 154
Tyndale, William, 4, 76

Uganda, 129
Unction, 88
Unitarianism, 29
Utrecht (Netherlands), 151

Van Buren, Paul Matthews, 151
Vatican Council II (1962–1965), 59, 64, 65
"Veni creator spiritus" (hymn), 28
Vestigia ecclesiae, 64–65, 66
Vincentian canon, 130, 153
Virgil (Publius Virgilius Maro), 18, 29
Virgin Birth, 45, 46, 47–48
Virginia, 128, 133
Virginity, 46, 47, 105
Virtue, moral, 71, 72
Virtues, theological, 6
Vogelsang, Erich Paul Friedrich, 61
Vows, 109

Wallace, Ronald Stewart, 151
War, 76, 80, 86
Waterloo, Battle of (1815), 21
Watson, Dr. John H. (character), 16
Weijenborg, Reinoud, 59
Wellington, Arthur Wellesley, Duke of, 22

Wesley, John, 98, 99, 114
Westphal, Joachim, 125, 174n9
Wicks, Jared, 59
Will, 54, 69, 70, 71, 98
William of Ockham. See Ockham.
Williams, Rowan Douglas, 127
Willis, Edward David, 150
Wittenberg (Germany), 55, 56, 82
Wolmar, Melchior, 151
Women, 27, 107–108, 110–114, 164. See also under Ordination.
Word (proclamation), 50, 64, 93, 94, 96, 99, 101–102, 109, 114
Word of God, 74, 75, 82, 83–84, 85, 89, 90, 94, 95, 96, 99, 100, 121, 139
Words, 7, 82, 83–84, 95
Wordsworth, William, 12
Works, 10–11, 50, 57
Worship, 27, 32, 35, 40, 89, 96, 116, 117, 129, 159

Yale University, 92, 172n1
Yeago, David Stuart, 64

Zechariah (father of John the Baptist), 51, 110
Zell, Katherine, 110, 112, 114
Zell, Matthew, 110
Zurich (Switzerland), 60, 87, 116, 118, 164
Zwickau (Germany), 82, 83
Zwickau Prophets, 82, 85, 89
Zwingli, Huldrych, 21, 75, 86–87, 89, 108, 116–126, 140, 155, 164, 166, 170n3, 172n10